Juvenile Risk and Needs Assessment

This book takes a comprehensive, analytic approach to understanding Juvenile Risk and Needs Assessment (JRNA), covering elements relevant to how the practice affects youths' cases and the juvenile justice system. The work draws on both analysis of the extensive research on risk and needs assessment in the juvenile justice system as well as data from the authors' recent work in the area. Authors Sullivan and Childs have extensive experience in teaching about and doing research on the juvenile justice system, including multiple studies on juvenile risk and needs assessment tools and their implementation.

This expansive, integrative book leaves readers with a realistic sense of "where things stand" on the theory, research, policy, and practice of JRNA. By bringing together existing ideas and assessing them in depth, it identifies possible future paths and sparks ideas for improving the juvenile justice response to delinquent and at-risk youths.

Juvenile Risk and Needs Assessment is essential reading for scholars of juvenile justice system impact and reform as well as practitioners engaged in youth and juvenile justice work ranging from the preventive to the rehabilitative stages.

Christopher J. Sullivan is Professor and Director of the School of Criminal Justice and Criminology at Texas State University. He received his doctorate from Rutgers University in 2005. His research interests include developmental and life-course criminology; juvenile delinquency and juvenile justice; and research and analytic methods. He has published more than 90 journal articles and book chapters on those and related topics. He is author of *Taking Juvenile Justice Seriously: Developmental Insights and System Challenges* (Temple University Press, 2019), which was selected as an Outstanding Contribution by the American Society of Criminology's Division of Developmental and Life Course Criminology in 2020. Dr. Sullivan has been named a 250th Anniversary Fellow at Rutgers University and a Fellow of the Graduate School at the University of Cincinnati for his research and has received award recognition for his mentoring and teaching of graduate students and academic service. He has been data analyst or Principal Investigator (PI) on several federally or state-funded projects in juvenile justice practice and policy. Professor Sullivan has been Co-Editor of the *Journal of Research in Crime and Delinquency* since 2017.

Kristina K. Childs is an Associate Professor in the Department of Criminal Justice at the University of Central Florida. She received her doctoral degree in Criminology from the University of South Florida in 2008. Then, she was a post-doctoral fellow for the John D. and Catherine T. MacArthur Foundation's Models for Change: Systems Reform in Juvenile Justice initiative in Louisiana. Her main research interests include juvenile risk and need assessment practices, evaluation of prevention and intervention programs for at-risk youths, and the effectiveness of mental health and de-escalation training and education for front-line juvenile justice decision-makers. She has published more than 25 academic articles and book chapters on juvenile justice issues. To support her research, she has received over $1 million in external grants from the National Institute of Justice, Substance Abuse and Mental Health Services Administration, and the Bureau of Justice Assistance.

Routledge Studies in Juvenile Justice and Delinquency

Juvenile justice matters are of critical concern in both the United States and around the world. Books in the *Routledge Studies in Juvenile Justice and Delinquency* series explore mechanisms, consequences, insights, and innovations in the field of juvenile justice and its responses to delinquency. Each monograph will examine new areas of empirical and theoretical inquiry, provide an agenda-setting discussion of important concepts and controversies surrounding juvenile justice and delinquency, and seek to encompass a transnational or global approach to the issues addressed. The series will be a resource for the international community of undergraduates, post-graduates, researchers, practitioners, and policymakers concerned with juveniles and families caught up in or at risk of engagement in delinquency and justice system involvement.

Series editor David L. Myers

Due Process Protections for Youth
Defense Counsel Policies and Disparity in the Juvenile Justice System
Emily K. Pelletier

Norms of Violence
Violent Socialization Processes and the Spillover Effect for Youth Crime
Aimée X. Delaney

Explaining Variation in Juvenile Punishment
The Role of Communities and Systems
Steven N. Zane

Youth Violence in Context
An Ecological Routine Activity Framework
Eileen M. Ahlin & Maria João Lobo Antunes

Juvenile Risk and Needs Assessment
Theory, Research, Policy, and Practice
Christopher J. Sullivan and Kristina K. Childs

Juvenile Risk and Needs Assessment

Theory, Research, Policy, and Practice

Christopher J. Sullivan and
Kristina K. Childs

Routledge
Taylor & Francis Group

NEW YORK AND LONDON

First published 2022
by Routledge
605 Third Avenue, New York, NY 10158

and by Routledge
2 Park Square, Milton Park, Abingdon, Oxon OX14 4RN

Routledge is an imprint of the Taylor & Francis Group, an informa business

Library of Congress Cataloging-in-Publication Data
Names: Sullivan, Christopher J., author. | Childs, Kristina K., author.
Title: Juvenile risk and needs assessment : theory, research, policy, and
practice / Christopher J. Sullivan and Kristina K. Childs.
Description: New York, NY : Routledge, 2022. |
Series: Routledge studies in juvenile justice and delinquency |
Includes bibliographical references and index.
Identifiers: LCCN 2021020200 (print) | LCCN 2021020201 (ebook) |
ISBN 9780367422776 (hbk) | ISBN 9781032107356 (pbk) |
ISBN 9780367823122 (ebk)
Subjects: LCSH: Juvenile justice, Administration of. | Juvenile
delinquency--Prevention. | Juvenile courts.
Classification: LCC HV9069 .S84 2022 (print) | LCC HV9069 (ebook) |
DDC 364.36--dc23
LC record available at https://lccn.loc.gov/2021020200
LC ebook record available at https://lccn.loc.gov/2021020201

ISBN: 978-0-367-42277-6 (hbk)
ISBN: 978-1-032-10735-6 (pbk)
ISBN: 978-0-367-82312-2 (ebk)

DOI: 10.4324/9780367823122

Typeset in Bembo
by Taylor & Francis Books

Contents

Illustrations

Figures

Tables

Chapter 1

Risk and Needs Assessment and Effective Juvenile Justice Practice

The operations of the juvenile justice system build on a series of discretionary decisions made about a diverse group of youths who have become involved in the system because of varying degrees of misbehavior. Like the adult criminal justice system, in the last few decades juvenile courts and corrections have largely moved from unstructured, professional judgment to relying more on structured assessment processes as a precursor to making placement and treatment decisions, theoretically limiting discretion and affecting the decisions made by juvenile justice actors. Referring to juvenile probation systems, Wachter (2015) reports that more than two-thirds of U.S. states have now adopted standardized statewide assessments and many others have regional or local assessment tools. He goes on to mention that risk assessments are often "the foundation of evidence-based practices, enhancing efforts to treat offenders, reduce recidivism, and ultimately increase public safety" (p. 1). More broadly, proponents of the Risk-Needs-Responsivity (RNR) model of intervention suggest that effective treatment requires systematic assessment as a first step (Bonta, 2002). Such usages heighten the importance of this aspect of the juvenile justice process as it can have cascading effects on a range of decisions by court and correctional personnel, which are expected to affect youth outcomes for the better.

Juvenile Risk and Needs Assessment (JRNA) tools frequently contribute to more systematic decision-making, but several dimensions of related policy and procedure require further examination and analysis to ensure that these processes are effective, efficient, and fair when implemented in the juvenile justice system. The recent wide-scale adoption of these tools in systems with a dual mission of ensuring child wellbeing and administration of justice necessitates a close look at their impact to consider what the process and outcomes mean for justice-involved youths, public safety, and agencies themselves. This is particularly important given the inherent variation in the cases and contexts in which the JRNA process is applied (Sullivan, 2019).

DOI: 10.4324/9780367823122-1

The Scope of JRNA

Risk factors are events or influences in the individual, family, peer group, or community that increase the likelihood that a youth will engage in delinquency or continue that behavior if it has already started (Loeber, 1990). Needs are related to risk factors, but more generally define aspects of the youths' disposition and environment that are important targets for intervention (Vieira, et al., 2009). Frequently, these are dynamic in that they could, theoretically, change because of intervention.

The assessment process involves three steps: (1) gathering information on youths' risks and needs, (2) synthesizing the information collected and deriving risk and need scores (e.g., risk level), and (3) using the assessment results to inform conclusions about juvenile justice cases and facilitate the most effective interventions. This is true whether a probation officer is trying to get a read on a youth by implicitly comparing them to other cases they have seen (i.e., unstructured assessment) *or* by asking a series of pre-determined questions that lead to a score or categorization of their risk and needs (i.e., structured assessment). Likewise, it is true if an intake official or magistrate is attempting to decide about detention based on the seriousness of the offense and questions the youth about his or her family situation *or* working from a standardized set of scores and the police report of the incident. Either way, the result of that process is some conclusion about "risk" for future delinquent behavior and intervention needs.

Assessment permeates the juvenile justice process. Cicourel (1967) and Emerson (1969) both carried out intensive observational and interview-focused studies of the juvenile justice system. In a study that included intensive observation of juvenile justice processes like court hearings and intake or investigation interviews with youths and families, Cicourel (1967, p. 310) asserts that probation officers "seek[s] to develop general theories about the family and the juvenile in order to reconstruct how the participants could have produced actions leading to 'trouble'." He also reports that the process informs the views of other court actors about the case and helps develop conclusions about potential future pathways for the youth. Emerson (1969, p. 101) described the process leading up to juvenile court decisions as one of making "categorizations" of the youth and their offense. This process involved the juvenile court actor's judgment about where the current offense fits into the youth's overall moral character. With that they constructed a makeshift narrative about the youth that led to differing points of emphasis when presenting the case before the court. In other words, was the offense a fleeting response to a social situation or, rather, part of a more enduring pattern of behavior?

Elements of these processes bear close resemblance to contemporary assessment practices as part of the "pitch" or "presentation" made by a court actor, like a probation officer, who is attempting to identify where a youth might be "placed within the sequence of stages of a typical delinquent career" (Emerson, 1969, p. 120). Scott and Steinberg (2009) frame the consideration of youths involved in juvenile justice as a practice of balancing attributions about delinquent choice and character where the conclusions reached about the two ultimately affect how cases are handled individually and as sets.

Such links between the specific and general, or the individual case and the average of a group, are a fundamental premise of assessment practices. In formal assessment, statistical averages are developed based on samples of cases and then used to develop scoring systems and cutoffs. Those scores and categorizations are in turn applied to decisions made in similar cases—presumably after the assessment tool is validated. This applies knowledge from prior samples to make decisions about future cases and groups and reflects a desire to situate cases in some broader frame of reference in identifying appropriate case dispositions and treatments for youths. The process is seemingly more systematic with contemporary assessment tools, but its main objective and many of its characteristics remain the same. Even objective assessments require translation of information from the youth, his or her family, and prior record material to a formal scoring process. This frequently involves judgments—based on underlying processes—like those described by Emerson or Cicourel, which in some ways stretch back to the early work of William Healy and colleagues in Chicago's Juvenile Court Clinic (Healy, 1912; 1913). In this way, identifying the nature of cases and generating ideas about how to best respond is and has always been a central focus of the juvenile justice process.

In contemporary practice, JRNA is used in jurisdictions across the country and touches multiple stages of the juvenile justice process within states and local settings. Ohio, for example, uses a risk assessment tool comprising common risk factor items, like history of school suspension, in domains such as education and employment, across diversion, detention, disposition, residential facility, and reentry stages (Latessa et al., 2009). Florida's Department of Juvenile Justice (FDJJ) uses a set of three assessments that cover prevention and diversion cases, a community supervision tool, and a residential assessment) (Florida Department of Juvenile Justice, 2014).[1] The first of the three targets cases that have not penetrated the system and therefore require early intervention. The Community Assessment Tool (CAT) is meant to determine the necessary depth of system intervention because of the youths' needs and likelihood of reoffending. The residential assessment (i.e., Residential Assessment for Youth [RAY]) guides services in secure facilities and helps to assess change and readiness for release from custody. Louisiana's Office of Juvenile Justice relies on the Structure Assessment of Violence Risk in Youth (SAVRY) to inform disposition, treatment, and release readiness decisions. Other stages of the system (i.e., diversion, detention, drug court, prevention) rely on a variety of structured and non-structured screening or assessment tools.

The use of the three-step assessment process dictates that multiple facets of a youth's experience in the juvenile court, corrections agencies, and services draw on their categorizations and scores. Of the approximately 750,000 youths who reach the juvenile justice system each year (Sickmund et al., 2020), nearly all are categorized based on some type of systematic assessment tool. If these assessments and broader systems work as intended, the results, at least in part, affect a variety of decisions made in resolving delinquency cases. The range of those possible decisions include whether to: (1) formally process the case, handle it informally, or not pursue it at all (diversion or prevention screening and assessment); (2) hold a youth in custody as the case progresses through the court process (detention assessments); (3) utilize community-based sanctions or residential placement (disposition assessments); (4) determine community supervision levels and treatment referrals (disposition or community assessments); (5) assign security levels, make housing placements and match youths to treatment and services (residential assessments); (6) identify necessary supervision levels and treatment needs as youths transition from residential facilities back to their community (reentry assessments); and (7) determine release readiness (e.g., release, reentry, or community assessments).

Considering this coverage across the juvenile justice system, the scoring and categorization of the assessment process can have a significant impact on the outcomes of juvenile justice cases ranging from the least to the most restrictive sanction, as well as the juvenile justice system's allocation of time and resources. These impacts are both immediate, as well as longer term in the sense that youths may be affected by decisions about whether they remain in the community (Gatti et al., 2009; Petrosino et al., 2013) or are placed in a detention facility during the court hearing process or in a residential commitment program (Steinhart, 2006; Wordes & Jones, 1998). The assessments are also meant to guide intervention allocation and intensity such that the results of the assessment process also impact the juvenile justice system's treatment objectives (Vieira et al., 2009; Vincent et al., 2012). Although specific protocols may vary by tools and across juvenile justice agencies, the step of conducting systematic risk and needs assessment is also insightful in understanding the processes utilized, the decisions that result, and the related case, youth, and system outcomes.

The introduction and development of systematic assessment processes are also meant to facilitate both general juvenile justice system-wide changes and specific usage of evidence-based interventions with youths. The Ohio Youth Assessment System (OYAS) described previously, for instance, is meant in part to facilitate shifts in placement trends at the local and state levels (Ohio Department of Youth Services, 2012). This is also the case in Louisiana where several local jurisdictions experienced a significant reduction in the use of out of home placements and an increase in the utilization of evidence-based treatment services after the introduction of the SAVRY (e.g., Childs et al., 2011). The Annie E. Casey Foundation's Juvenile Detention Alternatives Initiative (JDAI), which is now operational in hundreds of counties and more than half of the states in the U.S. (The Annie E. Casey Foundation, 2014), is largely predicated on the use of risk assessment as a factor in case-level decision-making to promote community-based alternatives to secure detention. Writing about the role of risk assessment in JDAI, Steinhart (2006, p. 5) describes the objectives and process as follows:

> Detention risk screening is a fundamental strategy used to achieve these detention reform objectives. Risk screening is the process of evaluating each arrested minor to determine the need for secure, locked confine-ment…The overall risk score is then used to guide the intake officer in making the critical decision whether to detain or release an arrested youth. RAIs [Risk Assessment Instruments] are locally designed, and they vary in scope and format from site to site.

JRNA is clearly now a part of both the juvenile justice system's recent transformation and reforms *and* its day-to-day operations. Depending on its effectiveness and efficiency, it can also serve as a means of moving some of those larger initiatives, like JDAI or justice reinvestment, into routine prac-tice. In Ohio, for example, the assessment processes described on p. 28 are an important input into efforts to reduce the population of youths com-mitted to state facilities and appropriately match youths to effective alter-natives (Gies, 2015). In Louisiana, the assessments are part of the broader statewide goals of increasing the use of alternatives to formal processing and evidence-based intervention and reducing out of home placements and disproportionate minority contact. In Florida, assessment results are incor-porated into statewide efforts to monitor intervention effectiveness and positive youth outcomes using the Standardized Program Evaluation Pro-tocol (SPEP, see Baglivio et al., 2018). This suggests that understanding JRNA requires a review not only of the tools themselves but also how they fit with and affect the processing of youths.

Reaching Conclusions

These cases and uses illustrate that, whether it is a general categorization of risk or a formal risk score, justice officials reach conclusions about a youth based on an assessment and, in turn, that process is used to inform individual case processing, disposition, and referral to treatment services—at least in most instances. At a broader level, the foundation for using these processes is that they are superior to previous approaches based more heavily on the unstructured professional judgment and discretion of juvenile justice per-sonnel. There is a great deal of logic and empirical support for such assertions, making it difficult to argue for less systematization when agencies are dealing with a high volume of cases with numerous, relatively unique risks and needs (and combinations of both) (Sullivan, 2019). However, this process generates two fundamental, big picture questions. First, how well does the process of reaching case-level conclusions work? Second, how is that information then used to reach appropriate decisions?

Given the imprimatur that comes with being "evidence-based," there is a danger in making too many assumptions about the value of the new assessment approach such that there is complacency in thoroughly investigating the internal properties of the tools, their usage in decision-making, best practices in implementation, and the degree to which there may be unanticipated consequences or tradeoffs that require further consideration. Attention to such detail is also relevant in how the empirical evidence about JRNA tool effectiveness is conveyed to those administering JRNAs in the field as well as those doing related policy and planning work (Manski, 2013). At this point, the reach of these tools suggests that these questions have largely been settled, but a closer look at the scope and depth of the evidence reveals more questions to investigate. This should not be an "either/or" question, but rather focus on continuous quality improvement so that agencies are effectively using these tools for better decision-making and youth outcomes (Hamilton et al., 2021).

Understudied Aspects of Juvenile Risk and Needs Assessment

With this increased, almost ubiquitous, usage of JRNA and perceptions that juvenile justice decisions are now more evidence based as a result, the stakes for JRNA are high. With their widespread use, these assessments fundamentally impact agency practice and planning, effective intervention, public safety, and youth development. Nevertheless, there are several places where the research base for JRNA effectiveness and usefulness could be expanded. Implementation facilitators and barriers still require elaboration; the utility of the tools beyond predicting recidivism could use more evaluation (i.e., usefulness for identifying and addressing needs); and questions of equity and fairness must be contended with as well. These types of questions arguably take less priority than initial validation of the tools, which largely reflects a simple "proof of concept" stage in a continuum of evidence development and implementation (Harrell, 2006), but are required to fully move the evidence into practice in a sustainable way.

A systematic assessment of this new and improved way of doing juvenile justice requires a multi-dimensional evaluation that incorporates its lesser-discussed and tested aspects. Such a holistic approach is critical to understanding how JRNA practices work for all relevant stakeholders, especially youth. With that, further insight on how JRNA is working now and the potential for future improvement can be obtained. Certainly, it is important to consider first order questions about whether a tool can produce useful predictions, but a wider lens for evaluating JRNA is needed to facilitate optimal and equitable decisions.

A Settled Research Area?

The widespread adoption of assessment tools reflects the perception that they are effective at predicting recidivism and making other pertinent case decisions and therefore are a net advantage in juvenile justice practice. In other words, they offer an evidence-based source of information about individual cases to feed into the juvenile justice decision process. Still, research suggests that there is important variation in effectiveness depending on the research and implementation context. For example, a meta-analysis revealed a good deal of variability in predictive validity (see Schwalbe, 2007) and a study of one state's assessment system found a great deal of local variability (McCafferty, 2016), perhaps due to differences in fidelity of implementation, variability in local populations, or other factors that are infrequently considered in predictive validity research.

Drawing firm insight from these initial findings remains a challenge due to the state of current research. Too often the emphasis in research on JRNA is heavy on "ends justifies means" questions focused on whether the overall risk score or level derived from the process is associated with recidivism (i.e., predictive validity). In this way, it is not unlike other areas of evaluation where research is weighted toward questions pertaining to a focal outcome (i.e., does this practice or program work?) with less attention on the questions of *how, where,* and *for whom* it works (Pawson & Tilley, 1998; Sampson et al., 2013; Wikström, 2008). In measurement and assessment theory and research, which is the origin of these assessment tools, several questions come up when discussing validity, including those related to content validity, external validity, and reliability in administering and scoring the tool.[2] The full range of questions has rarely been addressed in JRNA studies, although they are essential for understanding how well JRNA will affect youths and alter system practices and decisions.

Good or poor predictive validity may emerge in several ways, but it is unclear why without looking further into the mechanisms by which risk and need information affects decisions and youth outcomes. In JRNA, the notion of heterogeneity in results within samples and across studies on a given tool is obscured—potentially to the detriment of both research and practice—without moving beyond merely analyzing the correlation between risk assessment information and recidivism. Without research into these mechanisms, it can be difficult to know what to make of those findings and a lot of lurking uncertainties could affect the quality of risk and needs assessment and related decisions. For example, does that same relationship between risk categories and recidivism hold true for multiple subgroups in the youth population or at different phases of the juvenile justice process? Do prediction errors, including false negatives and false positives, occur at similar rates for boys compared to girls or youths at different developmental stages? Are services available to meet the needs of all young offenders, regardless of extralegal factors? The information gathered from the assessment is not just meant to score or categorize but rather to better treat youth and improve their outcomes. The assessment is a measure at one end of a process and then recidivism is captured at the other end. This carries little insight on the process by which assessment information may be used to facilitate better decision-making and system responses to delinquent youths.

While some have studied how assessment tools work with respect to juvenile court and treatment decisions (Vieira et al., 2009; Vincent et al., 2012), the degree to which this process works as intended and where it fits relative to other influences on juvenile justice decision-making is still relatively unclear. That question certainly has not been systematically evaluated with each major tool and implementation context in the field to the same extent as predictive validity. This means that the basic question of whether decisions are in fact made differently with these tools than without are also unresolved and the logic model underlying their implementation has not been fully investigated (e.g., are detention decisions more appropriate after introduction of a systematic assessment tool? Does the assessment enhance individualized matching of youths to treatment?). As Baird and his colleagues (2013, p. 120) argue, "when the ultimate purpose of risk assessment is to reduce a youth's risk of recidivism, predictive utility is a necessary—but not sufficient—measure of success."

A more thorough consideration of the evidence requires greater attention to existing research questions, as well as expanding the scope of the research agenda on JRNA to touch on pieces of the evaluation process that have received little attention to date. This involves evaluation of the usage and results of the tools themselves and their subcomponents as well as the implementation of assessment and usage in applied juvenile justice settings. These inquiries must consider not only the items and constructs of interest, but also investigate the relevant information gathering process used to generate a score or categorization of youths and follow it forward in its use. A study of JRNA implementation by Sullivan and colleagues (2019) found that administrators of the same assessment tool sometimes used different material to gather information prior to scoring the assessment. For example, some relied heavily on previous officially recorded information, others put more stock in youth self-reports, and all varied in the extent to which they accessed and used collateral information. This inherently embeds some variability and subjectivity into scores and risk levels, which are typically considered to be more objective than professional judgments. The degree of evidence-based support for JRNA requires a more deliberate evaluation of its potential implications, incorporating potential alternatives or enhancements to current practice where it falls short.

This elaboration of the evidence base is especially relevant if agencies hope to use the information gathered from these assessments for any purposes besides simply projecting risk. For instance, if the subdomains of family or educational needs do not have face, content, or predictive validity, the results cannot effectively inform needs in that specific area. The whole assessment is important, but the parts must be in order as well if it is to effectively inform the range of decisions that are meant to follow from the results. Therefore, holistic research on JRNA requires evaluation that reflects its varied uses in the juvenile justice system. Similarly, if the summary and domain-based information in the tool does not enhance treatment matching then it may not impact case, agency, or system-level outcomes— regardless of its predictive validity.

To some extent, the research and adoption of these tools has only indirectly maintained its contact with the initial principles of this line of research and theory. While many of the tools utilized in JRNA do have origins in psychological assessment and therefore draw in part on those foundations, the lack of a strong measurement tradition in criminology and criminal justice to rival psychometrics undoubtedly has an impact on the strength of assessment methods in the justice system (Sullivan & McGloin, 2014). This is detrimental from the standpoint of thoroughly considering initial questions around effectiveness and identifying secondary evaluation questions that may be relevant to contemporary policies and practice for JRNA. Revisiting measurement theory and research first developed and elaborated in early work on systematic assessment by Meehl (1954) and other pioneers in this field is beneficial as a reminder that how the assessment is conducted and used is just as important as the fact that one is used at all. Other fields like education and psychology utilize standardized testing and assessment with youth development (Kazdin, 2005; Messick, 1984; Meyer et al., 2001) and therefore provide a point of comparison, and perhaps insight, when thinking about the application of systematic assessment in the juvenile justice system. The construction and use of assessment information also requires attention to basic premises of inferences about central tendency, variability, and covariation in statistical estimation, which are relevant to all empirical research in crime and justice settings (Maltz, 1994), but take on specific connotations and have practical implications in the case of JRNA.

Relatedly, since moving research to practice is only partly about the evidence for the assessment (e.g., predictive validity), it is difficult to know how these tools work without more insight on implementation and real-world application. The movement toward this new routine practice in JRNA certainly alters how information gathering on youths is achieved and affects how it is packaged for later decision-making. Developing a better sense of how these tools operate in the real world requires a greater focus on research about implementation drivers like staff buy-in, staff skills and training relative to assessment processes, and systems for decision-making support (Fixsen et al., 2009; Vincent et al., 2012; 2018). While there has been considerable emphasis on elements of validity in each tool, it is inherently part of a package with accompanying policies and practices to improve decision-making. Even when using a validated assessment instrument, the quality of implementation and usage in the field determines its effectiveness. Consequently, JRNA implementation requires close consideration both as a means of understanding the gap between assessment in theory and in practice and offering insight on obstacles and promotive factors in moving research into practice effectively in the future.

Assuming it works as intended, the introduction of a systematic assessment tool for JRNA is a unique technology transfer process as it inherently shifts some of the process of forming judgments and acting on them from individualized professional judgment to empirically established benchmarks. In that sense, this implementation process may differ from introducing a new treatment program, as the intent is to embed the tool and related practice entirely in the day-to-day activities of juvenile justice personnel. This requires a more intensive look at not just the validity of tools, which is currently a bit narrow in and of itself, but also greater depth in determining their effects on the day-to-day decision-making of juvenile justice actors. This includes attention to sustainability, optimization of use, and continuous quality improvement that must occur in agencies to ensure that the tool is used effectively. Developing and testing a tool is just one part of the evaluation life cycle of JRNA.

Labels, Judgment, and Assessment of Youths

The premise of assessment and its usage aligns with broader attempts to address delinquent behavior. The reaction to delinquency, which is frequently fleeting in its occurrence (Farrington, 1986; Moffitt, 1993; Sweeten et al., 2013), can exacerbate or elongate a delinquent career. From this standpoint, the label or score that comes with the assessment process (e.g., "high risk") is an inherent object of interest. Beyond questions of fairness and the long-held belief in youths' malleability by the juvenile justice system, there is also the possibility that such assessments may backfire and increase the likelihood of recidivism through subsequent social responses and reflected self-appraisals of youths (Lemert, 1951; Liberman et al., 2014; Paternoster & Iovanni, 1989). These designations also have policy connotations as the language applied to delinquency cases individually or more broadly can signal an orientation toward their treatment by framing the problem at hand. Singer (1996, p. 15) discusses the "distinct classes of labels" that may be applied to juveniles and how that process affects broad policy and responses to individual cases. All of this means that in reacting to justice-involved youths—especially those who are very young or have limited prior delinquency histories—the labels produced in the assessment processes and the associated consequences require careful analysis.

This question of labeling raises an operational issue in assessment practices. While researchers recommend reassessment to track and characterize change (Douglas & Skeem, 2005) and some agencies certainly require that in their systems (see, e.g., Baglivio, 2009), the commonality of such reassessment has not been studied that often. Without such updating, original conclusions may persist in a fixed way and affect subsequent decisions. This also raises questions about the different ways that system actors assess risk and make decisions about it. They may form impressions based on the pattern of results that emerge—even if there are elements of that scoring that tend to build on stability in risk. For example, continued inclusion of items that are more historic in nature, like prior juvenile justice contact, inherently builds stability into observed risk scores regardless of continued reassessment. Questions about whether (1) resources to address identified risks and needs are available and (2) assessments are appropriately updated over time to capture potential change therefore are important in fully evaluating the usage and impact of JRNA.

These points about labeling suggest that the system generally will reach a characterization—even implicitly—for each case, but it is nevertheless important to consider what that means given the presumption that it is based on systematic research or evidence. Evaluation of assessment tools and subsequent decisions therefore must be mindful of ideas and research about the formation of judgments, how they affect decisions, and their persistence or potential for change (Bell et al., 1988; Tversky & Kahneman, 1974). As the dissemination and use of assessment tools has advanced in recent decades, so too has the research on how individuals and professionals make decisions. Consequently, insight from research on decision theory and bounded rationality is useful in considering how the results of these tools might affect individual cases. So, for example, the objective of these tools is to ensure more rational and systematic decision-making, but there is also evidence to suggest that (in)numeracy affects how people frame risk and the resultant decisions (Reyna et al., 2009), which is particularly pertinent in the implementation and usage of JRNA (i.e., since it is based on statistical estimates).

Increasing evidence from cognitive psychology and behavioral economics suggests that fully understanding the reality of decision making is more challenging than when assuming a closed-system, purely rational model of human decision making that ignores the pull of emotion and subjectivity (Lerner et al., 2015; Simon, 1967). The underlying logic of risk and needs assessment in the justice system assumes that the introduction of systematic information into the process will improve the quality of decisions by reducing the subjectivity that plays a role in discretionary decisions. The decision-maker's assimilation and use of the assessment information, therefore, is one aspect of a system of interrelated parts that surrounds the use of JRNA, as opposed to a fully independent data point or intervention (Dhami, 2003). While this is an untapped area of research in JRNA usage, it does suggest the need for more work on the fit of structured assessment into existing frameworks for juvenile justice decisions.

Better insight on human cognition and its between-individual variation has the potential to improve understanding of how people make decisions (Thaler, 2000). This is necessary in the case of JRNA as seminal work on the movement of research to practice suggests that—even in cases where decision-makers incorporate science—they may not do so in the ways anticipated by researchers (Weiss & Bucuvalas, 1980). The evolution of JRNA means that juvenile justice personnel have insight and, frequently, intensive training on how to identify risk and need and systematically collate that information. Frequently, however, the JRNA administrator is not the same person making the case decisions. Even so, those involved still filter that information through heuristics and biases. This is evident when practitioners compare the results of the assessment process against their own professional view of a youth's risk level (Guy et al., 2014; Sullivan et al., 2019).

Research, Technology, and Fairness in JRNA Usage

Technological advances in risk assessment and predictive modeling have made assessments more practical, but fundamental questions about the quality and certainty of those predictions remain despite any advances in the research on JRNA. Often, these come down to questions about the information used in scoring, its production, and its implications for fairness in decision-making. Schwalbe (2007) reviewed 28 studies of the predictive validity of juvenile risk assessments. He found moderate predictive strength for juvenile recidivism based on the use of information from risk assessments. The main study association of 0.25 on a correlation scale (range: 00 to 1.0) and a test of aggregate predictive strength (AUC [Area Under the Curve] = .64 with .50 being akin to a "coin flip" determination of the likelihood of reoffending) were strong relative to previous research, but still far from perfectly predictive. The AUC value indicates that, if 100 youths were assessed and followed up, probabilistically 64 percent of the time a randomly chosen youth from that sample "indicated for" the chosen outcome (i.e., recidivated) will have a higher score than a youth "not indicated" for that outcome (Rice & Harris, 1995; Schwalbe, 2007). While this is a relative improvement over the 50 percent that comes with a simple coin flip, it nevertheless raises some research and value-based questions about the use of JRNA given that 36 of those 100 cases could tie or have reversed rankings on their assessment scores.[3]

The effectiveness of assessment tools is driven in part by the degree to which within-group variation (e.g., low, moderate, and high risk) is minimized and between-group variation is maximized (Gottfredson, 1987). That is the only way to be certain that the individual case is reasonably reflective of the broader characterization of the statistically generated group. This within-group variation also has important implications for fairness. Although juvenile justice system personnel, who can disregard the assessment information in whole or part, make those decisions, each youth and case still possess its own nuances that may be informative for placement and treatment decisions. Many strands of assessment practice inherently change the emphasis from properties of individual cases to outcomes of previous statistically generated groups. Silver and Miller (2002, p. 152) identify the potential problems with this approach:

> Actuarial risk assessment tools classify a heterogeneous population into more or less homogenous subgroups, transforming the unit of analysis from the individual to the aggregate. Individuality is reduced to a combination of risk factors that based on their associations with other factors in the population aggregate, reflect various levels of risk...To be placed in a particular risk category, it is enough to display the appropriate combination of characteristics identified as risk markers. The individual is transformed from an autonomous subject who may or may not choose to engage in a particular behavior to a nexus of factors made meaningful by the levels of risk they represent in the aggregate.

A full assessment of the risk assessment process therefore requires a consideration of this interdependence between the case and the group in decision-making.

Too frequently, questions about the equity and appropriateness of structured assessment are secondary in research and practice, even though similar questions have come up in previous policy discussions involving prediction in justice decision-making (see, e.g., Auerhahn, 1999; Greenwood & Abrahamse, 1982). This is problematic due to the implications of applying JRNA-based labels for immediate decisions about youths (e.g., high or low risk) as well as their later implications for juvenile justice involvement and other aspects of youths' lives, like peer relationships and educational attainment. With that, a comprehensive consideration of JRNA requires some emphasis on the nature of the information gathered and its use from the perspective of its fairness—particularly among disadvantaged or vulnerable subgroups or those who may not fit as well with the objectives of a given tool.

The question of inappropriate, race-correlated factors perpetuating disproportionate minority contact is particularly salient in the juvenile justice system. Most existing research pertaining to risk and needs assessment and race focus primarily on predictive validity (i.e., does the tool predict equally well for different groups? see, e.g., Baglivio & Jackowski, 2013; Vincent et al., 2011). These studies yield mixed findings, but generally support the use of the tools across different subgroups. Evidence of similar predictive validity informs the basic fairness of use question, but other aspects of the information gathering and assessment process can affect equity as well. For example, whether there is measurement invariance across groups determines similarity in assessing risk and need across the groups. This in turn has implications for whether specific risk and needs domains work similarly across subgroups as well as the degree to which the assessment captures the same nature and degree of risk (i.e., is the nature and impact of family risk analogous across different race groups?). The relationship between race and socioeconomic status (SES), for instance, suggests that family structure and process risk indicators may have differential prevalence and potentially different impacts on behavior for different race and SES groups.

The limited research on this question requires greater attention to the possibility that these assessments may be differentially predictive or are tapping distinct risk profiles across groups. These questions inherently move the conversation from merely whether the tools "work" on some benchmark to what their use means for the fairness of decisions made in the juvenile justice system (and how they impact cases). This was the main impetus for former U.S. Attorney General Eric Holder to recommend that the federal Sentencing Commission study the impact of the use of risk assessment in sentencing criminal defendants (Horwitz, 2014). The need to balance effectiveness and appropriateness stretches back to the origins of the juvenile court as improving youths' long-term life chances was a priority alongside short-term public safety goals (Bernard & Kurlychek, 2010; Scott & Steinberg, 2009; Tanenhaus, 2004). Some approaches, like incarceration for incapacitation purposes, may be effective for short-term crime control, but have problematic residual outcomes over the long-term including increased risk of chronic offending, poor educational and economic outcomes, and higher system costs. Thus, juvenile risk assessment may engender potential unintended consequences—despite acceptable predictive validity.

These questions speak to the limits of a fully technocratic, research-based approach to handling justice-involved youths. Or, at the very least they serve as reminders of the need for thorough study of where and when research can contribute to the operations of the juvenile justice system—and the limitations of that evidence—with an eye toward expanding the information used and the voices heard in adoption and implementation processes. At this stage, the research on JRNA is highly focused on its benefits without nearly as much consideration of costs, challenges, or unintended consequences.

Given the current scope of use and possible impacts of JRNA, it is a good time to assess, synthesize, and reach firmer conclusions about the various information inputs into these processes. We must closely analyze the nature and process of JRNA in its implications for individual cases, justice-involved youths, and allocation of agency resources. Mitigation of concerns like those of Silver and Miller (2002) is possible if the risk and needs assessment process leads to better placements and more access to treatment for most youths. Addressing this at the case level requires enumeration of routine safety valves for those instances that do not fit the statistical regularities behind the development and usage of JRNAs. These cost versus benefit questions await answers. In fact, they seem to be asked only occasionally, which leaves a gap in fully understanding the implications of JRNA practices. This gap detracts from the potential optimal use of JRNA in these impactful system decisions.

A More Complete Consideration of JRNA

The research on JRNA is extensive, but by no means exhaustive or definitive in answering the questions that must be resolved to enhance practice and consider other facets of procedures and uses that should factor into policy discussions. Given the juxtaposition of widespread adoption and numerous unanswered, but potentially important questions, this book will evaluate JRNA from a multi-faceted viewpoint to develop a deeper sense of where the practice currently stands and identify potential future improvements—in effect answering some of the questions highlighted earlier and identifying important lines of inquiry for the future. At this point, the field testing and policy analysis phases of studying JRNAs, which were identified in Harrell's (2006) continuum of evaluation for dissemination, have not been fully accomplished. This continuum progresses from first establishing potential efficacy to assessment of prospects for scaling up/generalizability and analyzing costs and benefits. Without addressing the full continuum, the available research remains limited and important questions surrounding optimal implementation and usage of JRNA await more definitive answers.

To set up our analysis, we develop a contextualized, multi-faceted framework for the JRNA process. We draw heavily on existing research that is both directly pertinent to JRNA topics as well as classic and contemporary work that is informative to its practice, but often overlooked. We will also conduct new analyses on questions important to improving the understanding of JRNA from a multi-faceted perspective. In doing so, we will consider several topics that appear infrequently in the research and discussion of JRNA. This includes implementation practices, moving beyond predictive validity in assessing tool performance, and providing clearer linkages from administration to scoring and categorization to subsequent decision-making. Following that analysis, we will then offer conclusions about the next generation of JRNA research, policy, and practice.

Chapter 2 will focus on the history and current application of JRNA by reviewing reports on practice and the related body of research. It also provides a critical look at the sampling, measurement, and analytic processes used in existing JRNA research to reach conclusions about the state of the evidence and its implications for practice. Chapter 3 builds on this initial description and key findings from the research synthesized in Chapter 2 by presenting the theoretical framework and guiding principles for the use of JRNA and then outlining the logic model embedded in the JRNA processes. Chapter 3 also reviews research on the relevant outcomes highlighted in the logic model and evaluates the different elements of JRNA research and practice. This chapter enumerates the main objectives of the JRNA process. These two chapters highlight areas of evaluation that warrant further consideration in the theory and practice of JRNA.

Chapter 4 focuses heavily on JRNA as a case study in implementation science allowing for an assessment not only of the scope of these practices but also the effectiveness and efficiency of implementation. Chapter 5 likewise focuses on practice but is more intent on considering broader implications relevant to the legal grounding for assessment, policies that structure and contextualize its use, and fairness and broader philosophical issues in its application.

Building on the synthesis of evidence to that point, Chapter 6 establishes the value of reintegrating underlying theoretical elements of the use of risk and needs assessment based on (1) decision-making theories, (2) extant justice research, and (3) principles of measurement and statistical analysis pertinent to the practice of JRNA (Chapter 6). In Chapter 7 we make several recommendations for the next phase of JRNA practice and research based on the preceding multi-faceted analysis and a consideration of benefits and possible downsides.

Given the scope of current usage, and its likely expansion in the future, JRNA has the potential to significantly impact youths and families, public safety, and juvenile justice practices. Seemingly, JRNA should produce effective and fair decisions, with efficiency in implementation for those who work in the system and related stakeholders. This effectiveness, fairness, and efficiency determines the net impact of the practice on a case-by-case basis as well as the system planning decisions made based on those conclusions. JRNA affects youths, communities, and the juvenile justice agencies that have adopted its practices (National Research Council, 2013). While the last few decades of research and practice have led to a greater grounding of juvenile justice assessment in evidence, that evidence should be studied systematically so that the label "evidence-based" can fully carry the meaning intended and not become a cloak for shortcomings in the foundations and usage of JRNA. Given the number of youths who encounter the juvenile justice system and their varying degrees of needs and potential risk, the stakes are high in ensuring that we thoroughly study such a ubiquitous practice to consider its current impacts and future potential.

Notes

1 The FDJJ revised their assessment instruments in 2019. Prior to this time, the FDJJ used the PACT as the primary community assessment tool. As a result, we refer to the CAT when discussing current FDJJ risk assessment protocols and we refer to the PACT when discussing FDJJ research or data prior to 2019.
2 Researchers do assess "responsivity" based on risk levels in the context of correctional treatment, but these questions generally receive less attention than simple predictive validity studies using recidivism as an outcome. Questions involving "for whom" can pertain to the assessment itself and the implementation setting.
3 This does not consider the other information available based on the overall risk and needs score or its various dimensions (e.g., substance use, educational risk). We assess this question more comprehensively later in the book.

References

Auerhahn, K. (1999). Selective incapacitation and the problem of prediction. *Criminology*, 37(4), 703–734.

Baglivio, M.T. (2009). The assessment of risk to recidivate among a juvenile offending population. *Journal of Criminal Justice*, 37(6), 596–607. doi:10.1016/j.jcrimjus.2009.09.008.

Baglivio, M.T., & Jackowski, K. (2013). Examining the validity of a juvenile offending risk assessment instrument across gender and race/ethnicity. *Youth Violence and Juvenile Justice*, 11(1), 26–43. doi:10.1177/1541204012440107.

Baglivio, M.T., Wolff, K.T., Howell, J.C., Jackowski, K., & Greenwald, M.A. (2018). The search for the holy grail: Criminogenic needs matching, intervention dosage, and subsequent recidivism among serious juvenile offenders in residential placement. *Journal of Criminal Justice*, 55, 46–57. doi:10.1016/j.jcrimjus.2018.02.001.

Baird, C., Healy, T., Johnson, K., Bogie, A., Dankert, E.W., & Scharenbroch, C. (2013). *A comparison of risk assessment instruments in juvenile justice*. Madison, WI: National Council on Crime and Delinquency. www.ojp.gov/pdffiles1/ojjdp/grants/244477.pdf.

Bell, D.E., Raiffa, H., & Tversky, A. (Eds.). (1988). *Decision making: Descriptive, normative, and prescriptive interactions*. Cambridge University Press.

Bernard, T.J., & Kurlychek, M.C. (2010). *The cycle of juvenile justice*. New York: Oxford University Press.

Bonta, J. (2002). Offender risk assessment: Guidelines for selection and use. *Criminal Justice and Behavior*, 29(4), 355–379. doi:10.1177/0093854802029004002.

Childs, K.K., Ryals, J., Frick, P.J., & Phillippi, S.W. (2011). *Jefferson parish youth outcomes study*. New Orleans, LA: MacArthur Foundation.

Cicourel, A.V. (1967). Fertility, family planning and the social organization of family life: Some methodological issues 1. *Journal of Social Issues*, 23(4), 57–81.

Dhami, M.K. (2003). Psychological models of professional decision making. *Psychological Science*, 14(2), 175–180.

Douglas, K.S., & Skeem, J.L. (2005). Violence risk assessment: Getting specific about being dynamic. *Psychology, Public Policy, and Law*, 11(3), 347–383. doi:10.1037/1076-8971.11.3.347.

Emerson, R.M. (1969). *Judging delinquents*. New Brunswick, NJ: Transaction Publishers.

Farrington, D.P. (1986). Age and crime. *Crime and Justice*, 7, 189–250. doi:10.1086/449114.

Fixsen, D.L., Blase, K.A., Naoom, S.F., & Wallace, F. (2009). Core implementation components. *Research on Social Work Practice*, 19, 531–540. doi:10.1177/1049731509335549.

Florida Department of Juvenile Justice (2014). *Pact Assessment System Overview*. Retrieved in June 2018 from www.djj.state.fl.us/docs/partners-providers-staff/pact-system-overview.pdf?sfvrsn=2.

Gatti, U., Tremblay, R.E., & Vitaro, F. (2009). Iatrogenic effect of juvenile justice. *Journal of Child Psychology and Psychiatry*, 50(8), 991–998.

Gies, R. (2015). *Changing the Footprint of Ohio's Juvenile Justice System*. Presentation given to University of Cincinnati School of Criminal Justice, Cincinnati, OH.

Greenwood, P.W., & Abrahamse, A.F. (1982). *Selective incapacitation* (pp. 11–26). Santa Monica, CA: Rand.

Gottfredson, D.M. (1987). Prediction and classification in criminal justice decision making. *Crime and Justice*, 9, 1–20. doi:10.1086/449130.

Guy, L.S., Nelson, R.J., Fusco-Morin, S.L., & Vincent, G.M. (2014). What do juvenile probation officers think of using the SAVRY and YLS/CMI for case management, and do they use the instruments properly? *International Journal of Forensic Mental Health*, 13(3), 227–241.

Hamilton, Z., Kigerl, A., & Kowalski, M. (2021). Prediction is local: The benefits of risk assessment optimization. *Justice Quarterly*, 1–23.

Harrell, A.V. (2006). Towards systematic knowledge building: An anti-crime research and development continuum. *Journal of Experimental Criminology*, 2(3), 339–344. doi:10.1007/s11292-006-9013-x.

Healy, W. (1912). Problem of causation of criminality. *Journal of the American Institute of Criminal Law and Criminology*, 2(6), 849–857.

Healy, W. (1913). Present day aims and methods in studying the offender. *Journal of the American Institute of Criminal Law and Criminology*, 4(2), 204–211. https://scholarlycommons.law.northwestern.edu/jclc/vol4/iss2/5.

Horwitz, S. (2014). Eric Holder: Basing sentences on data analysis could prove unfair to minorities, August 1, *Washington Post*. Available at www.washingtonpost.com/world/national-security/us-attorney-general-eric-holder-urges-against-data-analysis-in-criminal-sentencing/2014/08/01/92d0f7ba-1990-11e4-85b6-c1451e622637_story.html.

Kazdin, A. (2005). Evidence-based assessment for children and adolescents: Issues in measurement development and clinical application. *Journal of Clinical Child and Adolescent Psychology*, 34(3), 548–558. doi:10.1207/s15374424jccp3403_10.

Latessa, E., Lovins, B., & Ostrowski, K. (2009). *The Ohio youth assessment system: Final report*. Cincinnati, OH: University of Cincinnati, Center for Criminal Justice Research.

Lemert, E. (1951). Primary and secondary deviation. *Crime and Critical Concepts in Sociology*, 3, 603–607.

Lerner, J.S., Li, Y., Valdesolo, P., & Kassam, K.S. (2015). Emotion and decision making. *Annual Review of Psychology*, 66, 799–823.

Liberman, A.M., Kirk, D.S., & Kim, K. (2014). Labeling effects of first juvenile arrests: Secondary deviance and secondary sanctioning. *Criminology*, 52(3), 345–370. doi:10.1111/1745-9125.12039.

Loeber, R. (1990). Development and risk factors of juvenile antisocial behavior and delinquency. *Clinical Psychology Review*, 10(1), 1–41.

Maltz, M.D. (1994). Deviating from the mean: The declining significance of significance. *Journal of Research in Crime and Delinquency*, 31(4), 434–463. doi:10.1177/0022427894031004005.

Manski, C.F. (2013). Status quo deference and policy choice under ambiguity. *Journal of Institutional and Theoretical Economics*, 169, 116–128. doi:10.1628/093245613X660474.

McCafferty, J.T. (2016). The importance of counties: Examining the predictive validity of a state juvenile risk assessment instrument. *Journal of Offender Rehabilitation*, 55(6), 377–395. doi:10.1080/10509674.2016.1194944.

Meehl, P.E. (1954). *Clinical versus statistical prediction: A theoretical analysis and a review of the evidence*. Minneapolis, MN: University of Minnesota Press.

Messick, S. (1984). *The psychology of educational measurement*. Princeton, NJ: Educational Testing Service.

Meyer, G.J., Finn, S.E., Eyde, L.D., Kay, G.G., Moreland, K.L., Dies, R.R., & Reed, G.M.J.A.p. (2001). Psychological testing and psychological assessment: A review of evidence and issues. *American Psychologist*, 56(2), 128–165. doi:10.1037/0003-066X.56.2.128.

Moffitt, T.E. (1993). Adolescence-limited and life-course-persistent antisocial behavior: A developmental taxonomy. *Psychological Review*, 100(4), 674–701. doi:10.1037/0033-295X.100.4.674.

National Research Council (2013). *Reforming juvenile justice: A developmental approach*. Washington, DC: National Academies Press.

Ohio Department of Youth Services (2012). *Ohio department of youth services, fiscal year 2011 annual report*. Columbus, OH: State of Ohio Department of Youth Services.

Paternoster, R., & Iovanni, L. (1989). The labeling perspective and delinquency: An elaboration of the theory and an assessment of the evidence. *Justice Quarterly*, 6(3), 359–394. doi:10.1080/07418828900090261.

Pawson, R., & Tilley, N. (1998). Caring communities, paradigm polemics, design debates. *Evaluation*, 4(1), 73–90.

Petrosino, A., Turpin-Petrosino, C., & Guckenburg, S. (2013). *Formal system processing of juveniles: Effects on delinquency, No. 9*. Washington, DC: U.S. Department of Justice, Office of Community Oriented Policing Services. www.njjn.org/uploads/digital-library/resource_1478.pdf.

Reyna, V.F., Nelson, W.L., Han, P.K., & Dieckmann, N.F. (2009). How numeracy influences risk comprehension and medical decision making. *Psychological Bulletin*, 135(6), 943. doi:10.1037/a0017327.

Rice, M.E., & Harris, G.T. (1995). Violent recidivism: Assessing predictive validity. *Journal of Consulting and Clinical Psychology*, 63(5), 737–748. doi:10.1037/0022-006X.63.5.737.

Sampson, R.J., Winship, C., & Knight, C. (2013). Overview of: "Translating causal claims: principles and strategies for policy-relevant criminology". *Criminology & Public Policy*, 12(4), 585–586. doi:10.1111/1745-9133.12028.

Schwalbe, C.S. (2007). Risk assessment for juvenile justice: A meta-analysis. *Law and Human Behavior*, 31(5), 449–462. doi:10.1007/s10979-006-9071-7.

Scott, E.S., & Steinberg, L.D. (2009). *Rethinking juvenile justice.* Cambridge, MA: Harvard University Press.

Sickmund, M., Sladky, A., & Kang, W. (2020). *Easy access to juvenile court statistics: 1985–2018.* Online. Available: www.ojjdp.gov/ojstatbb/ezajcs/.

Silver, E., & Miller, L.L. (2002). A cautionary note on the use of actuarial risk assessment tools for social control. *Crime & Delinquency,* 48(1), 138–161. doi:10.1177/0011128702048001006.

Simon, H.A. (1967). Motivational and emotional controls of cognition. *Psychological Review,* 74(1), 29–39.

Singer, S.I. (1996). *Recriminalizing delinquency: Violent juvenile crime and juvenile justice reform.* New York: Cambridge University Press.

Steinhart, D. (2006). *Juvenile detention risk assessment: A practice guide to juvenile detention reform.* Annie E. Casey Foundation. www.aecf.org/m/resourceimg/aecf-juve niledetentionriskassessment1–2006.pdf.

Sullivan, C.J. (2019). *Taking juvenile justice seriously: Developmental insights and system challenges.* Philadelphia, PA: Temple University Press.

Sullivan, C.J., & McGloin, J.M. (2014). Looking back to move forward some thoughts on measuring crime and delinquency over the past 50 years. *Journal of Research in Crime and Delinquency,* 51(4), 445–466. doi:10.1177/0022427813520446.

Sullivan, C.J., Strange, C., Sullivan, C., Newsome, J., Lugo, M., Mueller, D., Petkus, A., Holmes, B., Lonergan, H., & McCafferty, J. (2019). *Multi-method study on risk assessment implementation and youth outcomes in the juvenile justice system.* Submitted to Office of Justice Programs, Office of Juvenile Justice and Delinquency Prevention, www.ojp.gov/pdffiles1/ojjdp/grants/252927.pdf.

Sweeten, G., Piquero, A., & Steinberg, L. (2013). Age and the explanation of crime, revisited. *Journal of Youth and Adolescence,* 42(6), 921–938. doi:10.1007/s10964-013-9926-4.

Tanenhaus, D. (2004). *Juvenile justice in the making.* New York: Oxford University Press.

Thaler, R.H. (2000). From homo economicus to homo sapiens. *Journal of Economic Perspectives,* 14(1), 133–141. doi:10.1257/jep.14.1.133.

The Annie E. Casey Foundation (2014). *2014 Juvenile Detention Alternatives Progress Report.* Baltimore, MD: Author. Retrieved from 2014 Juvenile Detention Alternatives Initiative Progress Report (aecf.org).

Tversky, A., & Kahneman, D. (1974). Judgment under uncertainty: Heuristics and biases. *science,* 185(4157), 1124–1131.

Vieira, T.A., Skilling, T.A., & Peterson-Badali, M. (2009). Matching court-ordered services with treatment needs: Predicting treatment success with young offenders. *Criminal Justice & Behavior,* 36(4), 385–401. doi:10.1177/0093854808331249.

Vincent, G.M., Chapman, J., & Cook, N.E. (2011). Risk-needs assessment in juvenile justice: Predictive validity of the SAVRY, racial differences, and the contribution of needs factors. *Criminal Justice & Behavior,* 38(1), 42–62. doi:10.1177/0093854810386000.

Vincent, G.M., Guy, L.S., Gershenson, B.G., & McCabe, P. (2012). Does risk assessment make a difference? Results of implementing the SAVRY in juvenile probation. *Behavioral Sciences & The Law,* 30(4), 384–405. doi:10.1002/bsl.2014.

Vincent, G., Sullivan, C.J., Sullivan, C., Guy, L., Latessa, E., Tyson, J., & Adams, B. (2018). *Studying drivers of risk and needs assessment instrument implementation in juvenile justice*. Washington, DC: Office of Juvenile Justice and Delinquency Prevention. http://nysap.us/assets/publications/risk/Studying%20Drivers%20of%20Risk%20and%20Needs%20Assessment%20Instrument%20Implementation%20in%20Juvenile%20Justice.pdf.

Wachter, A. (2015). *Statewide risk assessment in juvenile probation*. Pittsburgh, PA: National Center for Juvenile Justice.

Weiss, C.H., & Bucuvalas, M.J. (1980). *Social science research and decision-making*. New York: Columbia University Press.

Wikström, P.-O. (2008). In search of causes and explanations of crime. In R. King & E. Wincup (Eds.), *Doing research on crime and justice* (2nd Ed., pp. 117–139). Oxford, UK: Oxford University Press.

Wordes, M., & Jones, S.M. (1998). Trends in juvenile detention and steps toward reform. *Crime & Delinquency*, 44(4), 544–560. doi:10.1177/0011128798044004005.

Chapter 2

Contemporary Juvenile Risk and Needs Assessment

The foundation of early juvenile justice systems was based on two goals: to protect public safety and to rehabilitate justice-involved youths (Bilchik, 1999). As a result, assessments of youths' risk for recidivism and potential for rehabilitation have been a central part of the juvenile justice system since its inception. The potential benefit of formal assessments of offenders' risk and needs came to the forefront in the early 1990s. Since that time, almost all states and local jurisdictions have relied on the use of formal, structured assessment instruments to assist in making juvenile court decisions (see Wachter, 2015). The move toward the use of structured assessment processes reflects three key factors: a significant rise in juvenile violent crime, the recognition of disproportionate decision-making, and the increased utilization of evidence-based practices in the criminal and juvenile justice systems. These issues exemplify the challenges and context faced by the juvenile justice system during the early to late 1990s and highlight how the implementation of JRNA can serve different functions and potentially ameliorate multiple problems within the system.

First, there was a significant rise in the juvenile violent crime rate. From 1985 to 1994, the rate of murder committed by juveniles increased exponentially, the number of juvenile murders that involved a handgun quadrupled, and arrests for serious violent crimes rose significantly (Fox, 1996). These substantial increases in serious youth violence were coupled with stable or decreasing rates of violence among adults. This led advocates and policy makers to call for improved juvenile justice practices for early identification of youths at risk for criminal and violent behavior as well as more intensive and punitive intervention programs for serious and chronic juvenile offenders (Loeber & Farrington, 1999; Wiebush et al., 1995). Support for this approach grew considerably during the 1990s and early 2000s as the juvenile justice system was moving from a punitive approach to a medicalized, evidence-based approach to responding to juvenile delinquency. Achieving these objectives requires use of knowledge and resources that starts with identifying the key risk factors for violent behavior and recidivism (Grisso et al., 2005). As a result, Andrews and colleagues' (1990)

DOI: 10.4324/9780367823122-2

Risk, Needs, Responsivity (RNR) model quickly gained recognition as a guide for efforts to link discretionary decisions with principles of effective intervention. This process entails identifying the risk level of each individual for future violent behavior (i.e., risk), identifying their criminogenic needs for targets of intervention (i.e., needs), and matching offenders' noncriminogenic characteristics to services modalities (i.e., responsivity). Structured risk/needs assessments were viewed by many as an effective strategy to accomplish these goals, and thus became an essential component of implementing the RNR model in justice system settings.

Second, recognition of disparities in juvenile justice decisions across race and ethnicity was also increasing in the 1990s (Kempf-Leonard, 2007). Official data during this time showed that a significantly larger percentage of youths from underrepresented race and ethnicity groups were processed in the juvenile justice system as compared to the general population. For example, national data from the early 1980s showed that minority youths comprised approximately one-third of the adolescent population in the United States but over half to two-thirds of youths in secure detention and residential commitment programs (Hsia et al., 2004). The rate of increase in delinquency cases among minority youths sent to juvenile court was more than double the rate of increase in delinquency cases among White youths. Such discrepancies were referred to as disproportionate minority contact (DMC) then and are now characterized as racial and ethnic disparities (RED).

The severity of racial inequality in the juvenile justice system was recognized by the federal government in the late 1980s with several initiatives including a report submitted to Congress by the Coalition for Juvenile Justice (National Coalition of State Juvenile Justice Advisory Group, 1989), the development of Office of Juvenile Justice Delinquency and Prevention's (OJJDP) technical assistance strategies to address DMC (OJJDP, 2009), and amendments of the Juvenile Justice Delinquency and Prevent Act (JJDP 1988, 1992) that required states to address DMC. Juvenile justice experts have long considered disproportionality to be a multi-faceted and challenging social problem (Cabaniss et al., 2007; Nellis, 2015). A handful of strategies have been identified as potentially effective ways to reduce these disparities. The use of standardized risk assessment procedures is among these strategies due to the removal of subjective decision making via use of systematic and objective assessment instruments (Cabaniss et al., 2007; Poulin et al., 2011).

Third, the movement toward evidence-based policy and practice was coming to the forefront of juvenile justice reform efforts. An evidence-based practice is a program or process that has been shown effective with scientific principles and rigorous research design. The movement was due, in part, to a shift in ideology from the "get-tough" philosophies of the 1980s and early 1990s to an approach centered on research, crime prevention, and cost-effectiveness (Hay et al., 2018; Lipsey et al., 2010). This shift was due to empirical research covering a range of topics including the introduction of the RNR framework of correctional effectiveness (Andrews et al., 1990), cost-benefit analyses of interventions for youths (Aos et al., 2001; Drake et al., 2009), public perceptions of the need for rehabilitation of youths involved in the juvenile justice system (Bishop, 2006; Nagin et al., 2006), and the iatrogenic effects of the unnecessary restrictiveness of juvenile sanctions (Fagan, 1991). Taken together, juvenile justice leaders began to realize the value in relying on policies and programs that have been shown to be effective in rehabilitating delinquent youths and reducing costs (i.e., evidence-based programs). Research supported the ability of the JRNA process to achieve the goals of classification, reduced disparities, and cost-effectiveness through systematizing and streamlining the decision-making process. Thus, the use of JRNA as an evidence-based practice spread quickly. The purpose of this chapter is to define key JRNA terminology, describe the three-step JRNA process, and summarize the research base. Then we highlight a few key limitations to existing research and set the stage for the analysis and discussion in the rest of the book.

JRNA Terminology

Risk is defined as the probability that an offender will engage in future violent or criminal behavior. It is often referred to as risk to reoffend or risk for recidivism, given that assessments of risk are conducted as part of juvenile justice system processing with youths who have committed, or have been accused of committing, at least one delinquent offense. Determinations of risk are often based on discrete categories such as low risk, moderate risk, or high risk. A *risk factor* is a variable, characteristic, or exposure that is associated with an increased probability of offending (Howell et al., 2014). The selection of risk factors for inclusion in assessment instruments is based on empirical research that shows a consistent and strong relationship to offending. Risk factors are broken down into two types: static and dynamic. *Static risk factors* represent historical factors that can no longer be changed. Examples of commonly measured static risk factors include prior criminal behavior, age of onset, and history of trauma or abuse. *Dynamic risk factors* are characteristics that carry the potential to change over time. Dynamic risk factors include interaction and identification with delinquent peers, family functioning, educational achievement/employment skills, substance use, mental health, and pro-criminal attitudes.

Due to their malleability, dynamic risk factors also capture criminogenic needs and are considered key areas for prevention and intervention planning. In JRNA research the dynamic risk factor and criminogenic need labels are often used interchangeably (see Hoge, 2002). Andrews et al. (1990, p. 31) define *criminogenic needs* as a subset of risk factors that "are dynamic attributes of offenders and their circumstances that, when changed, are associated with changes in the chances of recidivism." The malleability of youths is a key tenet of juvenile justice policy and practice so characterizing these dynamic, changeable risk factors is an essential step.

Protective factors, or assets, represent characteristics of the youths and their environment that may reduce the effects of risk factors on behavior. DeMatteo and Marczyk (2005) define protective factors as "external or internal influences or conditions that decrease the likelihood of a negative outcome or enhance the likelihood of a positive outcome" (p. 21). According to Hoge (2002, p. 385), protective factors are based on the concept of resilience, which stems from robust empirical observations that some youths who experience multiple or serious risk factors do not engage in criminal or violent behavior while others that experience the same or similar risk factors do engage in these behaviors. Resilience is a phenomenon characterized by good outcomes despite serious threats to adaptation or development (Masten, 2001). Research suggests that the presence of multiple protective factors can reduce the likelihood of antisocial behavior (Werner, 2000). This occurs through a buffering effect where the protective factors lessen the impact that risk factors have on behavior. Quality parenting, cognitive skills, self-esteem, and attitudes or motivations are considered key protective factors for reducing the impact of risk factors on behavior (see Luthar et al., 2000; Masten, 2001; Newsome & Sullivan, 2014). Thus, the presence of such assets, in the face of adversity, reduces the likelihood of future antisocial behavior.

A Brief History of JRNA

The juvenile justice system has primarily used three methods to assess risk. The first method is *clinical judgment* which involves the gathering of information from multiple sources (e.g., prior history, youth, or parent) and then relying on experience, knowledge, and skills to make judgments about risk and needs. This method of assessing risk is often referred to as unstructured clinical judgment because practitioners are not afforded much guidance in making these decisions (Bonta, 1996; Andrews et al., 2006). This form of assessment was evident in the clinic established around the time of the origins Cook County (IL) Juvenile Court (Bronner, 1925; Healy, 1913) but is not routinely practiced today.

The second method is *actuarial assessment* which involves statistical synthesis and aggregation of varied indicators of behaviors, attitudes, or circumstances, based on a set of responses to a list of predetermined questions that measure those risk factors. This more systematic version of assessment developed heavily from the measurement and prediction research conducted in the middle part of the 20th century (Cronbach & Meehl, 1955; Lazarsfeld, 1955; Meehl, 1954). Typically, a formula is used to calculate a score or categorization that is in turn linked to some probability of future behavior. Essentially, conclusions based on actuarial assessments tell the practitioner that if a youth scores X, he or she has a certain probability of reoffending (Latessa & Lovins, 2010, p. 210). These tools do allow for practitioner override of subsequent risk levels should the conclusion from the assessment process disagree with court standards in some identifiable way (Shlonsky & Wagner, 2005), but how that occurs varies across agencies (Sullivan et al., 2019).

The third, and most recently developed, method for assessing risk for future behavior is *structured professional judgment* (SPJ). SPJ assessments try to blend the advantages of both the actuarial and clinical judgment approaches. This method involves a series of predetermined questions that measure empirically identified risk factors for delinquent behavior. Risk level is determined using defined guidelines that assist the professional in making their assessment. Therefore, SPJ allows practitioners to make a systematic assessment of the risk factors most relevant to each unique case. The SPJ approach explicitly draws both on actuarial and clinical approaches to assessment, making it a more open system of information gathering and use than the former alone. Intensive training on youth development, empirical research, and key mitigating and aggravating circumstances is critical to ensuring appropriate structured judgments (Borum, 2003; Vincent, 2006).

A large body of research has been devoted to examining the performance of these assessment methods for estimating risk to reoffend. Existing evidence overwhelmingly suggests that actuarial methods provide more accurate assessments of risk compared to unstructured clinical judgments (Ægisdóttir et al., 2006; Grove et al., 2000; Shlonsky & Wagner, 2005). This finding has been consistent across different system-involved populations, including adults and juveniles, and assessment instruments. Studies comparing actuarial assessments to SPJ assessments are rarer than comparisons of actuarial and clinical judgments. In general, the existing studies suggest that actuarial and SPJ measures of risk show similar levels of accuracy in predicting future behavior (Guy, 2008; Yang et al., 2010). Among JRNA instruments, compared to actuarial methods, the SPJ framework has been shown to be a more accurate tool when predicting future behavior (Pedersen et al., 2010; Hilterman et al., 2014), particularly when it comes to predicting violence (Lodewijks et al., 2008; Hoge, 2002).

Generations of Criminogenic Risk and Needs Assessment Instruments

Four generations of criminogenic risk assessment instruments have been identified (Howell et al., 2014; Schwalbe, 2007). These generations vary in the type of assessment method used (i.e., clinical judgment, actuarial judgment, SPJ) and their inclusion of criminogenic risk, needs, and protective factors. First-generation assessments are based on clinical, or unstructured, judgments. Results are often based on professional opinions that were derived from a series of standardized questions but the information gathering process is not completed systematically or objectively. Today, the use of first-generation assessments is rare in the juvenile justice system (Wachter, 2015). Second-generation instruments are actuarial in nature and rely almost exclusively on static risk factors with an emphasis on criminal history items (e.g., type of prior offenses, number of prior arrests, age of onset). These assessments focus on prediction and classification (Schwalbe, 2008). Second-generation assessment instruments are considered atheoretical due to their emphasis on static risk factors that cannot be changed with intervention (Andrews et al., 2006).

Compared to first- and second-generation assessments, third-generation instruments are considered more theoretically and empirically informed (Howell et al., 2014; Andrews et al., 2006). These assessments assess both static and dynamic risk factors to make predictions about risk and to inform intervention planning. Therefore, third-generation assessment instruments consider both classification (overall results) and the specific risk factors identified, their relationship to recidivism, and their potential to change with proper intervention. Third-generation instruments serve two functions: predicting risk to reoffend and identifying intervention needs. The Youth Level of Service/Case Management (YLS/CMI, Hoge & Andrews, 2002) is one common third-generation assessment instrument used by juvenile justice agencies. This instrument measures eight domains of risk including prior criminal history, family circumstances, education and employment, peer relations, substance abuse, leisure and recreation, personality and behavior, and attitudes/orientation. Items are given point values and summed to create an overall risk level based on predetermined numeric categories and practitioners consider results within each domain to determine intervention needs.

Fourth-generation assessments measure static and dynamic risk as well as protective factors or assets. These assessments enhance juvenile justice practitioners' ability to match youths' criminogenic needs to their treatment plans while also considering their level and type of resiliency. Another goal of fourth-generation instruments is reassessment at regular intervals to guide services and supervision throughout the juvenile justice process (Andrews et al., 2006). Fourth-generation assessments can be actuarial or rely on SPJ. One example of a popular fourth-generation risk assessment instrument is the Structured Assessment of Violence Risk in Youth (SAVRY, Borum et al., 2006). The SAVRY relies on SPJ and measures four domains: historical (static) risk factors, individual risk factors (dynamic), social/contextual risk factors (dynamic), and protective factors (assets). Thus, administrators collect information on risk, needs, and assets, and then make structured decisions regarding risk level and intervention needs.

JRNA Process

The three key steps in the JRNA process are depicted in Figure 2.1. Information gathering is the first step in the process. Information gathering

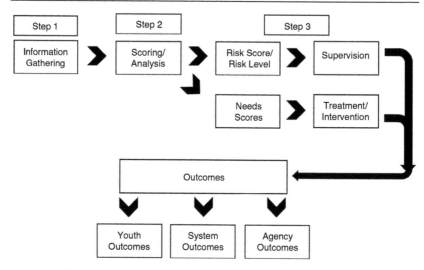

Figure 2.1 Three-step JRNA Process

involves collecting data from youths, their families, and other sources such as teachers, counselors, or school records to assess the presence and severity of each item on the instrument. Assessment instruments are comprised of a pool of individual items found to be robust predictors of delinquent behavior. Each item is then combined with other related items to create specific risk domains. For example, the SAVRY includes 30 items that represent four domains: historical risk, individual risk, social/contextual risk, and protective factors. The CAT measures 12 domains: prior criminal history, gender, school history and school status, use of free time, employment, relationship quality, family and living arrangements, alcohol and drug use, mental health, attitudes/behavior, aggression, and skills. The structure of juvenile assessment instruments suggests that risk is a multi-dimensional, higher-order construct where the assessment items represent the observed indicators, the domain scores represent relevant first-order latent constructs, and risk to reoffend is a higher-order latent construct based on multiple risk domains (or dimensions). Thus, targeting high scoring domains (i.e., first-order constructs) through intervention should reduce overall risk (i.e., higher-order construct) given their interdependence.

During the second step, scoring and analysis, the domain scores are used to estimate the overall risk level and to identify specific criminogenic need areas. Scoring and analysis is guided by structured professional judgments (i.e., SAVRY) or actuarial formulas or algorithms based on item responses (i.e., CAT). Some scoring procedures consider both static and dynamic risk factors while others rely solely on static risk factors to estimate an offender's risk for recidivism. The third and final step involves a two-pronged approach where the risk level is used to make supervision decisions and dynamic risk domain scores are used to drive programmatic or intervention recommendations. This last step of the process has received the most attention among juvenile justice policy makers due to the systemization it brings to the decision-making process. However, the quality or accuracy of this step is based on the quality and accuracy of the first two steps (information gathering and scoring). More specifically, poor information gathering and inaccurate estimates of risk can be detrimental to case processing decisions. Together, these three steps are expected to lead to a variety of positive outcomes including improved well-being and desistance from delinquent behavior (youth outcomes), reductions in out of home placement and racial and ethnic disparities (system outcomes), and monetary and resource savings (agency outcomes).

The Various Functions of JRNA

Today, JRNA serves several different functions across multiple decision-making levels. Most often discussed is the use of JRNA results to inform key youth-level decisions such as case processing and intervention planning (i.e., Step 3 of the JRNA process). However, these results, when aggregated across youths and/or jurisdictions, can also provide valuable information regarding resource allocation, community needs, and program effectiveness.

Case Decisions and Performance

The most discussed role of JRNA focuses on the use of assessment results to inform juvenile justice case-processing decisions. These decisions are often based on the overall judgment of risk obtained through the assessment process (i.e., Step 2 in Figure 2.1). Like the assessment of risk and needs, these case-level decisions are unique to each youth and are frequently driven by information beyond the assessment results (e.g., agency resources). JRNA is used at multiple stages of the juvenile justice system to make decisions about pretrial detention, diversion, disposition, and release readiness. For example, the assessment of risk and needs is common among probation departments to assist in making post-adjudication recommendations to the court about appropriate sanctions such as community or residential placements. This process is often based on a predetermined graduated sanctions model where decisions are indexed to a table that combines a youth's risk level determined by the assessment process, seriousness of the current offense, and prior adjudications or other contacts with the juvenile justice system.

More recently, with the increased utilization of third- and fourth-generation instruments, JRNA results are also incorporated into case planning and intervention recommendations. The information about youths' criminogenic needs and protective factors gathered through the assessment process facilitates the matching of intervention services to their needs. Reliance on assessment results—compared to unstructured assessments of needs—provides a more objective and systematic method for effective linkages of juveniles' unique needs and the available services. Service matrices that connect identified criminogenic needs with available intervention options formalize these processes (Hussemann & Liberman, 2017; Ryals, 2013).

JRNA instruments can also facilitate the continual, systematic assessment of change while the youth is under juvenile justice supervision. Most JRNAs used today are not intended to be administered in a discrete manner, for example only prior to or just after adjudication. Instead, JRNAs are intended to be administered on a routine basis to monitor progress toward goals, changes in criminogenic needs, and readiness for release. The authors of the SAVRY, for example, suggest that repeated assessments at regular intervals are important to focus on changes in dynamic risk factors that may alter the youth's risk level (Borum et al., 2006, p. 19). In Louisiana, SAVRY reassessments are mandated every six months for youths on probation, parole, or in non-secure custody. The FDJJ requires that an assessment be conducted every 90 days on all youths placed on probation or in residential programs. Sullivan and colleagues (2019) found that three states' policies for use of the OYAS typically included fixed intervals for follow-up assessment as well, but awareness of policies and the rationale for reassessment varied across staff. When fully applied, these reassessments allow decision-makers to make systematic and objective decisions regarding possible changes or additions to a youth's intervention plan, consider whether interventions are working as intended, and determine that the youth has progressed enough to reduce sanction restrictiveness or be released from custody.

Agency Decisions and Optimal Performance

Beyond the more obvious case-level functions of JRNA outlined in Figure 2.1, important agency or jurisdictional decisions are informed by JRNA results (see Vincent, Guy, Gershenson, & McCabe, 2012). To be used effectively, this requires summarizing or aggregating assessment results to produce group-based estimates of risk levels as well as the commonly identified static risk factors and criminogenic needs. These aggregated assessment data can help juvenile justice administrators allocate resources effectively. This may include personnel assignments, identifying hiring needs, setting caseload size, or determining training and intervention needs. These data can also help establish and evaluate treatment provider contracts, contributions to collaborative partnerships, and associated costs for staff, infrastructure, and materials. The reliance on the results of JRNA data to inform agency-level decisions such as resource allocation is an effective management tool to improve cost-savings and meet community needs. This is referred to as data-driven decision-making (i.e., the use of data to inform policy, practice, and fiscal decisions at the agency level). Some juvenile justice reform initiatives offer evidence that this data-driven approach to decision making (i.e., use of assessment data) improves agency practices and leads to increased cost-savings (see Vincent, Guy, Gershenson, & McCabe, 2012, for example).

Probation agencies typically assign probation officers to either regular, intensive, or specialized (e.g., sex offender) caseloads. Decisions about intensity of supervision are often based on risk level. Thus, by monitoring trends in risk levels and types of probation cases over time, administrators can alter caseload assignments as needed. Theoretically, this ensures that employee time and effort is being used in the most efficient and effective manner. Agency-level intervention decisions help ensure that the right services are available to youths and families based on their identified needs. This is a key element to ensuring effective matching of youths' needs to their treatment plans. By monitoring trends in the most common criminogenic needs of youths entering the system, agency administrators can assess the appropriateness of investments in and partnerships with service providers used to make intervention referrals and/or develop and provide in-house programming. In addition, using agency-level data on changes in criminogenic needs (i.e., the number/percent of offenders that showed improvement in needs over time), as measured through continual administration of assessment instruments (see p. 30), can also provide helpful information regarding intensity, dosage, and intervention effectiveness at a program level. Securing empirical evidence that agency resources are being devoted to the most appropriate services—and that these services are effective at reducing youths' needs—embodies effective leadership and resource allocation. A study of JRNA implementation across three states found that these agency-level uses of JRNA were least prevalent relative to assigning risk levels for individual cases from the perspective of those in the field and therefore probably reflect a higher order of implementation and usage of these tools and practices (Sullivan et al., 2019).

Studies of JRNA Performance

Existing research on the use of JRNA has primarily focused on three general areas: predictive validity, incremental validity, and differences in predictive validity across socio-demographic groups. Each of these areas is concerned with testing the performance of a tool either among full samples of justice-involved youths, across subgroups of youths, or across the various domains measured. Prior to reviewing existing research on JRNA performance, a short review of the methodology used in these studies is necessary to contextualize the state of the research.

Most JRNA studies rely on officially recorded data on all youths assessed at a given stage of the juvenile justice process (e.g., probation). Data on the assessment results, current offense, demographic characteristics, and recidivism are drawn from the jurisdiction's case management system and used to examine instrument performance. The most common operationalization of recidivism is as a dichotomous indicator for whether the event (i.e., re-offense) occurred or did not occur. However, studies vary in the operationalization of recidivism in three important ways. First, there is variation in the types of recidivism measured, specifically, whether general recidivism is the only dependent variable or violent recidivism and general recidivism are measured separately in the same study. The type of reoffending measured is important to consider because some studies have found differences in predictive strength across general, violent, and nonviolent reoffending (see Olver et al., 2009). Second, the time frame for recidivism varies across studies. For example, in Schwalbe's (2007) meta-analysis, he identified studies with follow-up time periods that ranged from 6 to 60 months. Third, definitions of recidivism are either based on a subsequent arrest, petition, or adjudication (see Pusch & Holtfreter, 2018 for examples). Such variations in the operationalization of the dependent variable can lead to important differences in tool performance since a larger proportion of youths will be re-arrested than re-adjudicated. There are also methodological inconsistencies in the timing of the assessment that can influence tests of predictive accuracy. For example, some studies rely on pre-disposition assessments to predict recidivism while other studies rely on assessments completed at the time of release from custody. This is an important distinction because pre-disposition assessments do not account for change that may occur as the result of intervention whereas post-disposition assessments are completed after intervention has occurred (Baglivio, 2009).

Predictive validity is the extent to which the risk assessment instrument can help to foresee recidivism up to some predetermined time, such as one year after release from juvenile corrections custody and supervision. Most often, predictive validity studies rely on either the overall risk level (low, moderate, high) determined by the instrument or a total risk score derived from the sum of its items to predict whether a juvenile reoffended. An association between greater risk and recidivism suggests that the instrument successfully predicts future behavior (i.e., predictive validity). The most common method for assessing the predictive accuracy of risk assessment instruments is the area under the receiver operating characteristic curve or "area under the curve" estimates (AUC, see Rice & Harris, 2005 for a detailed explanation of this method). The AUC illustrates the probability that a score (i.e., risk level) from a randomly selected case from one population (i.e., youths who reoffend) will be significantly higher than a score (i.e., risk level) of a randomly selected case from a different population (i.e., youths who did not reoffend). AUC values range from 0 (perfect negative prediction) to 1.0 (perfect positive prediction). Values less than .50 represent poor predictive ability, AUCs between .55 and .65 are considered small effects, AUCs between .66 and .75 are considered moderate effects, and AUCs over .75 are considered large effects or high predictive ability (Rice & Harris, 2005). Although the large majority of JRNA studies rely on AUC values to test predictive accuracy, this analysis procedure is limited. Mainly, AUC estimates test bivariate associations and therefore do not consider exogenous factors that carry the potential to influence the correlation between risk level and recidivism. Examples of such factors include characteristics of the offense, youth, and practitioner administering the instrument as well as the environmental conditions in which the information was gathered, participants involved in the three-step JRNA process, and the reliability of the information collected.

Reviews of risk/needs assessment instruments used in both the juvenile and adult systems provide general support for the predictive validity of structured assessment instruments (Edens et al., 2007; Fazel et al., 2012; Schmidt et al., 2011; Singh et al., 2011). To date, two reviews that focus exclusively on the use of assessment instruments in the juvenile justice system have been conducted. In his meta-analysis, Schwalbe (2007) found that, compared to instruments that focus solely on risk classification (i.e., second generation), instruments that focused on risk classification and intervention planning (i.e., third generation) had significantly greater AUC values (i.e., about .04 points higher on the scale from 0 to 1.0). Olver et al. (2009) conducted a meta-analysis of 49 empirical studies examining the predictive validity of three of the most widely used juvenile assessment instruments: the YLS/CMI which is an actuarial-based instrument that provides a cumulative risk score for general recidivism based on eight scales (Hoge & Andrews, 2002); the Psychopathy Checklist: Youth Version (PCL: YV) which captures the severity of psychopathic traits based on interpersonal, affective, behavioral, and antisocial domains (Forth et al., 2003); and the SAVRY which is based on SPJ and measures four domains representing historical, individual, social/contextual, and protective factors (Borum et al., 2006). Their results provided support for the accuracy of all three tools in predicting violent, nonviolent, and general recidivism (r ranged from .16 to .32).

In addition to these meta-analyses, many studies, examining a wide range of third and fourth juvenile justice risk assessment instruments (e.g., SAVRY, PCL: YV, YLS/CMI, PACT, YASI [Youth Assessment and Screening Instrument]) have been conducted. These studies either focus on one specific instrument (Baglivio, 2009; Borum et al., 2010; McGrath & Thompson, 2012; Vincent et al., 2011) or compare the predictive validity of two or more instruments (Catchpole & Gretton, 2003; Hilterman et al., 2014; Schmidt et al., 2011; Welsh et al., 2008; Perrault et al., 2017). Across these studies, AUC values typically range from .58 to .77 for general reoffending and .51 to .81 for violent reoffending. Taken together, the findings from existing research on predictive validity suggest three key findings: (1) there are moderate levels of predictive validity across JRNA studies; (2) third- and fourth-generation risk/needs assessment instruments reveal stronger predictive validity compared to first- and second-generation instruments; and (3) there is significant variation in predictive validity across studies, instruments, and the type of reoffending measured (e.g., violent reoffending versus general reoffending).

Incremental validity measures the extent to which one measure or item increases the predictive ability beyond that of other existing measures. Incremental validity has been assessed in terms of whether incorporating dynamic risk factors (i.e., criminogenic needs) increases the ability to predict future behavior above and beyond static risk factors. These studies have highlighted the contribution that the assessment of dynamic risk factors provides in predicting reoffending among youthful offenders (Douglas & Skeem, 2005; Perrault et al., 2017). Dynamic risk factors have been shown to independently predict recidivism and improve the level of prediction for the full instrument (Clarke et al., 2017; McGrath & Thompson, 2012; Vincent et al., 2011; Gammelgård et al., 2015). These findings have been documented across studies, populations, and assessment instruments. This is most likely due to their ability to capture the constellation of individual and contextual risk factors unique to each youth's developmental trajectory, which are therefore potential targets for intervention and support.

More recently, with the introduction of fourth-generation risk assessment instruments, studies have begun to examine the incremental contribution of protective factors, or assets, to the prediction of reoffending. Assuming they are empirically useful, juvenile justice and treatment personnel can capitalize on these assets in developing case plans for justice-involved youths (Butts et al., 2005). The relative contribution of protective factors to predictive validity remains unclear based on the handful of studies that have been conducted on this topic. For example, findings regarding the incremental validity of the protective items measured on the SAVRY are mixed. Penney et al. (2010) and Hilterman et al. (2014) did not find evidence of incremental validity once scores from the SAVRY protective factors were incorporated into analyses predicting reoffending. However, Lodewijks and colleagues (2010), Rennie and Dolan (2010), and Shepherd et al. (2016) found support for increased prediction after including scores from the SAVRY protective domain into their analyses. Thus, further research on the incremental validity of protective factors, above and beyond static and dynamic risk factors, is needed. In addition, examining whether the protective factors contribute through a "buffering effect" or have a direct effect on recidivism is also important to understanding the role these measures play in an instrument's predictive ability (Soderstrom et al., 2020).

JRNA Validity Across Youth Subgroups

Both predictive validity and incremental validity have been examined across subgroups of delinquent youths (Bonta & Andrews, 2012; McGrath & Thompson, 2012; Vincent et al., 2011). Understanding how JRNA instruments perform across race/ethnicity, gender, and age is important to ensuring equitable assessments of risk and case processing decisions based on these assessments (e.g., disposition). Fewer studies analyze heterogeneity in predictive validity across subgroups compared to general populations of justice-involved youths. The small pool of studies find similar levels of predictive accuracy across race/ethnicity and gender but inconclusive results for age or developmental stage.

Race/Ethnicity and JRNA Predictive Validity

Scholars offer several reasons for examining racial and ethnic differences in the accuracy of risk assessment instruments. Perrault et al. (2017) explain that marginalized groups, such as youth of color, have been posited to score higher on risk assessment instruments due to increased exposure to risk and social inequality, rather than higher propensity for delinquent behavior. Basing judgments of risk on static factors, such as prior criminal history, may therefore place youths from such groups at a disadvantage due to observed biases in previous arrest or court decisions that have been found in previous research (e.g., Leiber et al., 2016; Peck & Jennings, 2016). In addition, differences in cultural values and socialization practices can potentially impact the level and nature of included risk factors across race and ethnicity subgroups.

On one hand, existing studies on racial differences in predictive validity generally suggest that risk levels tend to be higher for minority groups and that there are differences in the presence of specific risk items across groups (Vincent & Viljoen, 2020). On the other hand, predictive accuracy has been shown to be relatively similar (Baglivio & Jackowski, 2013; Chapman et al., 2006; McCafferty et al., 2017; McGrath & Thompson, 2012; Olver et al., 2009; Schwalbe et al., 2006). For example, Perrault et al. (2017) compared the predictive accuracy of the SAVRY and YLS/CMI and found no significant differences in the strength of prediction across White and Black youths. However, their results did reveal significant differences in overall risk level and several static (e.g., suicide attempts) and dynamic (e.g., substance use, disorganized community) items across these groups. When racial differences in the incremental validity of the dynamic risk factors was assessed, similar dynamic risk factors showed improvements in prediction over static risk factors for both groups. Thus, although there is evidence of racial differences in the indicated level and type of risk and needs factors, the ability of these JRNA instruments to predict recidivism (i.e., predictive validity) generally has held up.

Gender and JRNA Predictive Validity

Studies involving gender-specific analyses of predictive validity have been conducted in recent years as well. Given that most samples of justice involved youths consist predominantly of boys, any differences in predictive accuracy that are specific to girls may get lost in analyses based on pooled samples of boys and girls. In addition, Odgers and colleagues (2005) point to several differences across delinquent girls and boys that may impact the measurement of risk and need and predictive validity. These include a lower base rate of serious forms of violent and nonviolent behavior among delinquent girls, gender differences in the form and target of violent behavior, differences in developmental trajectories for boys and girls, and a lack of gender-specific studies measuring the psychometric properties of risk assessment instruments. A great deal of theoretical and empirical attention has been devoted to highlighting the need for gender responsive practices in juvenile justice settings. These practices are based on the notion of "gendered" risk factors or pathways to delinquency and exposure to risk factors across boys and girls (Belknap & Holsinger, 2006; Holsinger, 2000). Victimization, abuse, and trauma are examples of risk factors considered critical to girls' delinquency trajectories, which may have differential prevalence and impacts across gender groups.

Several studies have compared the performance of risk/needs assessment instruments across gender. Findings from both juvenile and adult samples suggest that the specific risk factors for reoffending differ across boys and girls, but the overall predictive accuracy is similar (Smith et al., 2009; Barnes et al., 2016; van der Knaap et al., 2012). These findings have also been confirmed across juvenile justice risk assessment instruments (i.e., SAVRY—Penney et al., 2010; Gammelgård et al., 2015; YLS/CMI—Thompson & McGrath, 2012; Campbell et al., 2014; Vaswani & Merone, 2014; PACT—Baglivio & Jackowski, 2013). Few studies have found predictive accuracy to be stronger for male juvenile offenders compared to female juvenile offenders (YLS/CMI—Schmidt et al., 2011; North Carolina Assessment of Risk [NCAR]—Schwalbe et al., 2006).

To date, three meta-analyses have been conducted on gender differences in the predictive validity of JRNA instruments. Schwalbe (2008) focused exclusively on juvenile justice risk assessment instruments. This study included results from 19 studies based on several different juvenile risk assessment instruments. Effects sizes for predicting general and violent recidivism were almost identical for boys (average $r = .26$) and girls (average $r = .27$). Olver et al. (2009) also broke down the results of the studies used in their meta-analyses, when possible, by gender. Results showed that the predictive accuracy of juvenile risk assessment instruments was comparable for both general recidivism ($r = .33$ for boys and .36 for girls) and violent recidivism ($r = .23$ for boys and .24 for girls). Most recently, Pusch and

Holtfreter (2018) examined gender differences in the predictive accuracy of the YLS/CMI based on 42 unique samples of justice-involved youths. Consistent with previous meta-analyses, effect sizes for general recidivism (boys, r = .28; girls, r = .25) and violent recidivism (boys, r = .30; girls, r = .25) did not significantly differ. Like the results on racial and ethnic differences in predictive validity, the existing evidence suggests that although girls and boys present different types of risk factors, the overall predictive accuracy is similar for the two groups.

Age and JRNA Predictive Validity

Compared to variations across race/ethnicity and gender, differences in the predictive accuracy of risk assessment instruments across age has not received as much empirical attention. Nevertheless, understanding how these instruments perform across different developmental stages carries important implications. Adolescent development plays a critical role in decisions to engage in behavior and can influence how individual and contextual risk factors impact behavior over time. Key risk factors can differ in salience across adolescence as well, which may impact assessment and predictive validity (Childs et al., 2010). It is therefore important to consider the degree to which there may be age differences in predictive validity of JRNA tools.

The few studies that have examined developmental differences in predictive accuracy have mixed results. Among juvenile sex offenders, Viljoen et al. (2009) found overall risk level predicted general recidivism among older adolescents (ages 16 and older) only. This finding was consistent across three different assessment instruments: The Estimate of Risk of Adolescent Sexual Recidivism (ERASOR), YLS/CMI, and PCL: YV. Vincent, Perrault, et al. (2012) compared the predictive validity of the SAVRY across three age groups: 12 and younger, 13–15, and 16–18. They found that the SAVRY risk rating significantly predicted general and violent reoffending among the 13–15 and 16–18 age groups (AUCs ranged from .62–.69) but did not predict recidivism among the youngest age group. Among a sample of juveniles placed on probation, Childs and Frick (2016) found that the SAVRY risk rating significantly predicted general and violent recidivism among the 13–15 age group but did not predict general or violent recidivism among the 16–18 age group. Thus, additional research is needed to clarify the role that age and developmental status play in the predictive accuracy of juvenile risk/needs assessment instruments.

Summary of JRNA Predictive Validity Studies

Numerous studies and a handful of meta-analyses have focused on the usefulness of JRNA in predicting future behavior. This body of work suggests that contemporary assessment instruments that are based on actuarial or structured professional judgments, and which include both static and dynamic risk factors, predict reoffending with moderate levels of accuracy and tend to perform similar across race/ethnicity and gender. However, the information that these studies provide is limited to predictions of future behavior which is only one component of understanding the benefits and limits of using JRNAs to make juvenile justice decisions. In the next section we outline several limitations to existing research needed to fully understand how well the risk assessment process operates in the context of juvenile justice processing.

The Limitations of JRNA Research

The rather narrow focus on predictive validity in prior JRNA studies leads to an incomplete understanding of how well JRNA works in practice. These limitations are related to inaccurate predictions of risk (i.e., false positives), implementation and fidelity, field reliability, psychometric properties, and potential practitioner effects. For example, the modest levels of predictive accuracy found across studies continue to be puzzling. As reported on p. 12, most studies yield estimates that provide evidence of moderate levels of prediction (i.e., AUC values below .75) but then conclude that these instruments effectively predict future behavior. From these results, researchers and practitioners conclude that the tools work. But looked at more critically, the same estimates also suggest that the tools produce false predictions in a rather large proportion of cases. Under prediction can lead to threats to public safety; over prediction can lead to unnecessary confinement or restrictions which carry a range of negative youth (iatrogenic effects) and system (costs) outcomes (Baglivio, 2009). A better understanding of these false predictions can also generate a more complete picture of the underlying processes that engender juvenile delinquency and recidivism (Sullivan, 2011).

Existing research on JRNA has also overlooked the importance of confirming the field reliability of these instruments. Field reliability measures the extent to which instruments are effective measures when conducted by practitioners as part of their routine procedures. This differs from most published tests of inter-rater reliability which are conducted in more controlled settings and often involve the collection of information through file reviews rather than in person (see Vincent, Guy, Fusco, & Gershenson, 2012). Overall, studies based on "laboratory-like settings" have shown high levels of reliability across juvenile risk/needs assessment instruments (Borum et al., 2010; National Council on Crime and Delinquency, 2014). However, these settings do not account for the environmental factors, political pressures, and time constraints that occur when conducting assessments in the field (Vincent, Guy, Fusco, & Gershenson, 2012). The unique circumstances that occur when conducting assessments in practice have led some experts to question whether risk/needs assessments can be completed reliably in practice (see Baird, 2009; National Council on Crime and Delinquency, 2014). It has been argued that practitioners' ability to rate dynamic risk factors should be a key area of concern (Perrault et al., 2017). This argument is based on the unique circumstances faced by justice-involved youths that carry the potential to lead to large variations, or interpretations, of the severity of risk factors and how they may or may not impact future behavior. For instance, when interviewing juvenile probation officers (JPOs) about their perceptions of the use of JRNA, Guy et al. (2014) found that JPOs reported difficulty in accurately rating some dynamic risk factors related to parenting, peers, and community disorganization. Furthermore, a large percentage of JPOs felt that youths should be rated "differently" based on their unique circumstances. These factors carry the potential to reduce the true reliability of JRNA in practice.

Just two studies of the field reliability of JRNA could be found. One study assessed the inter-rater reliability of the SAVRY based one juvenile probation officer and one trained researcher during interviews of youths in the field. Good inter-rater reliability was found across all four domains of the SAVRY and the overall risk rating (see Vincent, Guy, Fusco, & Gershenson, 2012). In contrast, Kennealy et al. (2017) found that only 59 percent of the staff included in their study of the California Youth Assessment and Screening Instrument (CA-YASI) scored the tool with accuracy and the dynamic subscales showed the lowest accuracy in ratings. Due to these inconsistent findings, replication studies using different instruments, samples, and raters are needed to provide a better assessment of the field reliability of juvenile risk assessment tools. The knowledge gained from these studies may provide valuable information regarding training needs, the implementation of policies or guidelines regarding administration of instruments, and context to the empirically identified inaccuracies in risk prediction.

From a methodological standpoint, without confirmation of good field reliability, tests of performance should be interpreted with caution. Since most studies are based on existing data drawn from case management systems, the ability to confirm the reliability of the assessment scores prior to assessing their predictive ability is lost. Therefore, it is possible that unreliable assessments are contributing to the moderate levels of accurate prediction found across studies. Thus, tests of field reliability and predictive accuracy within a single study are necessary. This requires greater attention to pilot testing in initial phases of the research and evaluation process to ensure that appropriate modifications are possible prior to wide-scale adoption and implementation of JRNA in a particular setting.

In addition to questions about predictive validity and reliability, studies assessing internal consistency and dimensionality are also lacking. Internal consistency is related to the cohesion of assessment items and dimensions.

Dimensionality is related to whether the items and/or domains measured on the instrument represent risk as a uni-dimensional or multi-dimensional construct and whether this is consistent across instruments, subgroups of youths who are assessed, and practitioners who administer the tool. Unfortunately, existing research has failed to examine these psychometric properties among JRNA instruments. The implications of this shortcoming have been explained in detail by Baird (2009). He specifically questions the relevance and particular downside of using items that are found to be unrelated to recidivism: "logically, we must conclude that if a factor is not related to recidivism in the first place, changes in that factor should have little to no impact on outcomes" (Baird, 2009, p. 3). He further argues that items lacking statistically significant associations with recidivism may in fact reduce the predictive accuracy of the tool and misguide practitioners in making case management decisions.

Later work by Baird and colleagues (2013) suggests that juvenile risk assessment should be simple and focused on first principles of predicting the likelihood of reoffending on the part of youths. Clearly juvenile justice agencies are using—and being advised by researchers to use—these tools for other objectives, however. For example, discussing the Youth Level of Service Inventory (YLSI), Hoge (2002, p. 391) states:

> A number of potential strengths are associated with the measure. First, it is based on the latest theory and research regarding the correlates and causes of criminal activity in young people. Second, the measure is designed to provide a direct link between the assessment of risks and needs and case planning.

Thus, research that assesses the cohesion among items, the relative importance of each individual item to its domain score and the overall rating of risk, and the value of each item and domain to case planning is needed. Furthermore, Lee (2013) argues that comparisons of risk levels and assessments of predictive validity across groups (e.g., gender, race) should be withheld until the psychometric properties of risk/needs assessment instruments overall and across groups are better understood. These questions inherently expand the demands of the research base beyond simply looking at risk levels and scores in relation to youth recidivism. It is likely that research into the field reliability of JRNA instruments as well as the internal consistency across items will provide valuable insight into existing questions of predictive accuracy, both within and across groups of justice-involved youths.

Chapter Summary

The existing research described in this chapter focuses on one piece of the "assessment puzzle" which is the performance of these instruments in predicting recidivism. This narrow focus underscores the need for a more holistic evaluation of the JRNA process. Such an evaluation requires moving beyond predictive validity to study how the results of the assessment are used in practice, implementation quality and outcomes, and broader issues of equity and fairness in JRNA processes. The information gleaned from these key areas will inform how JRNA benefits juvenile justice decision-making and helps to identify its shortcomings.

The purpose of JRNA is to provide a holistic, systematic, and structured way of fairly considering youths' risk for recidivism and intervention needs that leads to equitable, fair, and effective juvenile justice decisions. Assessment of the usefulness of JRNA instruments should be approached in the same manner—holistically, systematically, and in a structured manner. Building on the existing body of research by focusing on implementation, psychometric properties, objectives beyond predicting recidivism, and practitioner impacts on the process provide critical avenues for future research to accomplish this approach. JRNA has become routine practice in most jurisdictions across the United States without a clear picture of how these strategies operate in practice and whether they are producing the intended youth and system-level results.

References

Ægisdóttir, S., White, M.J., Spengler, P.M., Maugherman, A.S., Anderson, L.A., Cook, R.S., Nichols, C.N., Lampropoulos, G.K., Walker, B.S., Cohen, G., & Rush, J.D. (2006). The meta-analysis of clinical judgment project: Fifty-six years of accumulated research on clinical versus statistical prediction. *Counseling Psychologist*, 34, 341–382. doi:10.1177/0011000005285875.

Andrews, D.A., Bonta, J., & Hoge, R.D. (1990). Classification for effective rehabilitation: Rediscovering psychology. *Criminal Justice and Behavior*, 17(1), 19–52. doi:10.1177/0093854890017001004.

Andrews, D.A., Bonta, J., & Wormith, J.S. (2006). The recent past and near future of risk and/or need assessment. *Crime & Delinquency*, 52(1), 7–27. doi:10.1177/0011128705281756.

Aos, S., Phipps, P., Barnoski, R., & Lieb, R. (2001). *The comparative costs and benefits of programs to reduce crime.* Olympia, WA: Washington State Institute of Public Policy. www.wsipp.wa.gov/ReportFile/756/Wsipp_The-Comparative-Costs-and-Benefits-of-Programs-to-Reduce-Crime-v-4-0_Full-Report.pdf.

Baglivio, M.T. (2009). The assessment of risk to recidivate among a juvenile offending population. *Journal of Criminal Justice*, 37(6), 596–607. doi:10.1016/j.jcrimjus.2009.09.008.

Baglivio, M.T., & Jackowski, K. (2013). Examining the validity of a juvenile offending risk assessment instrument across gender and race/ethnicity. *Youth Violence and Juvenile Justice*, 11(1), 26–43. doi:10.1177/1541204012440107.

Baird, C. (2009). *A question of evidence: A critique of risk assessment models used in the justice system.* Madison, WI: National Council on Crime and Delinquency. www.

evidentchange.org/publications/a-question-of-evidence-a-critique-of-risk-assessm ent-models-used-in-the-justice-system.

Baird, C., Healy, T., Johnson, K., Bogie, A., Dankert, E.W., & Scharenbroch, C. (2013). *A comparison of risk assessment instruments in juvenile justice.* Madison, WI: National Council on Crime and Delinquency. www.ojp.gov/pdffiles1/ojjdp/gra nts/244477.pdf.

Barnes, A.R., Campbell, N.A., Anderson, V.R., Campbell, C.A., Onifade, E., & Davidson, W.S. (2016). Validity of initial, exit, and dynamic juvenile risk assessment: An examination across gender and race/ethnicity. *Journal of Offender Rehabilitation*, 55(1), 21–38. doi:10.1080/10509674.2015.1107004.

Belknap, J., & Holsinger, K. (2006). The gendered nature of risk factors for delinquency. *Feminist Criminology*, 1(1), 48–71. doi:10.1177/1557085105282897.

Bilchik, S. (1999). *Juvenile justice: A century of change.* Washington, DC: Office of Juvenile and Delinquency Prevention. Available online at www.ncjrs.gov/p dffiles1/ojjdp/178995.

Bishop, D.M. (2006). Public opinion and juvenile justice policy: Myths and misconceptions. *Criminology & Public Policy*, 5, 653–644.

Bonta, J. (1996). Risk-needs assessment and treatment. In A.T. Harland (Ed.), *Choosing correctional options that work: Defining the demand and evaluating the supply* (pp. 18–32). Thousand Oaks, CA: Sage.

Bonta, J., & Andrews, D. (2012). Viewing offender assessment and rehabilitation through the lens of the risk-needs-responsivity model. In R. McNiel & C. Trotter (Eds.), *Offender supervision* (pp. 45–66). New York: Routledge.

Borum, R. (2003). Managing at-risk juvenile offenders in the community: Putting evidence-based principles into practice. *Journal of Contemporary Criminal Justice*, 19 (1), 114–137. doi:10.1177/1043986202239745.

Borum, R., Bartel, P., & Forth, A. (2006). *Structured Assessment of Violence Risk in Youth (SAVRY).* Lutz, FL: Psychological Assessment Resources.

Borum, R., Lodewikjs, H., Bartel, P., & Forth, A. (2010). Structured Assessment of Violence Risk in Youth (SAVRY). In K. Douglas & R. Otto (Eds.), *Handbook of violence risk assessment* (pp. 63–80). New York: Routledge.

Bronner, A. (1925). The contribution of science to a program for treatment of juvenile delinquency. In J. Addams (Ed.), *The child, the clinic, and the court: A group of papers* (pp. 75–92). New York: New Republic.

Butts, J., Mayer, S., & Ruth, G. (2005). *Focusing juvenile justice on positive youth development.* Chicago, IL: Chapin Hall Center for Children at the University of Chicago.

Cabaniss, E.R., Frabutt, J.M., Kendrick, M.H., & Arbuckle, M.B. (2007). Reducing disproportionate minority contact in the juvenile justice system: Promising practices. *Aggression and Violent Behavior*, 12(4), 393–401. doi:10.1016/j.avb.2006.09.004.

Campbell, C., Onifade, E., Barnes, A., Peterson, J., Anderson, V., Davidson, W., & Gordon, D. (2014). Screening offenders: The exploration of a youth level of service/case management inventory (YLS/CMI) brief screener. *Journal of Offender Rehabilitation*, 53(1), 19–34. doi:10.1080/10509674.2013.861314.

Catchpole, R.E., & Gretton, H.M. (2003). The predictive validity of risk assessment with violent young offenders: A 1-year examination of criminal outcome. *Criminal Justice & Behavior*, 30(6), 688–708. doi:10.1177/0093854803256455.

Chapman, J.F., Desai, R.A., Falzer, P.R., & Borum, R. (2006). Violence risk and race in a sample of youth in juvenile detention: The potential to reduce disproportionate minority confinement. *Youth Violence and Juvenile Justice*, 4(2), 170–184. doi:10.1177/1541204006286316.

Childs, K.K., & Frick, P.J. (2016). Age differences in the Structured Assessment of Violence Risk in Youth (SAVRY). *International Journal of Forensic Mental Health*, 15(3), 211–221. doi:10.1080/14999013.2016.1152618.

Childs, K.K., Sullivan, C.J., & Gulledge, L.M. (2010). Delinquent behavior across adolescence: Investigating the shifting salience of key criminological predictors. *Deviant Behavior*, 32(1), 64–100. doi:10.1080/01639621003748498.

Clarke, M.C., Peterson-Badali, M., & Skilling, T.A. (2017). The relationship between changes in dynamic risk factors and the predictive validity of risk assessments among youth offenders. *Criminal Justice & Behavior*, 44(10), 1340–1355. doi:10.1177/0093854817719915.

Cronbach, L.J., & Meehl, P.E. (1955). Construct validity in psychological tests. *Psychological Bulletin*, 52(4), 281–302. doi:10.1037/h0040957.

DeMatteo, D., & Marczyk, G. (2005). Risk factors, protective factors, and the prevention of antisocial behavior among juveniles. In K. Heilbrun, N. Sevin Goldstein, & R. Redding (Eds.), *Juvenile delinquency: Prevention, Assessment, and Intervention* (pp. 19–44). New York: Oxford University Press.

Douglas, K.S., & Skeem, J.L. (2005). Violence risk assessment: Getting specific about being dynamic. *Psychology, Public Policy, and Law*, 11(3), 347. https://doi.org/10.1037/1076-8971.11.3.347.

Drake, E.K., Aos, S., & Miller, M.G. (2009). Evidence-based public policy options to reduce crime and criminal justice costs: Implications in Washington State. *Victims and Offenders*, 4(2), 170–196.

Edens, J.F., Campbell, J.S., & Weir, J.M. (2007). Youth psychopathy and criminal recidivism: A meta-analysis of the psychopathy checklist measures. *Law and Human Behavior*, 31(1), 53–75. doi:10.1007/s10979–10006–9019-y.

Fagan, J. (1991). Community-based treatment for mentally disordered juvenile offenders. *Journal of Clinical Child and Adolescent Psychology*, 20(1), 42–50. doi:10.1207/s15374424jccp2001_6.

Fazel, S., Singh, J.P., Doll, H., & Grann, M. (2012). Use of risk assessment instruments to predict violence and antisocial behaviour in 73 samples involving 24,827 people: Systematic review and meta-analysis. *British Medical Journal*, 345, 1–12. doi:10.1136/bmj.e4692.

Forth, A.E., Kosson, D.S., & Hare, R.D. (2003). *Hare Psychopathy Checklist-Revised: Youth Version*. Toronto, ON: Multi-Health Systems.

Fox, J.A. (1996). *Trends in juvenile violence: A report to the United States Attorney General on current and future rates of juvenile offending* (pp. 1–15). Washington, DC: US Department of Justice, Bureau of Justice Statistics. www.bjs.gov/content/pub/pdf/tjvfox.pdf.

Gammelgård, M., Koivisto, A.M., Eronen, M., & Kaltiala-Heino, R. (2015). Predictive validity of the structured assessment of violence risk in youth: A 4-year follow-up. *Criminal Behaviour and Mental Health*, 25(3), 192–206. doi:10.1002/cbm.1921.

Grisso, T., Vincent, G., & Seagrave, D. (Eds.). (2005). *Mental health screening and assessment in juvenile justice*. New York: Guilford Press.

Grove, W.M., Zald, D.H., Lebow, B.S., Snitz, B.E., & Nelson, C. (2000). Clinical versus mechanical prediction: A meta-analysis. *Psychological Assessment*, 12, 1–19. doi:10.1037//1040–3590.12.1.19.

Guy, L. (2008). *Performance indicators of the Structured Professional Judgment approach to assessing risk for violent to others: A meta-analytic survey*. Unpublished Manuscript. Retrieved in October 2018 from www.summit.sfu.ca.

Guy, L.S., Nelson, R.J., Fusco-Morin, S.L., & Vincent, G.M. (2014). What do juvenile probation officers think of using the SAVRY and YLS/CMI for case management, and do they use the instruments properly? *International Journal of Forensic Mental Health*, 13(3), 227–241. doi:10.1080/14999013.2014.939789.

Hay, C., Ladwig, S., & Campion, B. (2018). Tracing the rise of evidence-based juvenile justice in Florida. *Victims & Offenders*, 13(3), 312–335.

Healy, W. (1913). Present day aims and methods in studying the offender. *Journal of the American Institute of Criminal Law and Criminology*, 4(2), 204–211. https://scholarlycommons.law.northwestern.edu/jclc/vol4/iss2/5.

Hilterman, E.L., Nicholls, T.L., & van Nieuwenhuizen, C. (2014). Predictive validity of risk assessments in juvenile offenders: Comparing the SAVRY, PCL: YV, and YLS/CMI with unstructured clinical assessments. *Assessment*, 21(3), 324–339. doi:10.1177/1073191113498113.

Hoge, R.D. (2002). Standardized instruments for assessing risk and need in youthful offenders. *Criminal Justice and Behavior*, 29(4), 380–396. doi:10.1177/009385480202900403.

Hoge, R.D., & Andrews, D.A. (2002). *Youth level of service/case management inventory users' manual*. North Tonawanda, MY: Multi-Health Systems.

Holsinger, K. (2000). Feminist perspectives on female offending: Examining real girls' lives. *Women & Criminal Justice*, 12(1), 23–52. doi:10.1300/J012v12n01_03.

Howell, J.C., Lipsey, M.W., & Wilson, J.J. (2014). *A handbook for evidence-based juvenile justice systems*. Lanham, MD: Lexington Books.

Hsia, H.M., Bridges, G.S., & McHale, R. (2004). *Disproportionate minority confinement: 2002 update*. Washington, DC: US Department of Justice, Office of Justice Programs, Office of Juvenile Justice and Delinquency Prevention. www.ojp.gov/pdffiles1/ojjdp/201240.pdf.

Hussemann, J., & Liberman, A. (2017). *Implementing evidence-based juvenile justice reforms: Demonstration Sites in OJJDP's Juvenile Justice Reform and Reinvestment Initiative*. Urban Institute, retrieved from Implementing Evidence-Based Juvenile Justice Reforms (urban.org).

Kempf-Leonard, K. (2007). Minority youths and juvenile justice: Disproportionate minority contact after nearly 20 years of reform efforts. *Youth Violence and Juvenile Justice*, 5(1), 71–87. doi:10.1177/1541204006295159.

Kennealy, P.J., Skeem, J.L., & Hernandez, I.R. (2017). Does staff see what experts see? Accuracy of front line staff in scoring juveniles' risk factors. *Psychological Assessment*, 29(1), 26–34. doi:10.1037/pas0000316.

Latessa, E.J., & Lovins, B. (2010). The role of offender risk assessment: A policy maker guide. *Victims and Offenders*, 5(3), 203–219. doi:10.1080/15564886.2010.485900.

Lazarsfeld, P.F. (1955). Why is so little known about the effects of television on children and what can be done? testimony before the Kefauver Committee on Juvenile Delinquency. *Public Opinion Quarterly*, 19(3), 243–251.

Lee, S.Y. (2013). Testing psychometric properties and the cross-ethnic construct validity of the Risk and Resiliency Checkup. *Youth Violence & Juvenile Justice*, 11, 165–177. doi:10.1177/1541204012460875.

Leiber, M.J., Peck, J.H., & Beaudry-Cyr, M. (2016). When does race and gender matter? The interrelationships between the gender of probation officers and juvenile court detention and intake outcomes. *Justice Quarterly*, 33(4), 614–641. doi:10.1080/07418825.2014.958185.

Lipsey, M.W., Howell, J.C., Kelly, M.R., Chapman, G., & Carver, D. (2010). *Improving the effectiveness of juvenile justice programs*. Washington DC: Center for Juvenile Justice Reform at Georgetown University. https://njjn.org/uploads/digital-library/CJJR_Lipsey_Improving-Effectiveness-of-Juvenile-Justice_2010.pdf.

Lodewijks, H.P., Doreleijers, T.A., de Ruiter, C., & Borum, R. (2008). Predictive validity of the Structured Assessment of Violence Risk in Youth (SAVRY) during residential treatment. *International Journal of Law and Psychiatry*, 31(3), 263–271. doi:10.1016/j.ijlp.2008.04.009.

Lodewijks, H.P., de Ruiter, C., & Doreleijers, T.A. (2010). The impact of protective factors in desistance from violent reoffending: A study in three samples of adolescent offenders. *Journal of Interpersonal Violence*, 25(3), 568–587.

Loeber, R., & Farrington, D.P. (1999). *Serious and violent juvenile offenders: Risk factors and successful interventions*. Thousand Oaks, CA: Sage.

Luthar, S.S., Cicchetti, D., & Becker, B. (2000). The construct of resilience: A critical evaluation and guidelines for future work. *Child Development*, 71(3), 543–562. doi:10.1111/1467-8624.00164.

Masten, A.S. (2001). Ordinary magic: Resilience processes in development. *American Psychologist*, 56(3), 227–238. doi:10.1037//0003-066X.56.3.227.

McCafferty, J., Newsome, J., & Sullivan, C.J. (2017). *Study of Arizona Youth Assessment System (AZYAS)-Residential*. Cincinnati, OH: University of Cincinnati Center for Criminal Justice Research.

McGrath, A., & Thompson, A.P. (2012). The relative predictive validity of the static and dynamic domain scores in risk-need assessment of juvenile offenders. *Criminal Justice & Behavior*, 39(3), 250–263. doi:10.1177/0093854811431917.

Meehl, P. E. (1954). *Clinical versus statistical prediction: A theoretical analysis and a review of the evidence*. Minneapolis, MN: University of Minnesota Press. doi:10.1037/11281-000.

Nagin, D.S., Piquero, A.R., Scott, E.S., & Steinberg, L. (2006). Public preferences for rehabilitation versus incarceration of juvenile offenders: Evidence from a contingent valuation survey. *Criminology & Public Policy*, 5(4), 627–651.

National Coalition of State Juvenile Justice Advisory Group (1989). *A report on the delicate balance*. A Delicate Balance.compressed.pdf (juvjustice.org).

National Council on Crime and Delinquency (2014). *NCCD compares juvenile justice risk. assessment instruments: A summary of the OJJDP-funded study*. San Diego, CA: National Council on Crime and Delinquency. www.evidentchange.org/sites/default/files/publication_pdf/fire_report_summary.pdf

Nellis, A. (2015). *A return to justice: Rethinking our approach to juveniles in the system*. Lanham, MD: Rowman & Littlefield.

Newsome, J., & Sullivan, C.J. (2014). Resilience and vulnerability in adolescents: Genetic influences on differential response to risk for delinquency. *Journal of Youth and Adolescence*, 43(7), 1080–1095. doi:10.1007/s10964-014-0108-9.

Odgers, C.L., Moretti, M.M., & Dickon, N.R. (2005). Examining the science and practice of violence risk assessment with female adolescents. *Law and Human Behavior*, 29(1), 7–27.

OJJDP (2009). *Disproportionate minority contact technical assistance manual* (4th Ed.). Washington, DC: Office of Juvenile Justice and Delinquency Prevention, U.S. Department of Justice.

Olver, M.E., Stockdale, K.C., & Wormith, J.S. (2009). Risk assessment with young offenders: A meta-analysis of three assessment measures. *Criminal Justice and Behavior*, 36(4), 329–353. doi:10.1177/0093854809331457.

Peck, J.H., & Jennings, W.G. (2016). A critical examination of "being Black" in the juvenile justice system. *Law & Human Behavior*, 40(3), 219–232. doi:10.1037/lhb0000180.

Pedersen, L., Rasmussen, K., & Elsass, P. (2010). Risk assessment: The value of structured professional judgments. *International Journal of Forensic Mental Health*, 9, 74–81. doi:10.1080/14999013.2010.499556.

Penney, S.R., Lee, Z., & Moretti, M.M. (2010). Gender differences in risk factors for violence: An examination of the predictive validity of the Structured Assessment of Violence Risk in Youth. *Aggressive Behavior*, 36(6), 390–404. doi:10.1002/ab.20352.

Perrault, R.T., Vincent, G.M., & Guy, L.S. (2017). Are risk assessments racially biased? Field study of the SAVRY and YLS/CMI in probation. *Psychological Assessment*, 29(6), 664–678. doi:10.1037/pas0000445.

Poulin, M., Orchowsky, S., & Iwama, J. (2011). Assessing DMC initiatives: A case study of two states. In N.Y. Parsons-Pollard (Ed.), *Disproportionate minority contact: Current issues and policies* (pp. 97–121). Durham, NC: Carolina Academic Press.

Pusch, N., & Holtfreter, K. (2018). Gender and risk assessment in juvenile offenders: A meta-analysis. *Criminal Justice & Behavior*, 45(1), 56–81. doi:10.1177%2F0093854817721720.

Rennie, C.E., & Dolan, M.C. (2010). The significance of protective factors in the assessment of risk. *Criminal Behavior & Mental Health*, 20(1), 8–22. doi:10.1002/cbm.750.

Rice, M.E., & Harris, G.T. (2005). Comparing effect sizes in follow-up studies: ROC Area, Cohen's d, and r. *Law and Human Behavior*, 29(5), 615–620. doi:10.1007/s10979-10005-6832-6837.

Ryals, J.S. (2013). *Probation Review Implementation: How Best Practices Meet Everyday Practices*. John D. and Catherine T. MacArthur Foundation's Models for Change initiative. Available at: http://rfknrcjj.org/resources/.

Schmidt, F., Campbell, M.A., & Houlding, C. (2011). Comparative analyses of the YLS/CMI, SAVRY, and PCL: YV in adolescent offenders: A 10-year follow-up into adulthood. *Youth Violence and Juvenile Justice*, 9(1), 23–42. doi:10.1177/1541204010371793.

Schwalbe, C.S. (2007). Risk assessment for juvenile justice: A meta-analysis. *Law and Human Behavior*, 31(5), 449–462. doi:10.1007/s10979-006-9071-7.

Schwalbe, C.S. (2008). A meta-analysis of juvenile justice risk assessment instruments: Predictive validity by gender. *Criminal Justice and Behavior*, 35(11), 1367–1381. doi:10.1177/0093854808324377.

Schwalbe, C.S., Fraser, M.W., Day, S.H., & Cooley, V. (2006). Classifying juvenile offenders according to risk of recidivism: Predictive validity, race/ethnicity, and gender. *Criminal Justice & Behavior*, 33(3), 305–324. doi:10.1177/0093854806286451.

Shepherd, S.M., Luebbers, S., & Ogloff, J.R. (2016). The role of protective factors and the relationship with recidivism for high-risk young people in detention. *Criminal Justice & Behavior*, 43(7), 863–878. doi:10.1177/0093854815626489.

Shlonsky, A., & Wagner, D. (2005). The next step: Integrating actuarial risk assessment and clinical judgment into an evidence-based practice framework in CPS case management. *Children and Youth Services Review*, 27, 409–427. doi:10.1016/j.childyouth.2004.11.007.

Singh, J.P., Grann, M., & Fazel, S. (2011). A comparative study of violence risk assessment tools: A systematic review and metaregression analysis of 68 studies involving 25,980 participants. *Clinical Psychology Review*, 31(3), 499–513. doi:10.1016/j.cpr.2010.11.009.

Smith, P., Cullen, F.T., & Latessa, E.J. (2009). Can 14,737 women be wrong? A meta-analysis of the LSI-R and recidivism for female offenders. *Criminology & Public Policy*, 8(1), 183–208. doi:10.1111/j.1745-9133.2009.00551.x.

Soderstrom, M.F., Childs, K.K., & Frick, P.J. (2020). The role of protective factors in the predictive accuracy of the Structured Assessment of Violence Risk in Youth (SAVRY). *Youth Violence and Juvenile Justice*, 18(1), 78–95. doi:10.1177/1541204019837329.

Sullivan, C.J. (2011). The utility of the deviant case in the development of criminological theory. *Criminology*, 49(3), 905–920. doi:10.1111/j.1745-9125.2011.00236.x.

Sullivan, C.J., Strange, C., Sullivan, C., Newsome, J., Lugo, M., Mueller, D., Petkus, A., Holmes, B., Lonergan, H., & McCafferty, J. (2019). *Multi-Method Study on Risk Assessment Implementation and Youth Outcomes in the Juvenile Justice System*. Submitted to Office of Justice Programs, Office of Juvenile Justice and Delinquency Prevention. www.ojp.gov/pdffiles1/ojjdp/grants/252927.pdf.

Thompson, A.P., & McGrath, A. (2012). Subgroup differences and implications for contemporary risk-need assessment with juvenile offenders. *Law and Human Behavior*, 36(4), 345–355. doi:10.1037/h0093930.

van der Knaap, L.M., Alberda, D.L., Oosterveld, P., & Born, M.P. (2012). The predictive validity of criminogenic needs for male and female offenders: Comparing the relative impact of needs in predicting recidivism. *Law and Human Behavior*, 36(5), 413–422. doi:10.1037/h0093932.

Vaswani, N., & Merone, L. (2014). Are there risks with risk assessment? A study of the predictive accuracy of the Youth Level of Service–Case Management Inventory with young offenders in Scotland. *The British Journal of Social Work*, 44(8), 2163–2181. doi:10.1093/bjsw/bct059.

Viljoen, J.L., Elkovitch, N., Scalora, M.J., & Ullman, D. (2009). Assessment of reoffense risk in adolescents who have committed sexual offenses: Predictive validity of the ERASOR, PCL: YV, YLS/CMI, and Static-99. *Criminal Justice & Behavior*, 36(10), 981–1000. doi:10.1177/0093854809340991.

Vincent, G.M. (2006). Psychopathy and violence risk assessment in youth. *Child and Adolescent Psychiatric Clinics*, 15(2), 407–428. doi:10.1016/j.chc.2005.12.001.

Vincent, G.M., & Viljoen, J.L. (2020). Racist algorithms or systemic problems? Risk assessments and racial disparities. *Criminal Justice and Behavior*, 47(12), 1576–1584. doi:10.1177/0093854820954501.

Vincent, G.M., Chapman, J., & Cook, N.E. (2011). Risk-needs assessment in juvenile justice: Predictive validity of the SAVRY, racial differences, and the contribution of needs factors. *Criminal Justice and Behavior*, 38(1), 42–62. doi:10.1177/0093854810386000.

Vincent, G.M., Guy, L.S., Fusco, S.L., & Gershenson, B.G. (2012). Field reliability of the SAVRY with juvenile probation officers: Implications for training. *Law and Human Behavior*, 36(3), 225–236.

Vincent, G.M., Guy, L.S., Gershenson, B.G., & McCabe, P. (2012). Does risk assessment make a difference? Results of implementing the SAVRY in juvenile probation. *Behavioral Sciences & the Law*, 30(4), 384–405. doi:10.1002/bsl.2014.

Vincent, G.M., Perrault, R.T., Guy, L.S., & Gershenson, B.G. (2012). Developmental issues in risk assessment: Implications for juvenile justice. *Victims & Offenders*, 7(4), 364–384. doi:10.1080/15564886.2012.713900.

Wachter, A. (2015). *Statewide risk assessment in juvenile probation*. Pittsburgh, PA: National Center for Juvenile Justice. http://modelsforchange.net/publications/836/Statewide_Risk_Assessment_in_Juvenile _ Probation.pdf.

Welsh, J.L., Schmidt, F., McKinnon, L., Chattha, H.K., & Meyers, J.R. (2008). A comparative study of adolescent risk assessment instruments: Predictive and incremental validity. *Assessment*, 15(1), 104–115. doi:10.1177/1073191107307966.

Werner, E. (2000). Protective factors and individual resilience. In J. Shonkoff & S. Meisels (Eds.), *Handbook of early childhood intervention*. Cambridge, UK: Cambridge University Press.

Wiebush, R.G., Baird, C., Krisberg, B., & Onek, D. (1995). Risk assessment and classification for serious, violent, and chronic juvenile offenders. *A sourcebook: Serious violent & chronic juvenile offenders*. Thousand Oaks, CA: SAGE Publications.

Yang, M., Wong, S.C.P., & Coid, J. (2010). The efficacy of violent prediction: A meta-analytic comparison of nine risk assessment tools. *Psychological Bulletin*, 136, 740–767. doi:10.1037/a0020473.

Chapter 3

Logic and Use of JRNA

There are multiple stages of the juvenile justice system where important decisions about cases are made. These decisions include whether a youth should be arrested, if the case should be diverted or formally processed by the juvenile court, if pretrial detention is necessary, whether an adjudicated youth should be placed on community supervision or in a residential program, selecting necessary intervention services to reduce the likelihood of recidivism, and whether the youth is ready to be released from juvenile justice supervision. Many of these decisions are informed by screening or assessment practices based on agency policy or state mandates. For instance, after an arrest is made, screening procedures may be used to assess a youth's likelihood of future criminal behavior, appearing in court, and need for a more in-depth assessment of criminogenic needs. Based on the results, screeners determine whether a juvenile should be sent home, placed on electronic monitoring, or placed in pretrial detention. Prosecutors or intake officers use screening and assessment instruments to determine whether a juvenile should be diverted or formally processed (Mears, 2012). If diverted, the specific type of diversion program may be selected based on the criminogenic needs identified through the assessment process.

Most commonly, JRNA is used after a juvenile has been adjudicated, but before a disposition has been determined. The purpose of JRNA at this stage is to assess the youth's potential for future delinquent or criminal behavior and identify targeted areas for intervention. The results of the JRNA are then matched with the appropriate sanction and the type and intensity of treatment service referrals. A juvenile's risk level helps determine whether a disposition of community probation or residential placement is best (i.e., risk-sanction match) and the identified criminogenic needs are used to pinpoint appropriate intervention programs (i.e., service-need match). JRNA is also used as a tool to monitor progress toward risk reduction during supervision. Decisions regarding decreases in intensity of supervision, additional intervention services, and release from supervision can be informed by observed changes in risk/needs over time.

Prior research has confirmed that the implementation of JRNA practices can lead to more objective decision-making practices (e.g., Baglivio et al.,

DOI: 10.4324/9780367823122-3

2015), reduced disparities (e.g., Nellis & Richardson, 2010), and reductions in restrictive placements (e.g., Vincent, Guy, Gershenson, & McCabe, 2012). However, most of these studies have focused on one outcome and/ or one jurisdiction at a time. The three-step process involves several components that occur sequentially (see Figure 2.1) but are also a function of the broader environment in which assessments are administered. The ways in which these processes work together to produce the expected youth- and agency-level benefits of JRNA have yet to be fully examined. Such an assessment of JRNA processes requires a thorough look at *how* the components of JRNA fit together and *why* the effectiveness of JRNA practices varies across different contexts (e.g., stages of juvenile justice system, youth, jurisdictions).

The importance of a comprehensive evaluation of how the three-step process works in practice is based upon the long-lasting impact that juvenile justice system decisions can have on youths. These effects are, in part, due to the wide range of developmental changes that occur during youths' involvement with the juvenile justice system and how life trajectories may be altered due to system experiences (Sullivan, 2019). For example, the potential iatrogenic effects of deep system involvement have been documented for quite some time (Gatti et al., 2009; Loughran et al., 2009; Petrosino et al., 2014). Thus, judgments of risk that influence detention or disposition decisions can have negative effects on future behavior, social adjustment, and educational and employment opportunities. Further compounding these iatrogenic effects is the potential for labeling a youth based on judgments of risk. Negative labels as "high risk" or "high need" can have lasting effects that turn into self-fulfilling prophecies, low confidence and self-efficacy, and secondary deviance.

The goal of this chapter is to provide an in-depth review of the logic of the three-step JRNA process that considers existing empirical research on how the components of JRNA are carried out in practice. We first describe the Risk-Needs-Responsivity (RNR) framework that provides the theoretical foundation for relying on risk and needs assessment practices to inform justice system decisions. Then, we describe the key activities involved in the JRNA process. To facilitate this discussion, we provide a logic model that links the three-step process presented in Chapter 2, RNR principles, and the expected outcomes of optimal JRNA usage.

Risk, Needs, and Responsivity

According to Andrews et al. (1990), the focus on retribution and punishment during the 1980s and 1990s was not effective in reducing recidivism rates. As a result, the RNR model was proposed as an alternative framework, based on the psychology of criminal conduct (i.e., social learning, cognitive, and personality theories), to guide offender rehabilitation in the juvenile and criminal justice systems (Bonta & Andrews, 2012; Brogan et al., 2015). The effectiveness of the RNR framework in reducing recidivism has been established in both the juvenile and criminal justice systems (Andrews & Bonta, 2010; Andrews et al., 2006; Wormith & Zidenberg, 2018). The model consists of three main principles: risk, needs, and responsivity. The fourth principle, professional override, ensures that decisions are appropriate given each offender's current circumstances. The RNR model makes the following arguments (see Andrews et al., 1990 and Bonta & Andrews, 2007 for detailed discussions):

Risk principle: Higher levels or more intensive services should be reserved for the highest risk cases. Empirical evidence suggests that placing lower risk youths in intensive services is not effective, increases the chances of negative outcomes, including recidivism, and is costly (e.g., Baglivio et al., 2015). Therefore, restrictive placement and other high-intensity programs should only be used for high risk youths who carry the greatest potential for change. Lower-level community placements and low intensity programs should be used for offenders who are less likely to reoffend. Thus, the risk principle involves matching the youth's risk level to the intensity of the sanction (i.e., risk-sanction match).

Needs principle: Services should be matched with criminogenic needs (i.e., service-need match). Changes in criminogenic needs should result in a lower risk for reoffending. Thus, when service referrals and intervention programs target identified criminogenic needs, the likelihood of correctional rehabilitation increases and the likelihood of recidivism decreases. Using empirical research on the strongest predictors of criminal behavior, Andrews et al. (2006) identified eight domains of criminogenic needs, referred to as the "Central Eight." Seven of the eight risk factors are dynamic risk factors and include pro-criminal attitudes, antisocial personality, deviant peers, criminal history, substance abuse, negative family relationships, employment/education, and use of free time. The needs principle asserts that identification of deficits in one or more of these areas represents a high priority for intervention services that specifically address the identified need(s).

Responsivity principle: Types of services (e.g., style, mode) should be linked to offender characteristics that are not directly associated with antisocial behavior but are relevant to the youth's response to interventions. Andrews et al. (1990) identified several responsivity factors that may impede the effectiveness of rehabilitation efforts that are not necessarily criminogenic. These include cognitive interpersonal skills, mental health, demographic characteristics, sensation-seeking, motivation to change, and social support.

Adherence to the RNR principles requires a comprehensive assessment of youths' risk and needs factors. JRNA is believed to be an effective method for gathering this information in a consistent and objective manner (Bonta

& Andrews, 2012). Therefore, the link between the RNR framework and correctional effectiveness is largely due to the use of standardized risk and needs assessment practices. As a result, the quality of the JRNA process, which involves a series of interconnected components, directly influences the effectiveness of juvenile justice efforts to treat and sanction youths. A logic model, grounded in the RNR framework, that connects the components of the JRNA process to the intended JRNA outcomes is presented in the following section.

JRNA Logic Model

A logic model presents the rationale behind a program or policy (MacPhee, 2009). In the case of JRNA, the model is used as a tool to efficiently communicate the elements of the JRNA process and how these elements work together to achieve the goal of the practice. There are generally five elements included in a logic model (see Kellogg Foundation, 1998 for more details). *Inputs* are the human and fiscal resources needed to accomplish the work. *Activities* represent the processes and procedures engaged in to achieve the goals. *Outputs* are the direct and tangible products produced by the activities. *Outcomes* are the specific changes that occur because of the program and are often separated into shorter- and longer-term outcomes. For example, in the JRNA logic model presented in Figure 3.1, short-term outcomes are accomplished within one year of JRNA implementation, intermediate outcomes are expected within three years of JRNA implementation, and long-term outcomes should occur within five or more years. *External factors* are elements that may impact the effectiveness of the JRNA process but are not directly controlled by the process. These factors are part of the external environment in which JRNA operates and can affect how well its components (input, output, outcomes) function together. Figure 3.1 presents the JRNA logic model.

Inputs

The resources that go into JRNA include the actual instrument(s) used, agency resources, various actors in the process, and applicable state mandates or jurisdictional policies. Each person that is involved in the process is integral to its effectiveness. For example, the youth and parent/guardian are necessary participants. Most of the information needed to complete the assessment is collected from the youth and their parent/guardian. The bottom-line effects of JRNA practices will fall on youths as they are centered in the assessments being made and the decisions that follow from that part of the process. Youths' families are also affected by treatment and sanction decisions as the responsibility for transportation, participation in services, and financial costs can often fall on parents or guardians. Aside from the youths and their families, frontline personnel who either gather

INPUTS	ACTIVITIES	OUTPUTS	SHORT-TERM OUTCOMES	INTERMEDIATE OUTCOMES	LONG-TERM OUTCOMES
JRNA instrument	Training on JRNA	Overall risk level	Service to need match	Reduced rates of out of home placements for low risk offenders	Improved offender wellbeing in justice-related and prosocial outcomes (e.g., school problems)
Frontline personnel	Administration of the JRNA tool	Dynamic need scores	Case level JJS processing decisions based on JRNA results	Aggregate risk/needs data describing population needs	Improved allocation of JJS resources to meet youth needs
Juvenile offender	Information gathering	Static risk factor scores	Systematic JJS decision making	Aggregate data on JJS program effectiveness	Reduced costs of intensive JJS placements
Parents/guardians	Scoring and analysis	Assessments of change in risk/needs factors	Identification of high risk offenders	Increase in rates of successful completion of JJ interventions	
Agency management	Linkage of JRNA risk/needs scores into JJS decisions			Reduced recidivism	
JJS decision-makers	Reassessment at defined intervals			Reduced disparities in JJS decision making	
Staff/personnel time					
Extended JJ network					
Agency resources					
Local policies					
State law, guidelines, and resources					
Federal guidelines and resources					

External Factors/Context

Youth/family: honesty during the JRNA process, cooperation, rapport with JRNA administrator, developmental characteristics of youths

Staff/personnel/decision-makers: attitudes and beliefs about JRNA, training on JRNA and adolescent development, interviewing skills, job satisfaction

Figure 3.1 Juvenile Risk and Need Assessment Logic Model

information about justice-involved youths or make decisions about their cases are key participants of the JRNA processes. The administrator of the assessment is a frontline staff member of the juvenile justice agency (e.g., juvenile probation officer) responsible for conducting the assessment and scoring the results. The staff member is often trained on JRNA best practices, scoring criteria, and motivational interviewing techniques. These practitioners are at the center of the JRNA process and therefore are a main driving force in its success or failure (see generally Fixsen et al., 2009).

Since the use of formal risk and needs assessment is meant to redirect justice system practices (Mears & Kelly, 1999; Vincent et al., 2016), agency management also plays a critical role in the JRNA process. Agency administrators include direct supervisors who are responsible for reviewing assessments and the associated decisions for fidelity and compliance. One or more upper-level employees usually serve as JRNA trainers or coordinators and are considered agency "experts" who are available for consultation. Upper-level management can also use JRNA data to inform administrative decisions (e.g., allocation of resources, staff needs) and ensure compliance with internal policies and broader jurisdictional or statewide mandates.

Juvenile justice decision-makers who are not directly involved in the administration of the assessment, but use the information gained from the assessment to inform their decisions, are also valuable resources. As the logic model suggests, the collection of data via a structured risk assessment is meant to inform decision-makers such that they are "end users" of the information who are not involved in administering the tool or directly involved with processes surrounding it. This includes judges and prosecutors who use the JRNA results to make decisions about delinquency cases. Since the use of JRNA results serves as one mechanism by which systems adhere to the RNR principles, the value placed on these results can impact the degree to which decisions are made in a systematic and unbiased manner that reflect the goals of the RNR framework.

Finally, a shift in operations and approach to different elements of case processing carries important implications for those in the networks of the juvenile justice system. A lot of services for youth are offered through private contractors and other nonprofit agencies. Therefore, those organizations are affected by this shift in practice and procedure, too (Howell et al., 2004; Maschi et al., 2008). Treatment agencies and personnel may be aware of the information contained in the assessment which can improve the services offered to youths and families. This may come via negotiated agreements developed to promote information sharing to inform treatment and progress monitoring (see Etten & Petrone, 1994; Mankey et al., 2006). Additionally, the use of JRNA data to evaluate these intervention programs, through monitoring change in risk domains prior to and after program participation effectiveness, can lead to increased oversight of the partner agencies' performance.

Agency resources include both time and money. Staff time is a necessary resource for JRNA. This includes the time it takes to train staff on JRNA policies and protocols, complete the assessment with the youth and parent/guardian, collect collateral information, score the instrument, and review the assessment with supervisors to ensure fidelity. These practices inherently reduce the time that staff can devote to performing other job responsibilities such as attendance at juvenile court proceedings, meeting with youths and families, professional development, and supervision checks. Staff time can also be quantified in terms of financial resources. Other financial resources include the cost of regularly offering training and professional development on JRNA, changing or updating electronic case management systems, and any costs associated with using the actual instrument (Vincent et al., 2016, p. 694). Finally, local policies and/or state mandates often provide clear guidance on JRNA best practices to promote consistency in the administration, scoring, and utilization of screening and assessment practices. These guidelines are essential resources for staff administering and scoring the instrument as well as ensuring that decision-makers are using the results in a systematic and unbiased manner. Mandates or policies are also frequently subject to federal oversight and/or training and technical assistance as funding awards to grantees can be made contingent on usage of certain practices, such as systematic risk and needs assessment. Importantly, each "input" included in the JRNA logic model interacts with other "inputs" to carry out the JRNA activities.

Activities

The activities that take place during the JRNA process include training staff, the administration of the instrument, information gathering (Step 1 of Figure 2.1), scoring and analysis (Step 2 of Figure 2.1) procedures, and the use of the assessment results to make system decisions that adhere to the RNR principles (Step 3 of Figure 2.1). These activities occur in sequential order (i.e., three-step process: gather information, score the assessment, incorporate into decisions) and rely on active participation from many of the JRNA inputs described earlier (i.e., frontline personnel, juvenile offender, parents/guardians, and juvenile justice system decision-makers). This means that the quality of each JRNA activity is a function of the various "inputs" involved.

Training

Staff training is necessary to ensure that the individuals who are responsible for administering and scoring the instrument are prepared to conduct the assessment in a trauma-informed and culturally sensitive manner. This involves educating staff on adolescent development and cognitive capacities, warning signs for important criminogenic risk factors (e.g., history of trauma, mental illness), and guidelines or techniques for scoring the assessment in a valid and reliable manner. Training also addresses how the information gathered and the associated assessment results (i.e., risk level, needs) are used to make case-level decisions, and in some cases, how the JRNA data will be used to make agency-level planning decisions (e.g., data-driven decision-making). Existing research indicates that training programs designed to educate professionals on risk assessment practices lead to improvements in knowledge about risk assessment, administration skills, and attitudes and confidence about using risk assessment instruments (Reynolds & Miles, 2009; Storey et al., 2011), but also that it is not sufficient to fully support implementation and sustainability (Vincent, Guy, & Grisso, 2012).

Information Gathering

The groundwork of the assessment process involves gathering information in a systematic, unbiased, and professional manner. Both the quality and type of information that is collected during the assessment process is directly incorporated into the scoring procedures. Successful administration of the assessment involves a conversation-like interview between the staff member collecting the information and the youth and parent/guardian providing the information. For example, the user's manual for the Washington State Juvenile Court Assessment (Barnoski, 2004; Barnoski & Markussen, 2005), which became the PACT, establishes that first a structured interview should be held with the youth and his/her family to gather relevant insight on risk and protective factors. The procedures manual also suggests contacting other agencies (e.g., schools, community treatment agencies) or collateral reporters (e.g., parents) to confirm the information provided during the interview process. This includes checks on both "denial responses" and "affirmative responses" (Barnoski, 2004, p. 23). Collecting collateral information is considered a JRNA best practice (Borum et al., 2006; Vincent, Guy, & Grisso, 2012). The purpose of gathering information from multiple sources is to ensure that only reliable information is considered during the scoring process and that a holistic assessment of the youth's circumstances is achieved. For example, communication with teachers may provide a more accurate assessment of the youth's school-related risk factors such as behavior at school, peers, and academic achievement. The assessor may also search through earlier records to confirm or elaborate on details from the interview with the youth.

Several factors can impact the quality of the information gathered. These factors are related to the characteristics of the youth and parent/guardian participating in the assessment and the professional administering the assessment. For example, how participants interpret the questions being asked can determine the validity of the information collected. Participants' interpretation may be dependent on their level of understanding of the questions being asked. Cultural differences in behavioral norms or language used to describe risk factors may impact the meaning attached to certain questions that are asked about a youth's family, peer, educational, and behavioral history. Differences in socialization experiences such as exposure to antisocial behavior can influence an individual's perceptions of what is relevant to the assessment and what is not. Youths may also interpret questions differently based on their level of cognitive functioning. Although most JRNA instruments are validated for use with youths aged 10 and older, the cognitive abilities of a 10-year-old are much different than the cognitive abilities of a 15-year-old (or a 17-year-old even more so). Furthermore, extant research suggests that juvenile offenders tend to have lower than average IQ, impulse control, and critical thinking skills (Lee & Prentice, 1988; McGloin & Pratt, 2003; Ray et al., 2016; Sigurdsson et al., 2001; Steinberg et al., 2015). These characteristics may increase the likelihood of insufficient understanding of the questions asked, poor memory, answering questions impulsively, or an inability to relay information in a coherent, descriptive manner.

Openness and honesty among youths are also integral to collecting accurate information. There is evidence to suggest that different adolescents might both underreport and overreport socially unacceptable behaviors such as engagement in delinquency and substance use (Buchan et al., 2002; Krohn et al., 2011). Using a large, nationally representative sample of adolescents (i.e., National Longitudinal Study of Adolescent and Adult Health), Fan et al. (2006) identified two different types of invalid survey responses. "Inaccurate responders" provided inconsistent results due to confusion or carelessness. "Jokesters" intentionally provided false information. Fan et al. (2006) also found that the tendency to fall into one category varied by the nature of the question. Several reasons why adolescents fail to disclose personal information during interviews have been identified including concerns over inappropriate police or court action, shame, parental awareness, and social desirability or self-preservation (deLara, 2012; Piquero et al., 2014; Spidel et al., 2011). Often it is assumed that higher risk adolescents (e.g., serious offenders) are less inclined to be open and honest (Krohn et al., 2011; Spidel et al., 2011). If this is the case, JRNA results could lead to underestimation of risk or a greater number of false negatives among those who are at high risk to reoffend and in need of intensive intervention services.

Rapport or the quality of communication between the administrator of the assessment and the offender can impact openness and honesty through the development of trust. For instance, one youth may be willing to provide detailed information about the frequency and intensity of parental conflict in the home while another youth may not be willing to share this information due to fear that a parent may find out. Such differences in the type and quality of information collected can lead to differences in overall assessments of family-related risk factors that could ultimately influence the determined level of risk and, in turn, the types of interventions needed. These perceptions can also affect the credence that is given to youth responses by juvenile justice personnel who administer these tools. If the assessor believes that the information from the interview is untrustworthy then they can look to collateral reporters or records to confirm the information offered by the youth.

The ways in which staff interpret the meaning of the items on the assessment can also impact the types of questions asked, source(s) of collateral information sought out, and the weight of the information considered for each item. For example, one administrator may interpret reports of parental conflict as "high risk" while another scores parental conflict as "low risk" given that two, biological parents are residing in the home (i.e., intact family considered a protective factor). Consistency in staff interpretations of what constitutes different levels of risk (i.e., low risk versus moderate risk) applies to both item responses and overall scoring procedures. Unfortunately, as discussed in Chapter 2, the reliability of JRNA scoring among practitioners in the field has not been fully established (Vincent, Guy, Fusco, & Gershenson, 2012). Variations in staff and youth interpretations threaten the reliability of the assessment results. If staff interpret the information differently than what the youth or other respondent intended, this can lead to inaccuracies. Thus, effective communication is critical to information gathering.

There is general agreement that the assessment of dynamic risk factors is a critical component of JRNA. Recall that the central tenet of the need principle is that dynamic risk factors that are criminogenic (i.e., empirically associated with recidivism) should be prioritized for intervention (Andrews et al., 2006; Andrews & Bonta, 2010; Caudy et al., 2013; Gendreau et al., 2006). Furthermore, existing research suggests that the collection of information related to dynamic risk factors, in addition to static risk factors, leads to a more comprehensive assessment. However, the process by which JRNA administrators determine that an existing, dynamic risk factor is or is not criminogenic has been debated. The RNR framework suggests a universal model of criminogenic needs (i.e., the "Central Eight") that is based on empirical research, and thus, applies to all offenders (Andrews & Bonta, 2010; Andrews et al., 2006; Bonta & Andrews, 2007; 2012). Others have argued that the risk factors that directly relate to delinquent behavior (i.e., criminogenic) vary by individual and that only considering the "Central Eight" promotes a "one size shoe fits all" approach to intervention (Ward et al., 2007, p. 320). As a result, information gathering should include both an assessment of the presence of dynamic risk factors and, of those present, which are high impact, criminogenic needs (Cording et al., 2016; Haqanee et al., 2015). It also should include reassessment at established time intervals to monitor progress and change (Baglivio et al., 2017; Douglas & Skeem, 2005).

Fourth-generation assessment instruments also include the collection of protective factors, or assets. These are characteristics that mitigate or reduce the impact of risk factors on behavior. Whether or not protective factors are assessed can impact the length of time it takes to complete the assessment and the types of questions that are asked during the information gathering process. For example, administrators may be less inclined to engage in follow-up questions or gather collateral information about risk factors if protective factors have been identified. Furthermore, some administrators may fail to consider protective factors while others integrate them in detail. Such differences can lead to variations in overall assessments of risk because, theoretically, protective factors reduce the effect of risk factors on behavior. This means that, when protective factors are identified during information gathering, estimates of risk may decline for a given case. If Case A and Case B have similar levels of risk and needs identified from a risk assessment instrument, but the administrator of Case A's assessment considers protective factors and the administrator of Case B's assessment does not, it is likely that Case A will be rated at a lower risk level than Case B given the presence of one or more protective factors that are expected to reduce the likelihood of reoffending.

There are two competing perspectives regarding the role of protective factors that could impact how professionals gather and assess information regarding existing strengths (see Serin et al., 2016; Polaschek, 2016; Rogers, 2000). The first perspective, referred to as the compensatory model, considers risk and protective factors as cumulative. Each risk factor increases the risk for reoffending and each protective factor reduces the risk for reoffending. The relationship between the risk and protective factors is not considered. The second perspective, the interactive model, considers protective factors only when they are in the presence of risk factors. That is, the importance of protective factors varies depending on the level and type of risk present. Protective factors then buffer the effects of risk factors on behavior (Lösel & Farrington, 2012; Rutter, 1985). According to Serin et al. (2016), this means that there are important differences between protective factors and assets. An asset, or strength, may not necessarily protect a youth from future criminal behavior. An asset only becomes a protective factor when it influences the choice to engage in prosocial, non-criminal behavior when faced with a criminal opportunity because it "protected" the individual from further delinquent behavior (Serin et al., 2016, p. 156). These differing perspectives can lead to differences in the ways in which information is gathered during the assessment process. Those that hold beliefs that align with the compensatory model may gather information regarding the presence of risk and assets separately without considering how they are related. Those whose beliefs align with the interactive model must gather information that helps to identify the presence of strength/assets and assess whether the existing asset(s) influences desistance.

Scoring and Analysis

Scoring is meant to be a systematic process whereby the same data synthesis and analytic procedures are used for every youth. The goal of this stage of the assessment process is objectivity and consistency in how the information gathered is used to estimate a youth's risk to reoffend and their intervention needs. It is standard practice to implement guidelines that outline how to determine a youth's score for each item and devote a portion of JRNA training protocols to this issue to ensure consistency in how ratings of risk are determined. Scoring involves assessing the presence or absence of each risk factor and, when present and applicable, its severity. The scoring of each item is completed during or after all information gathering activities are complete (e.g., interview with youth and parent/guardian, collection of collateral information). Once each item is scored, the overall risk score and level are determined. Some JRNA instruments rely on dichotomous indicators representing the presence or absence of each risk factor included on the assessment (e.g., YLS/CMI, OYAS) and other instruments measure degrees of risk for each item (e.g., SAVRY, PACT).

Several factors can influence exactly how objective JRNA scoring procedures are carried out in practice. One key characteristic of this component is professional discretion regarding how the information is used to derive scores. This includes choosing the specific information that was collected during the assessment interview with the youth and parent/guardian that will be considered during scoring, if and how much collateral information is collected and considered, adherence to scoring policies and procedures (i.e., fidelity), inclusion of protective factors, and the consideration of other, noncriminogenic needs that are not measured on the assessment (Basanta et al., 2018). Discretion can serve as a threat to the reliability of the JRNA process when staff vary in their use of different sources of information or the weight that they give to different items. Discretion can also jeopardize the expected "objectivity" of JRNA results when these variations in scoring practices are based on staff perceptions or biases regarding offenders' risk and needs. On the other hand, when used correctly, discretion can help account for the unique circumstances of each youth to improve the available information and subsequent decision making (Guy et al., 2014; Childs et al., 2014). Either way, training on RNR principles and JRNA best practices is essential to reducing the use of discretion during JRNA scoring (Kennealy et al., 2017).

The use of actuarial scoring procedures, where the risk score is derived via predetermined rules, limits discretion in scoring practices because, in theory, the same formula is applied in the same manner for each case. The use of structured professional judgment (SPJ), whereby the risk score is derived through professional judgment based on evidence-based guidelines, is characterized by greater discretion due to the reliance of practitioners' judgements of the youth's circumstances. The SPJ framework allows administrators, based on their professional judgment and empirically established criteria, to consider each youth's unique constellation of risk factors. In other words, the SPJ framework allows the administrator to consider the "totality of the circumstances" for each case. Guy et al. (2014, p. 229) argue that SPJ allows administrators to consider the individual manifestation of each risk item (e.g., for mental health problems: type or display of mental health symptoms; for substance use: type of substances used) and the relevance of each risk item to the offender's overall risk for reoffending (e.g., impact of the mental health symptom on potential future behavior; reasons for use of substances). Thus, SPJ involves the use of discretion regarding the type of information used to assess risk, whether and how manifestation and relevance are considered, and which items are considered to have the most impact on future behavior. Actuarial scoring practices, based on a standardized and quantitative scoring system, do not offer this flexibility. Therefore, actuarial assessments may lead to more consistent and objective scoring practices, but do not allow for customizing the JRNA results to the youth's unique circumstances.

All JRNAs rely on predetermined risk categories, regardless of scoring procedure. Reliance on fixed categories of risk (e.g., low risk, moderate risk, high risk) can give the illusion of clear differences across risk scores, leading to the reification of risk categories that do not actually represent real or concrete differences in risk and needs. Often, however, the distinction in values or levels of specific risk factors may be unclear. For example, take a juvenile who receives a score of 11 on an actuarial assessment instrument. The predetermined categories for risk level are low risk equals 0–6, moderate risk equals 7–10, and high risk equals 11–14. There is a meaningful (and obvious) difference in the label "moderate risk" or "high risk" but there may not be a meaningful or obvious difference in a risk score of 10 versus a risk score of 11, especially when the range of the scale is 0–14. Additionally, the intensity of the placement associated with each risk category could be vastly different based on a one-point difference in "risk."

Reification can also lead to negative labeling of youths by system actors and family members which can lead to further harmful consequences such as low self-esteem, criminal embeddedness, and entrenched engagement in antisocial behavior (Becker, 1963; Bernburg et al., 2006; Hagan, 1993). This extends to cases within the same risk level because the variation within risk categories and the nature of the specific risk factors contributing to the risk score can vary considerably and in ways that should inform case decisions about youths involved in the juvenile justice system.

Linking JRNA Results to Juvenile Justice Decision Making

Consistent with the RNR framework, the risk and needs scores are then incorporated into recommendations to the judge, graduated sanction matrices, case management planning, and referrals to intervention services. These recommendations and the associated JRNA scores are considered by various decision-makers (e.g., judges, prosecutors) to inform their decisions about placements and services. The utilization of the JRNA results by juvenile justice decision-makers can vary from complete discretion regarding when and how the decision-maker will use the JRNA results to mandated decision-making policies based on disposition or treatment matrices that identify prescribed dispositions and/or intervention programs (i.e., see local policies as an input in the logic model). For example, some jurisdictions provide guidelines on how to use the JRNA results when making recommendations to the judge but do not have formalized policies that link particular risk levels and mandatory dispositions. Other jurisdictions rely on mandated disposition matrices that specify which sanctions should be given to a youth based on their risk score and other offense-related characteristics. For example, the Florida Department of Juvenile Justice (2014) has implemented guidelines for disposition decisions based on a matrix that considers each youth's most serious current offense and the assessed risk to reoffend level. The matrix consists of a 4 X 4 table where current offense is represented in the rows and is broken down into offenses eligible for civil citation (nonviolent, first-time misdemeanors), minor offenses (i.e., misdemeanor offenses), serious offenses (i.e., felony offenses that do not include violence), and violent offenses (violent felony offenses). Risk level is represented in the columns and represents low risk, moderate risk, moderate-high risk, and high risk. The joint distributions include recommended dispositions that are broken down by level of restrictiveness. Level 1 includes alternatives to arrest, Level 2 includes diversion, Level 3 includes community supervision options, Level 4 includes non-secure residential commitment, and Level 5 includes secure residential commitment. Validation studies suggest that high adherence to the matrix during decision making (>90%) lowers rates of restrictive placements and reduces recidivism rates (Baglivio et al., 2015; Lehmann et al., 2020). This represents the flow of the inputs, activities, and outcomes specified in the logic model. Local policies (inputs) drive how juvenile justice system decision-makers (inputs) integrate the risk/needs scores into case-processing decisions (activity) that influence rates of out of home placements and recidivism (outcomes).

The ways in which the JRNA results are used during the decision-making process may vary by decision-maker, case circumstances (e.g., offense, prior history), and organization. Juvenile court judges who do not support the use of JRNA may not be inclined to use the results of the assessment during dispositional decision making while juvenile court judges that support JRNA may base their dispositional decisions entirely on the results. In this case, one judge may make dispositional decisions systematically while the other judge may be considering other, potentially extra-legal, factors that are unique to each case. Furthermore, organizations that rely on mandated policies regarding how JRNA results should be used, like FDJJ's disposition matrix, are more likely to experience consistent decision-making practices across decision-makers compared to organizations that do not rely on formal policies specifying how and when JRNA results should be used. Inconsistent use of JRNA results by system actors can jeopardize some benefits of JRNA including objectivity, systematic decision making, and proper matching of risk and needs to services (i.e., outputs of the logic model).

Studies of the juvenile and adult correctional systems that have examined whether JRNA results are used to match identified criminogenic needs to service and case management plans suggest that adherence to the needs principle is mixed. The consistency of adherence varies across studies and criminogenic needs (Bonta et al., 2008; Vieira et al., 2009; Luong & Wormith, 2011). Nelson and Vincent (2018) found that, following implementation of the SAVRY, less than 50 percent of criminogenic needs identified were matched with an intervention and that matching varied by the specific need. For instance, 74 percent of youths with substance use needs were matched but only 41 percent of youths with an educational need were matched. Furthermore, under-prescription of needs was observed more frequently than over-prescription. For example, 59 to 75 percent of moderate or high risk youths experienced under-prescription for at least one identified criminogenic need. Using the YLS/CMI, Vitopoulos et al. (2012) found high rates of service matching to employment and education needs but substantially lower rates of matching for other criminogenic needs such as family, substance use, and use of leisure time. Peterson-Badali et al. (2015) found lower rates of service to need matching using the YLS/CMI. Among their sample of 148 juveniles assessed at a mental health facility, 11 to 57 percent had their needs matched to the service recommendations included in their clinical report. There are several caveats to consider when making conclusions about service to need matching (Miller & Maloney, 2013). Inconsistency in the rate of occurrence of service to need matching varies across studies and across criminogenic need domains measured within a single study. One potential reason for variations in service to need matching is limited availability of programs that match one or more criminogenic needs (Haqanee et al., 2015; Shook & Sarri, 2007) and the relative emphasis given to training juvenile justice personnel on information gathering and scoring versus utilization of risk/needs information in case management (Sullivan et al., 2019), which potentially stems from an actual lack of available programs or a gap in knowledge of those programs among staff. An additional explanation for variation in matching needs to services is gaps in the ways in which the assessment information is translated into case management plans effectively which is closely related to training effectiveness and other implementation components discussed in Chapter 4.

Reassessment

Reassessment is also a core component of the JRNA process. This means that the JRNA activities described on p. 28 occur multiple times while a youth is under juvenile justice supervision. The purpose of reassessment is to monitor progress toward risk reduction and the enrichment of strengths/ protective factors while under juvenile justice supervision or custody (Baglivio et al., 2018). The level of change observed across assessment time points is then used to inform decisions about changes to supervision intensity, intervention goals, and readiness for release. Reassessment at defined intervals (e.g., every 90 days) represents a reliable mechanism to assess progress or changes during supervision. Relying on the same risk assessment items and scoring procedures across time ensures that assessments of change are based on the same criteria.

The assess-reassess process can also lead to unintended consequences that threaten the validity of the information provided. Staff expectancies based on previous assessments is one consequence. This can lead to selective information gathering or the selective use of information in accordance with these expectations. After multiple assessments over an extended period, youths may become familiar with the assessment questions and the ways in which the information is used to make decisions. As a result, youths may be prepared to provide information that will demonstrate positive progression and reduced risk. Maturation can also impact the validity of results. Adolescence is characterized by developmental changes in cognitive abilities, reasoning, and knowledge of interview questions that may influence how youths respond to the assessment process after their initial assessment. Staff turnover might mean that assessments are administered by multiple staff during a youth's involvement in the system. As discussed on p. 58, administrators may interpret information, use discretion, and rate risk and needs differently. Such testing effects can lead to inaccurate assessments of change in criminogenic needs.

The activities involved in the JRNA process represent a series of steps that occur consecutively in a linked fashion. For instance, the collection of accurate item-level information increases the likelihood of accurate estimations or risk, which in turn increases the likelihood of appropriate case-level decisions. Effective communication among youths and staff, proper training and education, policies or guidelines for best practices, objectivity, and consistency throughout the process (and across different inputs) are integral to ensuring that the JRNA process is occurring as intended. When this happens, the short-term outcomes, which include matching youth risk levels with case-processing decisions, linking criminogenic needs with intervention services, reducing biased decision-making practices, and ensuring the proper allocation of resources to higher risk cases can be achieved.

Outputs

The interaction among JRNA "inputs" and "activities" leads to valuable and unbiased products that are referred to as outputs. JRNA outputs include the final overall risk score, separate scores for dynamic and static risk domains, and measures of change in criminogenic needs based on two or more administrations of the assessment. These products are then used to make decisions that align with the RNR principles (i.e., short-term outcomes). Thus, the estimates of risk and need (i.e., outputs) serve as the catalyst to accomplishing the intended outcomes. Outputs can also be used in aggregate form to guide agency-level, data-driven decisions. Thus, the outputs developed through the JRNA process are used to educate decision-makers about individual cases, population trends, and agency needs.

Outcomes

JRNA outcomes represent the benefits of implementing JRNA practices. Our logic model breaks these benefits down into short-term (e.g., within one year), intermediate (e.g., within three years), and long-term (e.g., within five years) benefits. Proximal outcomes (i.e., short-term) reflect the ways in which JRNA can improve juvenile justice system practices. For case-level decisions, proximal benefits include better matching of youths' risk level to appropriate sanctioning decisions and matching youths' needs to intervention services. This means that one of the major short-term outcomes of JRNA is achieving adherence to the RNR framework. Appropriate risk-sanction and needs-service matches (key activities in the logic model) increase the likelihood of successful completion of juvenile justice interventions and reduces the likelihood of recidivism through the receipt of appropriate levels of supervision and targeted intervention (Andrews et al., 1990; Baglivio et al., 2015; 2018; Luong & Wormith, 2011; Peterson-Badali et al., 2015). Adherence to the RNR principles (i.e., short-term outcomes) increases the odds that the intermediate outcomes will be achieved. More specifically, adherence to the risk principle will reduce the likelihood of low or moderate risk for youths receiving an out of home placement. Adherence to all three principles will increase a youth's chances for engaging in effective interventions, successfully completing supervision terms, and desisting from antisocial behavior. As a result, improved youth wellbeing and positive youth outcomes across multiple domains including justice-related and prosocial outcomes will be sustained (i.e., long-term JRNA outcomes).

Consistent empirical evidence indicates that the correspondence of criminogenic needs and service recommendations is associated with lower rates of recidivism (Bonta & Andrews, 2012; Luong & Wormith, 2011; Vitopoulos et al., 2012). Peterson-Badali et al. (2015) found that 40 percent of youths with an identified need on the family domain of the YLS/CMI that was matched with services recidivated compared to 72 percent of youths that did not have their identified family need matched. Similar differences were found among youths with matched personality needs compared to youths with unmatched personality needs and youths with matched education/employment needs and youths with unmatched education/employment needs. Vieira et al. (2009) found that the odds of recidivism among youths with a low correspondence between needs and services was considerably greater than youths with a high correspondence among needs and services. Baglivio et al. (2018) examined whether matching criminogenic needs with services led to reductions in risk scores and later recidivism. Among a sample of 1,678 juvenile offenders released from residential placement in Florida, Baglivio et al. (2018) found that 73 percent of youths had their criminogenic needs matched with one or more services. Matching services led to significantly better drug/alcohol and aggression outcomes at release. However, when youths participated in a matched service for an adequate duration of time (based on Standardized Program Evaluation Protocol (SPEP), see Lipsey et al., 2007), they found significantly better outcomes across several domains including current relationships, alcohol and drug use, attitudes, aggression, social skills, and recidivism.

Nelson and Vincent (2018) focused specifically on one SPJ assessment, the SAVRY, and how well needs were matched to services. Their study was based on a sample of 452 youth cases in three probation offices in one state. The sites used a standardized implementation procedure involving training on the SPJ process and associated case management process and shifts in procedures and data collection procedures. The researchers assessed matching by employing the service matrices developed in each of their sites. They then determined whether the youth was under- or over-placed compared to the needs identified in their assessment results. While their study suggested that there was an improvement in the number of needs addressed over what was seen in previous research, they found that more than half of the youths in the sample did not receive a service that they needed, but that this varied across different areas of need. For example, substance use needs were reasonably well matched while educational and emotional health needs were "under-prescribed."

Together these studies provide preliminary support for the potential of JRNA processes to produce short-term outcomes that are part of the underlying logic of these practices, mainly adherence to the RNR principles. These studies also suggest that when risk assessment scores are used to make decisions about sanctions and service referrals, fewer restrictive placements are used and recidivism is reduced (Luong & Wormith, 2011; Peterson-Badali et al., 2015; Vincent, Guy, Gershenson, & McCabe, 2012).

Over time, intermediate and long-term changes in aggregate or agency-level practices should also be observed. For example, systematic decision making based on the RNR principles has been shown to reduce biased and unstructured decisions (e.g., Baglivio et al., 2015; also see Brogan et al., 2015 and Bonta & Andrews, 2012 for a review). Consequently, reduced rates of racial and ethnic disparities in juvenile justice decision-making practices should be observed over time. Aggregate JRNA data can also help administrators to understand population risk and need characteristics and to measure program and agency-level effectiveness through the assessment of change in risk/needs observed across different juvenile justice interventions.

The agency-level data can be used to drive decisions regarding the sustainment of existing intervention programs and the identification for new programs that address unmet needs. The continual assessment of aggregate JRNA data to monitor population needs and program effectiveness (i.e., intermediate outcome) will ensure proper allocation of resources and that available services effectively address youth needs (i.e., long-term outcomes). Relatedly, reserving intensive and costly interventions for higher risk offenders (i.e., intermediate outcome) can reduce the costs associated with these restrictive programs (i.e., longer-term outcome). These funds can then be properly allocated to the programmatic areas where deficits are identified (i.e., long-term outcomes). Using aggregate JRNA data, such deficits can be identified, targeted, and monitored to ensure that financial and staff resources are being directed to the appropriate programs and services. Thus, agency leaders and community stakeholders can develop a data-driven process for continual assessment of population needs, services available to meet those needs, and the effectiveness of existing services using aggregate JRNA data. In sum, the long-term outcomes of JRNA include offender rehabilitation and system efficiency. Over time, accomplishing the short-term (i.e., adherence to RNR principles) and intermediate outcomes (e.g., improving success rates, reducing recidivism) will presumably lead to positive youth outcomes across a variety of domains (e.g., education, employment, behavioral health, and relationship quality) and agency-level fiscal and operational outcomes (e.g., reduce disparities, allocation of resources). Preliminary evidence does suggest that the JRNA activities outlined in the logic model can lead to positive short-term (e.g., service to need matching) and intermediate (e.g., reduced rates of restrictive placements) outcomes. The long-term youth outcomes of JRNA have yet to be examined. For instance, whether JRNA practices lead to improvements in or sustainment of prosocial outcomes such as substance use, aggression, delinquent behavior, and attitudes later in life is an essential component to understanding the longevity of the benefits of JRNA for youths involved in the system.

External Factors Influencing the Use of JRNA

The external factors at the bottom of the logic model (Figure 3.1) represent the characteristics of the environment in which the JRNA process, and the

RNR principles, operate. These characteristics influence the quality of inputs, activities, and outputs, which in turn determine the quality of the outcomes. As Bonta and Andrews (2012, p. 35) note:

> It is one thing for scientists to demonstrate that a risk instrument or a treatment program can work; it is a very different matter to make it work in correctional agencies with a diverse workforce in terms of education, values and experiences, conflicting criminal justice policies, and management practices that are not conducive to selecting and training staff in effective assessment techniques.

External factors include characteristics of the staff administering the assessment, youths and parents/guardians participating in the assessment, the juvenile justice organization, and the broader socio-political climate. We provide a few examples of external factors that affect the success of the three-step JRNA process and return to the ways in which environmental and organizational conditions influence implementation of JRNA processes in Chapter 4.

Very little research has been conducted on how different characteristics of youths and staff affect the ability of JRNA processes to achieve the intended outcomes. One example is considering the setting in which the assessment instrument is administered (e.g., home, assessment center, probation office). Understanding how the surroundings in which the assessment is administered impacts youth and family cooperation, for example, is important to improving the likelihood of openness and honesty. This requires research examining whether assessments conducted in the youth's home where other family members may be listening produce the same level of measurement validity and predictive value as assessments conducted in an office with no one else around. Similarly, cultural competence and affinity between juvenile justice personnel and youths and family members may also affect the willingness of youths and parents to disclose, as well as the potential for scoring differences. Research on the factors that lead to a positive therapeutic alliance, which represents the relationship between the adolescent client and their therapist, suggests that both the setting of the intervention and the therapist's cultural awareness are important facilitators of openness, honesty, and engagement (Asnaani & Hofmann, 2012; Carpenter et al., 2018; Johnson et al., 2002; Vasquez, 2007). Given the similarities in the therapist–client relationship and the JRNA assessor–offender relationship (e.g., interviews, assessment of risk/needs), it is likely that these contextual factors also impact the quality of the assessment process. Attention to such influences can also provide more insight about field reliability.

Existing evidence suggests that support for JRNA, compliance with JRNA policies, and confidence to accurately administer and score JRNAs varies across professionals (Guy et al., 2014; Miller & Maloney, 2013). One's beliefs about the usefulness of assessment practices, or staff buy-in, is an important predictor of whether JRNA instruments are used as intended (Guy et al., 2014; Miller & Maloney, 2013; Shook & Sarri, 2007; Vincent, Paiva-Salisbury, et al., 2012). Investment from both upper-level management (e.g., direct supervisors, directors) and juvenile justice decision-makers (e.g., judges) facilitates an environment that is supportive of JRNA practices for frontline staff who are primarily responsible for implementation. Vincent et al. (2016, p. 694) explain that the implementation of JRNA practices "…makes no difference in jurisdictions where judges do not buy into the process and make all case management decisions." Not only can the weight given to JRNA results during case-level decision making impact the quality of the decisions that are made, but it can also affect staff's perception of the worth placed on their work by key actors in the process (and whether it makes sense for them to engage in extra effort to learn and use the assessment process with fidelity). This is demonstrated when decision-makers use the JRNA results to make decisions about placements and interventions that adhere to the RNR principles.

The clarity of agency-level policies and protocols for JRNA, as well as the enforcement of these policies and protocols by administrators, can also increase the likelihood of effective JRNA practices. Key elements to JRNA policies and procedures include the scoring of JRNA, gathering collateral information, required intervals for completion of reassessments (e.g., every six months), fidelity checks by supervisors, continual training or professional development, and the utilization of matrices that link the JRNA results with sanction and intervention decisions that adhere to the RNR principles.

Caseload size varies across staff within an agency and across agencies. Higher caseloads result in less time available to devote to JRNA. This can lead to rushed assessments that threaten the validity of the JRNA results, omission of key points in case planning, or staff choosing to skip a follow-up assessment to save time. Most juvenile justice practitioners are responsible for the completion of a large amount of paperwork including case notes for every visit with a youth, intervention referrals and follow-up, regular client updates to supervisors and the juvenile court, and written recommendations to the judge. Guy et al. (2014) found that the length of time it takes to complete the SAVRY was a consistent theme that negatively impacted JPOs' feelings toward the use of JRNA.

The availability and quality of programs and services carries significant weight in the ability to accomplish service to need matching (Haqanee et al., 2015). In jurisdictions where there is a wide range of programs and services available to justice-involved youths, adherence to the RNR principles is easier to achieve. Even when appropriate services exist, the quality of these programs varies across contexts, however (Belenko et al., 2017; Chuang & Wells, 2010). This is due to several factors including collaboration across agencies, information sharing about youths' needs, and broader county or statewide resources for adolescent behavioral health needs. Some of the most effective juvenile justice interventions (e.g., "brand-name" evidence-based programs such as

Multisystemic Therapy) are also the most expensive (Drake et al., 2009; Welsh et al., 2014). Therefore, jurisdictions with fewer resources often experience a shortage of available services that effectively target youths' risks and needs and consider important responsivity factors (e.g., mental health, gender). Without an assortment of intervention programs that vary in both intensity and targeted needs, it is difficult for staff to make referrals that adhere to the RNR principles which undermines the logic of the JRNA process.

Chapter Summary

Comprehensive studies of the JRNA logic model, or more specifically, how the components of the logic model work together to produce the expected outcomes, are relatively rare. The studies that have been conducted tend to focus on Step 3 of the JRNA process (see Figure 2.1) or the degree to which the JRNA results lead to systematic decisions that link the risk score to the severity of the sanction (i.e., RNR risk principle) or the identified criminogenic needs with case plans and service recommendations (i.e., RNR need principle). Some of these studies also examine whether recidivism rates vary based on the degree of adherence to one or more of these principles. In general, research from both the juvenile and adult justice systems indicates that the utilization of standardized assessment practices reduces rates of restrictive placements for low and moderate risk offenders and lowers recidivism (Andrews & Dowden, 2006; Dowden & Andrews, 2000; Lipsey, 2009; Lowenkamp et al., 2006).

The environment in which JRNA processes are embedded determines how successful an agency is at carrying out the logic model. Unfortunately, however, research to date has failed to consider the contextual factors that can influence these processes. Put another way, studies that consider the array of external factors highlighted in the JRNA logic model and how these operate, individually and jointly, to influence the quality of the three-step JRNA process are rare. This is because many existing JRNA studies are carried out in one jurisdiction, and, therefore, preclude an examination of how differences in context (i.e., external factors) may affect the JRNA process. There is evidence to suggest that JRNA processes and usage differ across environments (Vincent et al., 2016), which underscores the importance of the characteristics of the environment in which JRNA is implemented. This means that a complete understanding of how the three-step JRNA process works in practice requires that the logic model be contextualized in the people, structures, policies, and procedures that surround it.

The complicated question that remains unanswered is what are the optimal environmental conditions that increase the likelihood that the implementation of JRNA activities will consistently lead to positive short-term, intermediate, and long-term outcomes. Potential answers to these questions can be gleaned from considering issues surrounding the implementation and fidelity to the JRNA logic model within organizations. The quality of implementation and fidelity to the model, no doubt, carry significant weight in understanding its effectiveness. In the next chapter we blend existing implementation science frameworks and research to consider risk and needs assessment in juvenile justice settings.

References

Andrews, D.A., & Bonta, J. (2010). Rehabilitating criminal justice policy and practice. *Psychology, Public Policy, and Law*, 16(1), 39–55. doi:10.1037/a0018362.

Andrews, D.A., & Dowden, C. (2006). Risk principle of case classification in correctional treatment: A meta-analytic investigation. *International Journal of Offender Therapy and Comparative Criminology*, 50(1), 88–100. doi:10.1177/0306624X05282556.

Andrews, D.A., Bonta, J., & Hoge, R.D. (1990). Classification for effective rehabilitation: Rediscovering psychology. *Criminal Justice and Behavior*, 17(1), 19–52. doi:10.1177/0093854890017001004.

Andrews, D.A., Bonta, J., & Wormith, J.S. (2006). The recent past and near future of risk and/or need assessment. *Crime & Delinquency*, 52(1), 7–27. doi:10.1177/0011128705281756.

Asnaani, A., & Hofmann, S.G. (2012). Collaboration in multicultural therapy: Establishing a strong therapeutic alliance across cultural lines. *Journal of Clinical Psychology*, 68(2), 187–197. doi:10.1002/jclp.21829.

Baglivio, M.T., Greenwald, M.A., & Russell, M. (2015). Assessing the implications of a structured decision-making tool for recidivism in a statewide analysis: Disposition matrix for court recommendations made by juvenile probation officers. *Criminology & Public Policy*, 14(1), 5–49. doi:10.1111/1745-9133.12108.

Baglivio, M.T., Wolff, K.T., Howell, J.C., Jackowski, K., & Greenwald, M.A. (2018). The search for the holy grail: Criminogenic needs matching, intervention dosage, and subsequent recidivism among serious juvenile offenders in residential placement. *Journal of Criminal Justice*, 55, 46–57. doi:10.1016/j.jcrimjus.2018.02.001.

Baglivio, M.T., Wolff, K.T., Jackowski, K., & Greenwald, M.A. (2017). A multilevel examination of risk/need change scores, community context, and successful reentry of committed juvenile offenders. *Youth Violence and Juvenile Justice*, 15(1), 38–61. doi:10.1177/1541204015596052.

Barnoski, R. (2004). *Washington State juvenile court assessment manual, version 2.1*. Olympia, WA: Washington State Institute for Public Policy.

Barnoski, R., & Markussen, S. (2005). Washington State juvenile court assessment. *Mental Health Screening and Assessment in Juvenile Justice*, 271–282.

Basanta, J.L., Fariña, F., & Arce, R. (2018). Risk-need-responsivity model: Contrasting criminogenic and noncriminogenic needs in high and low risk juvenile offenders. *Children and Youth Services Review*, 85, 137–142. doi:10.1016/j.childyouth.2017.12.024.

Becker, H. (1963). *Outsiders*. New York: Free Press.

Belenko, S., Knight, D., Wasserman, G.A., Dennis, M.L., Wiley, T., Taxman, F.S., Oser, C., Dembo, R., Robertson, A., & Sales, J. (2017). The Juvenile Justice Behavioral Health Services Cascade: A new framework for measuring unmet substance use treatment services needs among adolescent offenders. *Journal of Substance Abuse Treatment*, 74, 80–91. doi:10.1016/j.jsat.2016.12.012.

Bernburg, J.G., Krohn, M.D., & Rivera, C.J. (2006). Official labeling, criminal embeddedness, and subsequent delinquency: A longitudinal test of labeling theory. *Journal of Research in Crime and Delinquency*, 43(1), 67–88. doi:10.1177/0022427805280068.

Bonta, J., & Andrews, D.A. (2007). Risk-need-responsivity model for offender assessment and rehabilitation. *Rehabilitation*, 6(1), 1–22. www.publicsafety.gc.ca/cnt/rsrcs/pblctns/rsk-nd-rspnsvty/rsk-nd-rspnsvty-eng.pdf.

Bonta, J., & Andrews, D. (2012). Viewing offender assessment and rehabilitation through the lens of the risk-needs-responsivity model. In F. McNeil, P. Raynor, & C. Trotter (Eds.), *Offender supervision: New directions in theory, research, and practice* (pp. 45–66). New York: Routledge.

Bonta, J., Rugge, T., Scott, T.L., Bourgon, G., & Yessine, A.K. (2008). Exploring the black box of community supervision. *Journal of Offender Rehabilitation*, 47(3), 248–270. doi:10.1080/10509670802134085.

Borum, R., Bartel, P., & Forth, A. (2006). *SAVRY: Structured assessment of violence risk in youth: Professional Manual*. Odessa, FL: PAR.

Brogan, L., Haney-Caron, E., NeMoyer, A., & DeMatteo, D. (2015). Applying the risk-needs-responsivity (RNR) model to juvenile justice. *Criminal Justice Review*, 40(3), 277–302. doi:10.1177/0734016814567312.

Buchan, B.J., Dennis, M.L., Tims, F.M., & Diamond, G.S. (2002). Cannabis use: Consistency and validity of self-report, on-site urine testing and laboratory testing. *Addiction*, 97, 98–108. doi:10.1046/j.1360-0443.97.s01.1.x.

Carpenter, A.L., Pincus, D.B., Furr, J.M., & Comer, J.S. (2018). Working from home: An initial pilot examination of videoconferencing-based cognitive behavioral therapy for anxious youth delivered to the home setting. *Behavior Therapy*, 49(6), 917–930. doi:10.1016/j.beth.2018.01.007.

Caudy, M.S., Durso, J.M., & Taxman, F.S. (2013). How well do dynamic needs predict recidivism? Implications for risk assessment and risk reduction. *Journal of Criminal Justice*, 41(6), 458–466. doi:10.1016/j.jcrimjus.2013.08.004.

Childs, K., Frick, P.J., Ryals Jr, J.S., Lingonblad, A., & Villio, M.J. (2014). A comparison of empirically based and structured professional judgment estimation of risk using the structured assessment of violence risk in youth. *Youth Violence and Juvenile Justice*, 12(1), 40–57. doi:10.1177/1541204013480368.

Chuang, E., & Wells, R. (2010). The role of inter-agency collaboration in facilitating receipt of behavioral health services for youth involved with child welfare and juvenile justice. *Children and Youth Services Review*, 32(12), 1814–1822. doi:10.1016/j.childyouth.2010.08.002.

Cording, J.R., Beggs Christofferson, S.M., & Grace, R.C. (2016). Challenges for the theory and application of dynamic risk factors. *Psychology, Crime & Law*, 22(1–2), 84–103. doi:10.1080/1068316X.2015.1111367.

deLara, E.W. (2012). Why adolescents don't disclose incidents of bullying and harassment. *Journal of School Violence*, 11(4), 288–305. doi:10.1080/15388220.2012.705931.

Douglas, K.S., & Skeem, J.L. (2005). Violence risk assessment: Getting specific about being dynamic. *Psychology, Public Policy, and Law*, 11(3), 347–383. doi:10.1037/1076-8971.11.3.347.

Dowden, C., & Andrews, D.A. (2000). Effective correctional treatment and violent reoffending: A meta-analysis. *Canadian Journal of Criminology*, 42, 449–467. doi:10.3138/cjcrim.42.4.449.

Drake, E.K., Aos, S., & Miller, M.G. (2009). Evidence-based public policy options to reduce crime and criminal justice costs: Implications in Washington State. *Victims and Offenders*, 4(2), 170–196. doi:10.1080/15564880802612615.

Etten, T.J., & Petrone, R.F. (1994). Sharing data and information in juvenile justice: Legal, ethical, and practical considerations. *Juvenile and Family Court Journal*, 45(3), 65–90. doi:10.1111/j.1755-6988.1994.tb01473.x.

Fan, X., Miller, B.C., Park, K.E., Winward, B.W., Christensen, M., Grotevant, H.D., & Tai, R.H. (2006). An exploratory study about inaccuracy and invalidity in adolescent self-report surveys. *Field Methods*, 18(3), 223–244. doi:10.1177/152822X06289161.

Fixsen, D.L., Blase, K.A., Naoom, S.F., & Wallace, F. (2009). Core implementation components. *Research on Social Work Practice*, 19, 531–540. doi:10.1177/1049731509335549.

Florida Department of Juvenile Justice (2014). *Pact assessment system overview*. Retrieved in June 2018 from www.djj.state.fl.us/docs/partners-providers-staff/pact-system-overview.pdf?sfvrsn=2.

Gatti, U., Tremblay, R.E., & Vitaro, F. (2009). Iatrogenic effect of juvenile justice. *Journal of Child Psychology and Psychiatry*, 50(8), 991–998.

Gendreau, P., Smith, P., & French, S.A. (2006). The theory of effective correctional intervention: Empirical status and future directions. *Taking Stock: The Status of Criminological Theory*, 15, 419–446.

Guy, L.S., Nelson, R.J., Fusco-Morin, S.L., & Vincent, G.M. (2014). What do juvenile probation officers think of using the SAVRY and YLS/CMI for case management, and do they use the instruments properly? *International Journal of Forensic Mental Health*, 13(3), 227–241. doi:10.1080/14999013.2014.939789.

Hagan, J. (1993). The social embeddedness of crime and unemployment. *Criminology*, 31(4), 465–491. doi:10.1111/j.1745-9125.1993.tb01138.x.

Haqanee, Z., Peterson-Badali, M., & Skilling, T. (2015). Making "what works" work: Examining probation officers' experiences addressing the criminogenic needs of juvenile offenders. *Journal of Offender Rehabilitation*, 54(1), 37–59. doi:10.1080/10509674.2014.980485.

Howell, J.C., Kelly, M.R., Palmer, J., & Mangum, R.L. (2004). Integrating child welfare, juvenile justice, and other agencies in a continuum of services. *Child Welfare*, 83(2), 143–156.

Johnson, L.N., Wright, D.W., & Ketring, S.A. (2002). The therapeutic alliance in home-based family therapy: Is it predictive of outcome? *Journal of Marital and Family Therapy*, 28(1), 93–102. doi:10.1111/j.1752-0606.2002.tb01177.x.

Kellogg Foundation (1998). *Using Logic Models to Bring Together Planning, Evaluation, and Action: Logic Model Development Guide*. Battle Creek, MI: W.K. Kellogg Foundation, untitled (aacu.org).

Kennealy, P.J., Skeem, J.L., & Hernandez, I.R. (2017). Does staff see what experts see? Accuracy of front-line staff in scoring juveniles' risk factors. *Psychological Assessment*, 29(1), 26–34. doi:10.1037/pas0000316.

Krohn, M.D., Thornberry, T.P., Lizotte, A.J., Bell, K.A., & Phillips, M.D. (2011). Self-report surveys within longitudinal panel designs. In D. Gadd, S. Karstedt, & S.F. Messner (Eds.), *The SAGE Handbook of Criminological Research* (pp. 23–35). Thousand Oaks, CA: Sage.

Lee, M., & Prentice, N.M. (1988). Interrelations of empathy, cognition, and moral reasoning with dimensions of juvenile delinquency. *Journal of Abnormal Child Psychology*, 16(2), 127–139. doi:10.1007/BF00913589.

Lehmann, P.S., Meldrum, R.C., & Greenwald, M.A. (2020). Upward departures from structured recommendations in juvenile court dispositions: The intersection of race, ethnicity, and gender. *Justice Quarterly*, 37(3), 514–540.

Lipsey, M.W. (2009). The primary factors that characterize effective interventions with juvenile offenders: A meta-analytic overview. *Victims and Offenders*, 4(2), 124–147. doi:10.1080/15564880802612573.

Lipsey, M.W., Howell, J.C., & Tidd, S.T. (2007). *The Standardized Program Evaluation Protocol (SPEP): A practical approach to evaluating and improving juvenile justice programs in North Carolina. Final evaluation report*. Nashville, TN: Vanderbilt University Center for Evaluation Research and Methodology.

Lösel, F., & Farrington, D.P. (2012). Direct protective and buffering protective factors in the development of youth violence. *American Journal of Preventive Medicine*, 43(2), S8–S23. doi:10.1016/j.amepre.2012.04.029.

Loughran, T.A., Mulvey, E.P., Schubert, C.A., Fagan, J., Piquero, A.R., & Losoya, S.H. (2009). Estimating a dose-response relationship between length of stay and future recidivism in serious juvenile offenders. *Criminology*, 47(3), 699–740.

Lowenkamp, C.T., Latessa, E.J., & Holsinger, A.M. (2006). The risk principle in action: What have we learned from 13,676 offenders and 97 correctional programs? *Crime & Delinquency*, 52(1), 77–93. doi:10.1177/0011128705281747.

Luong, D., & Wormith, J.S. (2011). Applying risk/need assessment to probation practice and its impact on the recidivism of young offenders. *Criminal Justice and Behavior*, 38(12), 1177–1199. doi:10.1177/0093854811421596.

MacPhee, M. (2009). Developing a practice-academic partnership logic model. *Nursing Outlook*, 57(3), 143–147. doi:10.1016/j.outlook.2008.08.003.

Mankey, J., Baca, P., Rondenell, S., Webb, M., & McHugh, D. (2006). *Guidelines for juvenile information sharing*. Washington, DC: Office of Juvenile Justice and Delinquency Prevention. www.promoteprevent.org/sites/www.promoteprevent.org/files/resources/215786_0.pdf.

Maschi, T., Hatcher, S.S., Schwalbe, C.S., & Rosato, N.S. (2008). Mapping the social service pathways of youth to and through the juvenile justice system: A comprehensive review. *Children and Youth Services Review*, 30(12), 1376–1385.

McGloin, J.M., & Pratt, T.C. (2003). Cognitive ability and delinquent behavior among inner-city youth: A life-course analysis of main, mediating, and interaction effects. *International Journal of Offender Therapy and Comparative Criminology*, 47(3), 253–271. doi:10.1177/0306624X03047003002.

Mears, D. (2012). The front end of the juvenile court: Intake and informal versus formal processing. In D.M. Bishop & B.C. Feld (Eds.), *The Oxford handbook of juvenile crime and juvenile justice* (pp. 1–35). New York: Oxford University Press.

Mears, D.P., & Kelly, W.R. (1999). Assessments and intake processes in juvenile justice processing: Emerging policy considerations. *Crime & Delinquency*, 45(4), 508–529. doi:10.1177/0011128799045004007.

Miller, J., & Maloney, C. (2013). Practitioner compliance with risk/needs assessment tools: A theoretical and empirical assessment. *Criminal Justice and Behavior*, 40(7), 716–736. doi:10.1177/0093854812468883.

Nellis, A., & Richardson, B. (2010). Getting beyond failure: Promising approaches for reducing DMC. *Youth Violence and Juvenile Justice*, 8(3), 266–276. doi:10.1177/1541204009361180.

Nelson, R.J., & Vincent, G.M. (2018). Matching services to criminogenic needs following comprehensive risk assessment implementation in juvenile probation. *Criminal Justice and Behavior*, 45(8), 1136–1153. doi:10.1177/0093854818780923.

Peterson-Badali, M., Skilling, T., & Haqanee, Z. (2015). Examining implementation of risk assessment in case management for youth in the justice system. *Criminal Justice and Behavior*, 42(3), 304–320. doi:10.1177/0093854814549595.

Petrosino, A., Turpin-Petrosino, C., & Guckenburg, S. (2014). The impact of juvenile system processing on delinquency. In D.P. Farrington, & J. Murray (Eds.), *Labeling theory: Empirical tests advances in criminological theory* (volume 18, pp. 113–147). New Brunswick, NJ: Transaction.

Piquero, A.R., Schubert, C.A., & Brame, R. (2014). Comparing official and self-report records of offending across gender and race/ethnicity in a longitudinal study of serious youthful offenders. *Journal of Research in Crime and Delinquency*, 51 (4), 526–556. doi:10.1177/0022427813520445.

Polaschek, D.L. (2016). Desistance and dynamic risk factors belong together. *Psychology, Crime & Law*, 22(1–2),171–189. doi:10.1080/1068316X.2015.1114114.

Ray, J.V., Thornton, L.C., Frick, P.J., Steinberg, L., & Cauffman, E. (2016). Impulse control and callous-unemotional traits distinguish patterns of delinquency and substance use in justice involved adolescents: Examining the moderating role of neighborhood context. *Journal of Abnormal Child Psychology*, 44(3), 599–611. doi:10.1007/s10802-015-0057-0.

Reynolds, K., & Miles, H.L. (2009). The effect of training on the quality of HCR-20 violence risk assessments in forensic secure services. *The Journal of Forensic Psychiatry & Psychology*, 20(3), 473–480. doi:10.1080/14789940802638366.

Rogers, R. (2000). The uncritical acceptance of risk assessment in forensic practice. *Law and Human Behavior*, 24(5), 595–605. doi:10.1023/A:1005575113507.

Rutter, M. (1985). Resilience in the face of adversity: Protective factors and resistance to psychiatric disorder. *The British Journal of Psychiatry*, 147(6), 598–611. doi:10.1192/bjp.147.6.598.

Serin, R.C., Chadwick, N., & Lloyd, C.D. (2016). Dynamic risk and protective factors. *Psychology, Crime & Law*, 22(1–2), 151–170. doi:10.1080/1068316X.2015.1112013.

Shook, J.J., & Sarri, R.C. (2007). Structured decision making in juvenile justice: Judges' and probation officers' perceptions and use. *Children and Youth Services Review*, 29(10), 1335–1351. https://doi.org/10.1016/j.childyouth.2007.05.008.

Sigurdsson, J.F., Gudjonsson, G.H., & Peersen, M. (2001). Differences in the cognitive ability and personality of desisters and re-offenders: A prospective study among young offenders. *Psychology, Crime & Law*, 7(1), 33–43. doi:10.1080/10683160108401781.

Spidel, A., Hervé, H., Greaves, C., & Yuille, J.C. (2011). 'Wasn't me!' A field study of the relationship between deceptive motivations and psychopathic traits in young offenders. *Legal and Criminological Psychology*, 16(2), 335–347. doi:10.1348/135532510X518722.

Steinberg, L.D., Cauffman, E., & Monahan, K. (2015). *Psychosocial maturity and desistance from crime in a sample of serious juvenile offenders*. Laurel, MD: US Department of Justice, Office of Justice Programs, Office of Juvenile Justice and Delinquency Prevention.

Storey, J.E., Gibas, A.L., Reeves, K.A., & Hart, S.D. (2011). Evaluation of a violence risk (threat) assessment training program for police and other criminal justice professionals. *Criminal Justice and Behavior*, 38(6), 554–564. doi:10.1177/0093854811403123.

Sullivan, C.J. (2019). *Taking juvenile justice seriously: Developmental insights and system challenges*. Philadelphia, PA: Temple University Press.

Sullivan, C.J., Strange, C.C., Sullivan, C.C., Lugo, M., Mueller, D., Petkus, A., Newsome, J., Holmes, B., Lonergan, H., & Gibbs, G. (2019). *A multi-state and multi-method study of juvenile risk assessment implementation, usage, and outcomes*. Final technical report submitted to the Office of Juvenile Justice and Delinquency Prevention. www.ojp.gov/pdffiles1/ojjdp/grants/252927.pdf.

Vasquez, M.J. (2007). Cultural difference and the therapeutic alliance: An evidence-based analysis. *American Psychologist*, 62(8), 878–885. doi:10.1037/0003-066X.62.8.878.

Vieira, T., Skilling, T., & Peterson-Badali, M. (2009). Matching court-ordered services with treatment needs. *Criminal Justice and Behavior*, 36, 385–401. doi:10.1177/0093854808331249.

Vincent, G.M., Guy, L.S., Fusco, S.L., & Gershenson, B.G. (2012). Field reliability of the SAVRY with juvenile probation officers: Implications for training. *Law and Human Behavior*, 36(3), 225–236. doi:10.1037/h0093974.

Vincent, G.M., Guy, L.S., Gershenson, B.G., & McCabe, P. (2012). Does risk assessment make a difference? Results of implementing the SAVRY in juvenile probation. *Behavioral Sciences & the Law*, 30(4), 384–405. doi:10.1002/bsl.2014.

Vincent, G.M., Guy, L.S., & Grisso, T. (2012). *Risk assessment in juvenile justice: A guidebook for implementation*. Implementation Science and Practice Advances Research Center Publications. Retrieved from https://escholarship.umassmed.edu/psych_cmhsr/573.

Vincent, G.M., Guy, L.S., Perrault, R.T., & Gershenson, B. (2016). Risk assessment matters, but only when implemented well: A multisite study in juvenile probation. *Law and Human Behavior*, 40(6), 683–696. doi:10.1037/lhb0000214.

Vincent, G.M., Paiva-Salisbury, M.L., Cook, N.E., Guy, L.S., & Perrault, R.T. (2012). Impact of risk/needs assessment on juvenile probation officers' decision making: Importance of implementation. *Psychology, Public Policy, and Law*, 18(4), 549. doi:10.1037/a0027186.

Vitopoulos, N.A., Peterson-Badali, M., & Skilling, T.A. (2012). The relationship between matching service to criminogenic need and recidivism in male and female youth: Examining the RNR principles in practice. *Criminal Justice and Behavior*, 39(8), 1025–1041.

Ward, T., Melser, J., & Yates, P.M. (2007). Reconstructing the Risk–Need–Responsivity model: A theoretical elaboration and evaluation. *Aggression and Violent Behavior*, 12(2), 208–228. doi:10.1016/j.avb.2006.07.001.

Welsh, B.C., Rocque, M., & Greenwood, P.W. (2014). Translating research into evidence-based practice in juvenile justice: brand-name programs, meta-analysis, and key issues. *Journal of Experimental Criminology*, 10(2), 207–225. doi:10.1007/s11292-013-9182-3.

Wormith, J.S., & Zidenberg, A.M. (2018). The historical roots, current status, and future applications of the Risk-Need-Responsivity Model (RNR). In *New Frontiers in Offender Treatment* (pp. 11–41). Cham: Springer.

Chapter 4

Implementation and Practice of Juvenile Risk and Needs Assessment

Young and colleagues (2006, p. 136) suggest that "the call to apply research-based knowledge has been made perhaps most persistently in the area of assessment." The results of impact studies—often focused on predictive validity—assume that the JRNA tool and accompanying process are implemented with fidelity. This is a strong assumption when considering the history of the adoption of evidence-based practices generally (Durlak & DuPre, 2008; Fixsen et al., 2009) or in justice settings specifically (Laub, 2016; Sullivan, 2019; Vincent et al., 2012).

Chapters 2 and 3 of this book show that these tools have been adopted and studied at several points in the juvenile justice system and identify the core practices relevant to their use. While research to date suggests that JRNA processes can improve juvenile justice practices and youth outcomes generally, there is far less clarity on the implementation of risk and needs assessment practices that must occur to ensure that the tools are used optimally (Vincent et al., 2012). The consequences of loss of fidelity with movement away from the logic or theory of how JRNA should work relative to the actual processes that occur when agencies introduce and adopt JRNA policies and protocols are not well understood. This leaves a crucial gap in understanding as the availability of even a well-validated tool is only one aspect of ensuring that JRNA ultimately impacts practice and case outcomes as intended (Sullivan, Strange, et al., 2019; Vincent et al., 2012).

Implementation and usage questions touch on several elements of the JRNA logic model presented earlier (see Figure 3.1), going beyond mere choices about what items to put on the tool or the scoring process, to instead focus on how people and organizations respond to the idea of structured risk assessment and the specific content of the tool being adopted. Stated differently, our logic model suggests that introducing JRNA into the juvenile court and corrections environment leads to the implementation of a package of interventions at multiple levels and that there are numerous inputs to consider in fully assessing how well the process works.

This chapter builds on the multi-dimensional framework presented in Figure 2.1 and the discussion in Chapter 3 to consider the ways in which juvenile justice agencies respond to the three-step JRNA process. This helps to fill a gap in understanding between the logic and practice of JRNA. We contemplate the

DOI: 10.4324/9780367823122-4

meaning of structured assessment as a practice to be implemented within juvenile justice organizations that are already stressed in case processing. We simultaneously consider the broader juvenile justice implementation landscape to connect that change in practice to system objectives in processing, sanctioning, and treating justice-involved youths. The later sections of this chapter assess the adoption, use, and sustainability of JRNA against some broader frameworks for implementation processes which offer external benchmarks to contextualize JRNA implementation. In doing so, we attempt to establish how JRNA is like and unlike other evidence-based practices that might be adopted in juvenile or criminal justice agencies. In turn, we consider what this review means for understanding JRNA policy and practice and the accompanying research base. Such a focus is necessary, in part, because there is relatively little formal implementation research available for JRNA (see Guy et al., 2014; Shook & Sarri, 2007; Vincent et al., 2012; Young et al., 2006). Though JRNA processes have been adopted and implemented extensively in the last few decades, writing about effectiveness and best practices in this area mainly consists of descriptions of processes in different implementation sites and/or information from surveys and interviews with practitioners and administrators involved with the process (Shook & Sarri, 2007; Sullivan, Strange, et al., 2019; Vincent et al., 2012; Young et al., 2006). Consequently, we discuss the available research and draw attention to work in general implementation science where relevant to JRNA as well.

The Implementation Environment Surrounding JRNA

Implementation of policy and practice in juvenile justice settings is somewhat unique because of the broader socio-political climate. Juvenile justice faces many intractable problems, including structural inequalities that affect the system caseload and the leverage points it might use to bring about change, and the relative lack of resources to fully match youths with all services that would be necessary to promote change (Lipsey et al., 2017; Sullivan, 2019; Walker et al., 2015). Politically, Bernard and Kurlychek (2010, p. 29) describe a process whereby policy and public opinion sway back and forth, responding to waves that then in turn affect how the justice system operates:

> Regardless of the type of policy in place, people remain convinced that juvenile crime is at an all-time high (whether it is or not) and that these rates are a recent occurrence…Instead of looking for times when juvenile delinquency was low and determining the societal factors that led to those low rates, we erroneously look back to policies that were in place thirty or so years ago.

This broader context cannot be divorced from the implementation of JRNA because its use in meeting the goals of the juvenile justice system involves multiple components, such as community support for alternatives to youth incarceration or funding for appropriate treatment programming. This means that even when some components are addressed successfully challenges remain in fully enacting the logic model that underlies JRNA implementation. This is because the full model requires both shifts in how information is gathered and processed as well as decision-making practices among system actors (Sullivan, Strange, et al., 2019; Young et al., 2006). In effect these different components are linked to one another in ways that are consequential for agencies' full adoption of JRNA and, subsequently, its effective use at the case level. As a result, adoption schemes for JRNA vary in ways that are relevant to understanding day-to-day practice and agency and case-level decision-making impacts. These are commonly tied to jurisdictional units as those naturally serve legal and policy functions in juvenile justice practice and procedures. Federal state or local agencies might affect adoption and implementation of JRNA practices. In turn, this higher-level public agency infrastructure can produce variation in the implementation, usage, and effectiveness of JRNA.

The three-step process presented in Figure 2.1 and the logic model presented in Figure 3.1 both occur within broader environmental circumstances that condition the effectiveness of the JRNA process in practice. As a result, a complete conceptual framework of the JRNA implementation process must also incorporate aspects of the environment in which the three-step process is embedded. Figure 4.1 provides a more precise

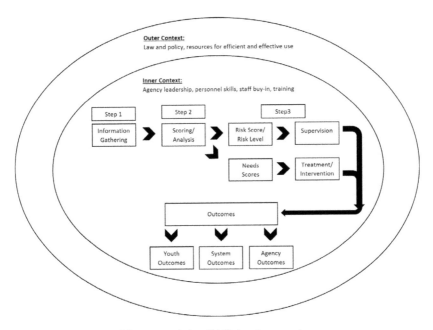

Figure 4.1 Conceptual Framework for JRNA Implementation

conceptual model of JRNA, including the components of the assessment process, desired outcomes, and the inner and outer contexts influencing the process.

Aarons and colleagues' (2011) Exploration, Adoption/Preparation, Implementation, and Sustainment (EPIS) framework is used in Figures 4.1 and 4.2 to delineate key aspects of JRNA implementation in the context of the juvenile justice system.[1] The authors establish an inner and outer context for implementation with each layer comprising multiple interrelated elements. This relates strongly to several inputs described in the logic model in Chapter 3, as well as the external factors included at the bottom of the logic model. It also builds on several aspects of prior work on implementation in JRNA (e.g., Sullivan, Strange, et al., 2019; Vincent et al., 2012). Figure 4.2 shows specific aspects of the implementation environment that require close consideration in evaluating JRNA and subsequent decision-making. It links multiple facets of implementation and connects them to the assessment process more specifically.

Outer Implementation Context: Public Infrastructure and JRNA Implementation

The outer implementation context in JRNA consists of those factors that may not have direct effects on the agencies and individuals implementing the tool, but which impact the likelihood of implementation success. This includes the broader political and administrative support and impetus for the move to formal assessments (e.g., legislative mandate versus administrative initiative), networks among agency leaders (including federal-state-local

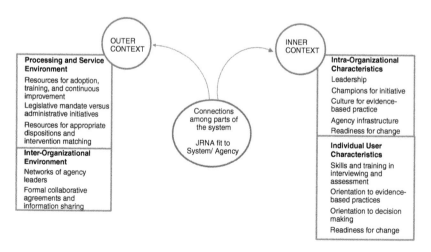

Figure 4.2 Implementation Context of Juvenile Risk and Needs Assessment

linkages in the context of JRNA initiatives), training and implementation resources, formal policy and practice guidance, and resources to support shifts in decision-making practices. Aarons and colleagues (2011, p. 7) suggest that this level in the implementation framework largely reflects "sociopolitical context" and "funding" streams for the initiative to be undertaken. Taken together, this can be both about *why* the initiative is being implemented around JRNA and *what* broad resources and supports are available to effectively do so. For example, JRNA implementation might be done to facilitate other changes to juvenile placement patterns and shifts in resource allocation that must occur to support that. This is what occurred in Ohio where the OYAS was used to facilitate the development and implementation of programs designed to offer alternatives to state residential placements (Sullivan, Park, & Holmes, 2019) and in Louisiana where the implementation of the SAVRY was found to reduce the use of out of home placements (Vincent et al., 2012).

Federal efforts toward implementation can take on multiple forms. One role is advisory where government agencies can suggest and promote standards of practice for the adoption and optimal use of risk and needs assessment in juvenile justice systems. Guy and colleagues (2014) note that the federal authorization of the Juvenile Justice and Delinquency Prevention Act (JJDPA) has included language specific to the use of risk and needs assessment practices for justice-involved youths. An agency like the Office of Juvenile Justice and Delinquency Prevention (OJJDP) can also provide or facilitate technical assistance and informational resources based on its mission of improving juvenile justice practice. In a grant-making capacity, Requests for Proposals (RFP) may also require agencies—implicitly or explicitly—to utilize JRNA practices as a means of capturing information about youths and then making decisions to meet conditions of funding. For example, Juvenile Drug Treatment Court (JDTC) Guidelines published by the Office of Juvenile Justice and Delinquency Prevention (2016) expect courts as a matter of routine practice to "assess all program participants for the risk of reoffending using a validated instrument" and "conduct comprehensive needs assessments that inform individualized case management" (p. 7). Guideline adherence in turn is expected to be part of funding and/or allocating technical training and assistance to ensure that JDTCs are meeting expectations.

Residing closer to individual juvenile courts and corrections agencies, states play a more direct role in the implementation process via several possible leverage points. States can take on roles similar to federal-level agencies in terms of funding and setting standards, but also can engage in some distinct, more direct practices to support adoption and implementation as well. For example, in Arizona state-level juvenile court and corrections agencies drove the decision to use an assessment tool and established the scope of who is assessed as well as its use in particular decisions. They also arranged for technical assistance and training for the assessment procedures and practices used in the 15 counties in the state.[2] In North Carolina and Florida, states have legislatively mandated the use of risk and needs assessment procedures for system-involved youths in effect assuring that these practices will be used at the local level (Howell, 2005).

Resource availability can affect implementation in multiple ways. The first way is common to most implementation processes. That is the degree to which agencies can effectively pay the cost to utilize the tool itself. Costs might include copyright-mandated use, training practices and subsequent follow-up and coaching, costs of evaluation and quality improvement procedures, and the development of information management systems that allow personnel to effectively access and use the assessments. This is necessary to develop a good sense of what each youth might require with respect to their risk and needs, providing an effective basis for matching to interventions. A variety of options is available so that agencies can identify one (or more) that best fits with their objectives. The selection of a specific instrument is both an initial decision on the part of the agency and one that should be revisited during its lifespan as continuous quality improvement and new knowledge may suggest a need for adjustments.

Resource availability is also important from the standpoint of appropriate usage. JRNA should identify high need areas for intervention on the part of the juvenile justice system and its affiliates. Referring back to Chapter 3, if the agency or community does not have quality anger management treatment options for a youth who is identified as having such needs then one aspect of the implementation-to-effective usage chain will be removed and the expectation for its positive performance would be undermined. Shook and Sarri (2007) studied 12 jurisdictions implementing a structured assessment process. Juvenile justice personnel (e.g., probation officers, judges, attorneys) reported that decision making around the assessment—including the use of professional judgment overrides—was often based on the availability of appropriate placements. For example, 20 percent of judges reported *not* placing a youth in the community—despite the assessment recommendation—because of a lack of available options. Twenty-seven percent of the probation officers surveyed responded in a similar way.

Inner Implementation Context: Agency and Staff Characteristics

The inner context in JRNA comprises factors at the agency and staff level that can impact case-level use and outcomes and is closer to *how* the initiative is implemented. Most on-the-ground implementation efforts occur within local agencies, including juvenile courts, detention facilities, and probation offices. In some instances, state officials make the decision to adopt a particular JRNA tool and identify training resources, policies, and procedures to support its implementation and use (Vincent et al., 2012).

This was the case in Ohio where the state developed its own risk assessment tool, the Ohio Youth Assessment System (OYAS), and then provided incentives and resources for its local adoption given its status as a "home rule" state (Gies, 2015; Lovins & Latessa, 2013; Sullivan, Park, & Holmes, 2019). The federal government and states may promote policy toward the use of JRNA but ultimately local practice and culture will be most influential in how well the process works. Direct implementation efforts occur at the local level of the ecological system. This is where youths are processed; intake and disposition interviews are conducted; risk and needs are identified; disposition and service allocation decisions are made; and treatment plans are established and executed. This is also where local norms, practices, and resources affect implementation (Exworthy, Berney, & Powell, 2002; Fixsen et al., 2009; Greenhalgh et al., 2004).

Tensions based on local practice and the decisions of juvenile justice personnel are illustrated by Lipsky's (1980) classic work on the "Street-Level Bureaucrat" where he identifies discretion and judgment on how to distribute the "nature, amount, and quality of benefits and sanctions provided by their agencies" as central to the daily routines of frontline workers who implement public policy (see also Miller & Trocchio, 2016). Zajac and colleagues (2015, p. 31; see also, Hawken, 2016) identify this imperative using the phrasing "all implementation is local" in considering dissemination of new programs. Finally, Fixsen et al. (2009, p. 532) assert that the "practitioner is the intervention" in discussing the types of services and contacts that are often at the heart of program implementation in human services or juvenile justice settings. With that, the inner implementation context requires the lion's share of the attention in thinking about prospects and challenges for implementation of JRNA practices (Aarons et al., 2011).

The inner context captures elements of the organizational environment as well as characteristics of agency staff that may affect adoption and implementation of both assessments and the decision-making schemes that should follow from them. At the "Intra-Organizational" level, several factors are essential in the implementation process. These include leadership that effectively supports implementation (and evaluation and continuous improvement afterwards), presence of champions from frontline ranks in the organization, a culture and infrastructure that is suitable to these initiatives, and agency readiness for change. This, for example, would mean that there is agency-level leadership willing to support the adoption and implementation of JRNA, but it should also be reinforced by mid-level management and line staff who identify the benefits of the practice for their work and recognize ways by which it can be integrated into day-to-day practice and updated/adjusted to improve practice. Agency infrastructure and readiness for change comprises the degree to which the new practice can be fully adopted given the totality of the operations of the agency. For instance, agencies may be culturally fit for JRNA practices but could be hindered if they seek to modify several aspects of their work at once as that strains agency resources and can diminish individual-level buy-in (Chung, Choi, & Du, 2017).

The other element of the inner context of JRNA implementation is based on the characteristics of individuals working within those agencies. Frontline staff will do the bulk of the work in routine use of JRNA practices. JRNA processes include establishing risk levels for recidivism, informing supervision level and approach, identifying treatment needs, developing a case and treatment plan, and monitoring change over time. Each of these tasks involve personnel groups that vary in several key characteristics including their skillsets, readiness to use JRNA, disposition toward it, and the degree to which they can assimilate the new approach into current practices. These staff characteristics are related to, but may also be somewhat distinct from, the individual readiness to change that will affect the success of implementation.

When linked to this inner context, the broader adoption framework created by different levels of government and the processes used for implementation can affect multiple important dimensions and stakeholders within juvenile justice. For example, if a move toward JRNA procedures is legislatively or administratively mandated from the state level, there inevitably is less question about whether a particular approach will be implemented but there may be greater challenges in how it will occur and the degree of heterogeneity in local practices and skillsets. Some aspects of the process may flow more smoothly (e.g., development of policy and procedure) while others, like obtaining staff buy-in or ensuring the availability of appropriate intervention services, are more challenging. A localized bottom-up approach will likely lead to greater differentiation in the tool(s) adopted and/or the practices behind its application to youths' cases. Ultimately either of these approaches is apt to be affected by the steps taken to identify what will be implemented and how that process should work (Greenhalgh et al., 2004). Very clearly the multiple components that must be introduced by systems, agencies, and individuals to effectively process and dispose of juvenile justice cases suggest the need for a well-thought-out implementation process that fits the implementation context well.

Implementation Frameworks and JRNA

The Exploration, Preparation, Implementation, Sustainment (EPIS) framework offers insight on the ways in which the outer and inner context for implementation come together to affect individual cases, aggregate practices and outcomes, and their sustainment over time (Aarons et al., 2011). These interdependencies show up in multiple ways as the impetus for the change at the inter-organizational level (e.g., state and local jurisdictions) inherently will affect the degree of readiness at the agency and individual staff level.

The strain on an agency implementing multiple evidence-based practices may be lessened if recommended changes are accompanied by resources from the state to train staff and provide programming to accompany shifts in decision-making practices. Similarly, while mandates from the state level to implement a JRNA process may be strong, they ultimately depend on local agency staff to effectively carry them out on a case-by-case basis. This interdependency is important as there is apt to be a great deal of variability in how implementation processes play out on the ground.

Building on that, Wandersman and colleagues' (2008) Interactive Systems Framework (ISF) can be linked to this account of the inner and outer context but focuses more on the roles that different groups play in the process of implementation. They describe three different "systems" that affect the process of moving evidence-based practice and policy into the field, which are also influenced by an outer context (Aarons et al., 2011). This environment could include macro policy, organizational climate, and funding. These systems are pertinent to JRNA implementation as they impact how key groups and individuals will interact with the process. For example, organizational climate is influential in how line staff react to change that comes with JRNA. The *Synthesis and Translation* element of the system refers to the process of making the evidence useable and translating it for use in the field. This might include gathering information to support the use of a structured risk and needs assessment process and conveying to users how and why it can work in their agency and case-level decision making.

The *Support* system moves past mere dissemination with an aim toward changing practice. This system provides training and technical assistance (TTA) for JRNA along two dimensions. First, this may require an effort to improve the foundation for effectively supporting the introduction of JRNA. This comprises building up motivation and interviewing and data gathering efficacy in those who will be working with the JRNA process. It will also include building needed partnerships and policies and procedures within the agency and with service providers and others in the network (Sridharan & Gillespie, 2004). The more specific aspect involves training users on the specifics of using the tool selected within the JRNA. This support might be provided by managers within an agency as well as outside contract agencies involved with the training and technical assistance process. The third aspect of the ISF is the *Delivery* system where the new practices are brought into the day-to-day operations of an agency. This might include the actual practice of interviewing a youth and their family, collecting record-based information, scoring the assessment, and then delivering the information to other decision-makers and/ or making decisions directly.

These three systems must work together effectively to support implementation. If information on the effectiveness of the assessment has not been adequately synthesized and translated for those in the field then it is unlikely to motivate practitioners and build capacity at the *Support* level.

Likewise, without adequate training at the Support level, then delivery will fall short in practice. Bringing these frameworks together, the growing insight on the implementation of a variety of different types of evidence-based policies and practices can be useful in understanding and informing efforts to implement JRNA consistent with the logic model and objectives described earlier.

Variability in JRNA Implementation

The nature and interaction of different facets of the implementation context—and its inputs and outputs—produce variation in how well the process works and, in turn, youth, agency, and system-level outcomes. The adoption scheme used to introduce and implement JRNA can promote or constrain some elements of variability that in turn affect case processing, juvenile justice personnel, and juvenile justice agencies. Local jurisdictions adopting and using their own tools and procedures would constitute maximum variability within states in these processes. This variability in turn may raise concerns about notions of justice by geography that are frequently mentioned in analysis of juvenile justice decision making and case outcomes (Bray et al., 2005; Feld, 1992; Krisberg et al., 1984). At the very least they suggest that the effectiveness of the structured assessment and decision-making process desired in implementation is apt to vary in whether it is fully realized across different places. This variability contributes to a desire to understand the implementation process systematically.

At the other end of the spectrum there are states that mandate (or nearly so) the use of a particular risk and needs assessment tool across jurisdictions. This was the case in two of the three states studied in the recent implementation study by Sullivan, Strange, and colleagues (2019). If implemented as intended, this creates the most implementation fidelity within a state. Even this can be a bit deceiving as there still may be variability within states that have adopted the same tool. McCafferty (2016), for example, studied 33 counties and 2,841 cases in Ohio. He found that, overall, there was a statistically significant, above average relationship between the OYAS risk score and recidivism (AUC = .68). Simultaneously, there was also considerable variability across the 33 study sites, with correlation values ranging from .00 to .43. Similarly, in Florida, an analysis of statewide data suggests that the association between PACT risk level and re-referral to FDJJ among a large sample of youths that completed probation (from 2007–2014) revealed some variation in AUC values across the 20 judicial circuits in Florida (ranging from .51 to .69). This means that predictive validity, which has long been thought to be the key indicator of an assessment's viability, differs across places that are believed to be implementing a fairly uniform process.

Similarly, in a study with more researcher control, Vincent and colleagues (2016) studied the impact of the implementation process on decisions about supervision and placement (and subsequent recidivism). Across six sites in two states (Louisiana and Pennsylvania), the authors found the most pronounced effects on supervision and placement decisions were from the sites that implemented the assessment processes with the greatest fidelity. Implementation fidelity was defined based on whether youths received appropriate assessments and their timing. For example, the site with the lowest implementation adherence, which also lacked buy-in from the judge, saw minimal impacts from the use of the tool. This implies that both immediate (inner) and more distal (outer) context can affect implementation processes and, in turn, youth outcomes via JRNA practices.

While these are important sources of variability, others must also be considered in characterizing effective JRNA implementation. For example, the potential for variability across agencies or states is obvious but there also may be variability in implementation within agencies as well. The notion of inter-rater reliability or consistency, for example, looks at whether similar cases will be scored in the same or similar ways across personnel in an agency (Baird et al., 2013). This speaks to the degree of variance or invariance in the overall or subdomain scores that might emerge in the assessment process. There are multiple steps in conducting an assessment, including interviewing, data gathering from collateral sources, and scoring (Barnoski, 2004). Any differences in procedure across those steps can produce variation in how the tool works toward meeting its goals. Additionally, research suggests that obtaining buy-in from judges and lawyers is central to effective implementation of JRNA (e.g., Vincent et al. 2016 described earlier). Without that, there can be slippage in the assessment-to-decision-making portion of the JRNA logic model. This potential variability identifies another source of adherence that must be accounted for in thinking about the theory and practice of risk and needs assessment. It also requires greater attention to the nature of the practice being implemented.

JRNA as an Innovation

Frequently the idea of technology transfer or diffusion of innovation is invoked when discussing the movement of theory and research into practice (Backer, 1995; Rogers, 2010). Therefore, a full analysis of JRNA must also consider *what* is being implemented and how that interacts with the implementation context. While there are certain parallels between the JRNA implementation eco-system and other juvenile justice interventions—and the implementation of innovative practices more generally—some differences are relevant for the broader discussion of JRNA in practice. As its logic model demonstrates, JRNA is a package of inputs and outputs involving information, individual and collective decision making, and disposition and treatment resources. In turn, this is generally more complex as an implementation challenge than if a discrete intervention is introduced into a set of treatment options used by a court or corrections agency.

The contrast between a treatment program and JRNA is implicit in the fact that the use of a formal assessment process is typically seen as a first step toward broader shifts in system decision making (Vincent et al., 2012; Young et al., 2006). For example, in Ohio the OYAS is viewed as a key driver of shifts in placement usage that led to more use of community-based alternatives to state-level placements in residential facilities (Gies, 2015; Sullivan, Park, & Holmes, 2019). To begin to establish an infrastructure for improving their juvenile justice performance, a Hawaii working group first established its criteria for selecting an assessment tool to adopt and implement statewide (Crime and Justice Institute, 2017). In that sense, JRNA is necessary precursor step and others, like disposition and placement decisions and available evidence-based programming, must fall into place appropriately for its objectives to be fully realized.

With its impacts on day-to-day practices and staff, the adoption of JRNA can impact all (or nearly all) cases that encounter the juvenile justice system and therefore it is different than a standard program targeted to a subsample of youths based on their characteristics and needs. Understanding the appropriate target population for a given innovation is essential in the implementation process (Welsh, Sullivan, & Olds, 2010). In the case of JRNA practices, the process is therefore affected by the overall variability in the level and type of risk and needs of youths that reach the juvenile justice system as these systems are often meant to be used with the entire population that reaches a particular stage of the process (e.g., intake, residential facility) (Sullivan, 2019). The target population is therefore important when considering the potential performance of an assessment system outside of the population or locale where it was originally validated. This might necessitate thoughtful adaptation to fit the new setting or population (Carroll et al., 2007; Lee et al., 2008).

When coupled with the intent of the JRNA logic model to link more precise information about the youth and their case to better dispositional and placement decisions and then improved outcomes, multiple components must align and work effectively together to promote the best possible outcomes for youths. Vincent and colleagues (2012, p. 25) note that "*risk assessment tools are NOT prescriptive...*will not tell the rater (also known as the assessor or user) exactly what course of action should be taken with the youth" (emphasis in original). A "technological" shift also comes in terms of how information is recorded, processed, used, and shared in a structured JRNA process.

While case records generally stay the same in terms of their blend of clinical notes and more static information such as number of previous juvenile court contacts and a risk score, JRNA practices can shift the nature of data gathering and processing in making juvenile court decisions by making it more structured. This inherently involves more guidelines and rules to follow, which means that practitioners may perceive a loss of discretion or autonomy—even if the decisions reached are largely similar. This can also bring differences in how information is stored. Vincent and colleagues (2018) identify information systems and data infrastructure as one important implementation driver in JRNA (see also Fixsen et al., 2013). One finding within that research was that dissatisfaction with the system used for inputting and storing information from the risk assessment process was related to overall satisfaction with the use of the tool among those who used it. Specifically, based on responses from juvenile justice personnel, Vincent and colleagues (2018) report that the association between views of the automated system implemented in OYAS states and overall satisfaction was .65.[3] This implies that practical impediments to implementation in service of practitioners' day-to-day work can have a general impact on the innovation being implemented and also exemplifies that JRNA really involves a holistic shift in agencies' "operating systems."

Key Implementation Components and JRNA

Implementation science suggests a few relevant procedures for rolling out new initiatives, ensuring they effectively take hold in the implementation setting, and sustaining them over time. These are worth analyzing in the context of JRNA practice, which blends an all-encompassing intervention designed to affect routine practice and a complex implementation environment. There are several implementation components that are worth discussing before broader consideration of how JRNA implementation might be organized and operationalized to consider how it will integrate into the routine practices of the juvenile justice system. These follow roughly from Fixsen and colleagues' (2009) "core implementation components," which they establish based on general work in social service implementation settings but focus very specifically on elements relevant to implementing and sustaining JRNA practices.

Considering Context and Assessing Readiness for Change

The context in which a policy or practice is promoted and adopted will have some enduring effects on its later implementation and use. This is also true of the existing practices and procedures of a given agency, which can create a degree of organizational inertia (Kelly & Amburgey, 1991) or path dependence (Sydow et al., 2009) that makes it difficult to enact new decision-making procedures. As noted on p. 88, both top-down mandated and bottom-up approaches to change in practice may be effective in their own ways—provided other core elements of implementation are considered. JRNA impacts both day-to-day activities of juvenile justice personnel and important agency-level decisions relevant to youths' cases. JRNA procedures are generally not being adopted anew and instead are intended to replace or enhance existing decision-making processes. This gives them a different character than the introduction of a standalone intervention or practice for the first time.

The complex implementation environment and the components that must be introduced and absorbed effectively to fully enact the logic of JRNA in the context of day-to-day decisions requires attention to readiness for change both at the individual and system level (see Backer, 1995). This is always the case in implementation of new initiatives but is particularly salient given the elements in JRNA, which are meant to promote change both in information gathering infrastructure and decision making. Implementation is especially complex with JRNA because each of the elements in the logic model can interact to the detriment of a particular case, caseload, or court docket. The fact that it is not merely an introduction of a practice or program but instead is intended to alter decision-making processes that have a deep-seated history in the juvenile justice system means that there may be an even greater perceived threat to the autonomy of practitioners. This goes back as far as early adoption of structured assessment practices (Meehl, 1954) and continues to affect the perspectives of some practitioners toward JRNA processes (Sullivan, Strange, et al., 2019).

A clear assessment of readiness for change in the adopting organization is a necessary early step for the implementation process—and one that is not always considered explicitly. Backer's (1995) work on this topic is instructive as he lays out a variety of methods (e.g., staff surveys or focus groups) that can be used in assessing readiness for innovative practices. He also discusses specific characteristics that might be sought in "social marketing" that accompany the implementation process. Importantly, he makes a distinction between the subtle promotion of a new practice (e.g., fully incorporate the practice into their work) and explicit promotion (e.g., tell their usage stories) by frontline staff. Backer suggests that assessing readiness for change in the relevant systems, taking stock of attitudes and skill-levels at multiple organizational levels, considering the existing approach to case- and organizational-level decision-making, and identifying potential obstacles and leverage points for implementation are necessary steps in implementation processes. Given the level of coverage of assessment practices and tools available now, it is likely that agencies might be moving to a new tool or seeking to improve current practice more so than trying to adopt these practices for the first time. The response to organizational needs will likely differ for an agency that is moving from one risk assessment tool to another as opposed to starting without an institutional history with JRNA.

Once the readiness to change in the implementation context is clear, agencies and relevant personnel must prepare for the change that will come with the introduction of the risk assessment tool (Vincent et al., 2012). As Backer (1995) points out, readiness is a dynamic property that manifests both at the individual and organizational level and therefore agencies can build it up in preparing for implementation. Vincent and colleagues (2012) identify three levels at which preparedness must happen: administrative level, operations level, and staff level. Administrative preparedness is geared toward those at a policy-making level who often are directing the process of adopting a risk assessment tool and then overseeing it (Vincent et al., 2012). These are often individuals who must exert their will to lead adoption and implementation. They also must be attentive to the climate for implementation and make prudent choices to ensure adoption, implementation, and sustainability. The operations level falls in the middle and involves those individuals and practices who oversee the day-to-day elements of casework with youths. They will likely have managerial responsibility for implementation and exert a strong impact on the organizational culture into which the tool will be introduced. They can also likely frame how the introduction of the tool may affect other daily practices in the agency. Line staff are directly involved in gathering information, scoring the assessment, and making decisions based on that information. Given that, their backgrounds, self-efficacy, training, and attitude toward JRNA will affect readiness to change and in turn determine how well the process is implemented (Fixsen et al., 2009).

Selecting Appropriate Tools

The processes of gaining buy-in and adopting JRNA illustrate that choices at early stages of adoption have important direct or indirect implications for the implementation process. For example, selecting an appropriate tool and process sets the stage for assessing individual youths and making decisions about their cases. Therefore, the fit between the tool and the setting also has implications for the implementation process and the later success of the introduction of JRNA into the environment (Miller & Lin, 2007). Stakeholder views, item inclusion, pragmatics of information gathering, and scoring procedures were identified as potential challenges to the implementation of a generic tool in New York City in Miller and Lin's study.

Bonta and colleagues (2001) suggest that staff be consulted and involved in identifying items, optimizing their wording, and determining how the appropriate information for an assessment tool will be gathered. They identify two options: choose a tool from among those that are published and available or develop one specifically tailored to their scenario (see also Vincent et al., 2012). This parallels broader selection for appropriate intervention fit for a given environment in ensuring readiness for implementation (Scaccia et al., 2015), which in turn fits into the notion that the context and mechanisms of a particular approach will ultimately drive its outcomes (Pawson & Tilley, 1997). It also reflects the imperative in JRNA that the tool should fit the objectives of the agency (or agencies) implementing it (Vincent, Guy, & Grisso, 2012). For example, a validated tool, such as Youth Assessment and Screening Instrument (YASI) or OYAS, differs from an approach that focuses on structured professional judgment. In turn these might be received differently by those in the field. The relevance of information from the tool may vary across individual juvenile justice and treatment personnel. So, for instance, probation officers may feel that a tool comprised predominantly of risk information allows them to appropriately establish a supervision level and case plan for youths. However, a tool that lacks quality information on youth needs is not apt to be very useful for a juvenile court's treatment coordinator or staff in treatment settings. The system may get into redundant—or even conflicting—assessment if care is not taken early in the process to ensure that an appropriate, goal-directed tool is selected for implementation. The transition from one system-wide assessment instrument (i.e., PACT) to three stage-specific assessment instruments in Florida (i.e., Prevention Assessment Tool, PAT; Community Assessment Tool, CAT; Residential Assessment for Youth, RAY) provides an example of ensuring a goal-directed tool is in place for youths referred to prevention programs, community placement, or residential treatment. As mentioned earlier, at this point most agencies are not adopting risk and needs assessment tools for the first time and therefore it is important to consider their value as a replacement for what is already in place or whether it may be "on top of" existing practices. These scenarios obviously have implications for needed training processes and obtaining staff buy-in for organizational change as those who are working with the assessment often have numerous other responsibilities (see, e.g., Viglione et al., 2018).

Rollout Processes, Staff Buy-In, and JRNA

Implementation takes time and deliberate effort if it is to be done well. If those who are leading the policy are not patient and systematic in introducing the JRNA system it will likely affect the degree to which the intervention is effectively implemented. This requires concerted attention to how stakeholders perceive the individuals leading the implementation as well as the process that is used. Champions for change must be selected very carefully to ensure that staff uptake of an initiative is not unduly affected by the person who is advocating for it (Vincent, Guy, Gershenson, & McCabe, 2012). This is consistent with the idea that potential champions for innovations within agencies be selected carefully and engage in a deliberate strategy in promoting it and obtaining feedback from stakeholders (Greenhalgh et al., 2004; Howell, 2005). For example, state-driven initiatives must have both administrative and local-level support for the new policy or practice to ensure that it is seamlessly adopted. It can therefore help to have a team of individuals to promote the use and identify strengths of the approach being implemented to meet the objectives of various stakeholders within and outside of the agency. Bonta and colleagues (2001) also suggest the use of implementation teams with a clear lead person to foster involvement and allow for centralized answers to potential questions from those in the field.

The rollout processes for risk and needs assessment tools can be characterized in multiple ways. This includes ways in which agencies arrive at choices about which JRNA tools they use in day-to-day practice, who made that decision, and how it is introduced to and engaged with by the various personnel who must carry it into the field as they investigate, process, and make decisions about justice-involved youths. As Greenhalgh et al. (2004) suggest, this has an important impact on how the implementation process will play out. In juvenile justice, for example, the process of a legislative change that leads to implementation may differ from a scenario where a new process is developed from the ground level up. The approach can affect the pace of adoption and implementation as well as juvenile justice personnel's predispositions toward it. How change happens has later implications for fidelity to the original intent of the innovation as well as the outcomes attained, implying that it is important to systematically plan and implement JRNA to maximize its potential. Ignoring this part of the process may lead to unsound assessments that lack face validity and can breed resentment among those practitioners who will implement the tool.

Sullivan, Strange, and colleagues (2019) studied implementation of a single assessment tool across three states at different stages of adoption and implementation. Their study included interviews with 217 purposively selected juvenile justice personnel at various stages of the juvenile justice system. The interviewees had varying roles with respect to the tool (e.g., agency leaders, assessment administrators, decision-makers who receive the information). To broaden the base of responses, they also included 1,103 personnel in those same states via a population-based web survey of their attitudes and JRNA practices. The response rate for the survey process was 32.4 percent. Respondents included staff from court ($n = 102$), correctional/secure treatment ($n = 132$), probation ($n = 592$), parole ($n = 7$), state-level administrators ($n = 8$), and individuals whose agency setting could not be inferred from their job title due to the anonymous nature of the survey data ($n = 157$) or whose job title was missing ($n = 15$).

Results of this study suggest that practitioners see some value in the JRNA process and agree that it has potential to meet key objectives in enhancing practice and promoting systematic decision making in juvenile justice. They saw the practice as broadly meeting the goals that it intends. Within that larger set of findings respondents showed less support for some JRNA practices, however—at least as currently used—such as for allocation of resources and making caseload decisions. This illustrates the nuance that comes with implementation as frontline users might agree in principle with their use but maybe have qualms about the implementation process. Among the important considerations in contextualizing staff perceptions and buy-in for innovative practices are staff experience, efficacy, and skill.

As a rule, technology transfer, or implementation, processes are even more crucial in human service or justice fields than in other contexts due to the fact the practitioners will have a great deal of responsibility—and therefore influence—over the day-to-day activities that operationalize the research evidence (Fixsen et al., 2009). Given the nature of the practice being implemented as far as the information gathering and decision-making inherent in JRNA, numerous juvenile justice personnel must be "on board" to achieve adoption as intended. Guy and colleagues (2014), for example, found that implementation was stymied unless judges bought in to using the assessment results. Similarly, in the Sullivan, Strange, et al. (2019) study of the implementation of the OYAS, practitioner attitudes varied on the usefulness of JRNA and the degree to which they thought buy-in was promoted and achieved in the implementation process. This in turn affected their views about the tool itself, meaning there was potential carryover from the implementation process to the actual performance of the tool. Specifically, among approximately 750 respondents, there were statistically significant correlations ranging from .25 to .38 between questions of whether the OYAS made their job easier and helped ensure better, fairer decision-making and the degree to which they perceived buy-in from staff in their agency.

Impact of Staff Attitudes and Buy-In

Miller and Trocchio (2016, p. 382) identify multiple "discretion points" relevant to how practitioners use risk and needs assessment. These include whether they complete the tool/process and the degree of time and effort that they invest; how they go about obtaining and interpreting relevant information in the process; and then how they use that assessment information in making decisions about disposition, placement, supervision, service matching, case planning, and case management. This means that a great deal of fidelity and adherence to the logic model of JRNA requires attention to individual work of frontline staff. Its salience is especially high in JRNA as people both conduct and score the assessment and then others must make decisions based on that assessment.

These elements of the implementation process underlying the JRNA logic model place a premium on practitioners' views about the assessment process. This includes their general disposition to risk and needs assessment as well as specific tools and procedures that are being used in their agency. It is distinct from attitudes toward other interventions, as regardless of how a probation officer might feel about a particular treatment program, they typically just refer youths to it as opposed to having to engage in it in a meaningful way themselves. This layer of separation creates a different dynamic in how their attitudes might affect the fidelity of implementation and use and, in turn, can impact individual and aggregate case outcomes.

While generally predisposed to the blend of helping and accountability inherent in the juvenile court (Bernard & Kurlychek, 2010; Sullivan, 2019), personnel in the juvenile justice system can have diverging views of the institutional mission that may affect implementation of JRNA. They may also have complex views of the treatment and sanction mission of the juvenile justice process (Viglione et al., 2018; Ward & Kupchik, 2009; 2010), which can affect the relative balance in weight of risk and needs as well as the degree to which they easily accept a perceived imposition on their existing data gathering, decision-making, and case management and supervision strategies. These views may cause some personnel to resist the implementation of JRNA if they perceive that it is lowering youths' actual risk by missing factors that their professional judgment suggest are important or that it is not conducive to their day-to-day casework for other reasons (e.g., they focus on screening or intake decisions and the tool used is intended to be a full case assessment). Even in cases where there is buy-in, it may occur mostly on the "risk" side of the assessment as opposed to the more complete risk and needs assessment that is necessary for appropriate treatment (and to recognize youths' strengths). In fact, the risk level or score is usually what is prioritized when the summary results of the assessment are considered in practice (as well as by researchers) and tends to hold the most weight when practitioners override the results of the assessment.

In a portion of the data from the multi-state implementation study by Sullivan, Strange, and colleagues (2019), there were a total of 213 overrides identified from 4,865 valid cases (4.4%) and only three of those were to a lower risk level (1.4%). This implies that practitioners may be predisposed to look at risk when they are unsure of a case attribution. This disposition might be exacerbated in cases where community-based resources for disposition and treatment are limited. Those interviewed and surveyed in that study also identified instances of both direct and indirect overrides of the risk assessment information. A direct override occurred within the bounds of the discretion of the assessor to place a youth into a different risk category based on their judgment. A more subtle, or indirect, override of the information came in how attorneys might use the information to make a case to a judge in court hearings. So, for example, a defense attorney might emphasize the assessment score more if the youth was assessed as "low risk," whereas the prosecutor might emphasize the results more in situations where the youth was designated as "high risk."

Shook and Sarri (2007) surveyed judges, lawyers, and probation officers in multiple states to try to understand their perspectives on structured professional judgment tools. In turn they help to identify some important considerations for implementing these tools in practice. They found that decisions about "overriding" the results of the assessment were often driven by resource availability such that a youth might be placed outside of their community if the appropriate services were not available. Overall, the authors concluded that there was a level of support for the use of these tools but also that the broader implementation context affects professionals' views. These views, then, feed back into their use in making appropriate decisions about youths' cases.

These studies of attitudes and the way that overrides tend to work illustrate that there are consequences for juvenile justice practitioners' knowledge about and orientation to elements of the JRNA logic model—both in scoring and decision making. Regardless of the specific steps in the process, buy-in must be obtained from staff as they will be administering the assessments and making routine decisions based on that information. Vincent and colleagues stress the value of identifying the ways in which the introduction of the assessment will help them to meet their daily goals while developing processes that ensure the tool is not an undue burden on them—or at least that they can identify some possible offsetting benefits. They argue that this is both the right approach to take and eventually will cause problems if it does not happen as part of assessing and building readiness for JRNA (see also Greenhalgh et al., 2004; Sullivan, Strange, et al., 2019).

Staff Experience and Skills

How JRNA tools and procedures are implemented matters in building and utilizing staff skills and efficacy. Some agencies engage in broad-based training of personnel while others only task certain personnel with conducting the assessments. These reflect generalized and more specialized, or decentralized and centralized, approaches to assessment (see Mears, 2012). This will inevitably have an impact on implementation strategy, process, and sustainability. A decentralized approach, which was most common among the agencies in the recent study of OYAS implementation across the juvenile justice system, means that a variety of juvenile justice personnel will conduct and use assessment information across their entire caseload or court docket. In a centralized system, the information is gathered and synthesized by a limited number of personnel and then dispersed to other parts of the system—including decision-makers like judges and treatment providers. This process is described in Mears (2012) and exemplified by the Juvenile Assessment Centers that are utilized across the state of Florida (see Dembo & Brown, 1994; Walters et al., 2005). This centralized approach has some clear benefits in building expertise and experience for appropriate use of assessment practices but also can concentrate a great deal of knowledge, responsibility, and buy-in for JRNA in a relatively small group of personnel within the whole system. This might also make the implementation system more susceptible to impacts from personnel turnover and risks potentially creating silos between the administration of the assessment process and its use in decision making. Whichever approach is taken, it should not hinder the overall climate for implementation or the ability to fully implement and sustain the JRNA process.

The evolution of risk and needs assessment processes over recent decades inherently suggests that what is asked of practitioners in the JRNA process differs from what was required of them previously. This means that aside from receptivity to the new approach, there may be barriers at the frontline staff level that have more to do with existing skillsets, experiences, and orientations to doing juvenile justice work. While turnover in juvenile justice staffing is relatively high, approaches to staffing ensure heterogeneity in how well different staff members will be able to carry out the processes associated with JRNA. However, in a survey conducted by Mears and colleagues (2010), the average tenure in juvenile justice for agency personnel was approximately 17 years with a standard deviation of 11 years. This suggests that there is a good deal of variability in the tenure of the staff who will be implementing initiatives like JRNA.

Promoting User Confidence and Efficacy

The different stakeholder groups described on p. 54 invariably come to the process with distinct orientations and concerns that depend on where they are positioned in the implementation process (i.e., what is their role in delivering the innovation?). With this, obtaining sustainable buy-in is affected by how the potential costs and benefits of JRNA are conveyed to relevant stakeholders based on the research at hand and its perceived applicability to their work (Nelson et al., 2006). Expression of the benefits of the new approach without any communication of uncertainty or the potential costs may engender more skepticism from those in the field. For instance, in the Sullivan, Strange, et al. (2019) implementation study, some interviewees indicated that they generally believed in the use of structured assessment but that it added considerable time to their work, which led them to question the cost and benefit of using the approach. For example, when asked an open-ended question about limitations/concerns with the OYAS, "time consuming" came up in 26 percent of responses. Respondents also frequently expressed concerns about the degree to which the tool was valid and reliable for their populations. In fact, this was the top concern mentioned by nearly half of 195 interviewees (Sullivan, Strange, et al., 2019). This suggests that these practitioners have some command of research concepts and underscores the need to adequately convey the certainties/uncertainties around the evidence in obtaining buy-in.

Young and colleagues (2006) evaluated the implementation of JRNA processes in Maryland's Juvenile Justice System and—among other recommendations—found that local validation and emphasis on fidelity in practice and quality assurance were central to effective practices. The data gathered in the study mainly entailed reviews of administrative reports. Among the implementation strategies identified in their study were a blending of insights from what would work in practice and the statistical considerations inherent in the use of actuarial instruments. Like the results from Miller and Lin (2007), they found that some practitioners felt as though youths' risk should not be impacted by familial delinquent or criminal behavior or experiences of neglect or abuse in the past. Other concerns stemmed from the belief that certain youth attitudes or prior behavior items are subjective, and therefore potentially unreliable, in how staff score them.

Young et al.'s study also identified similar barriers to implementation as identified in other studies. For example, staff expressed skepticism in changes to practice that were perceived to be handed down from higher level agency administrators and the system (e.g., state mandates). Staff also lacked a clear connection between the JRNA initiative and existing practice. Each of these is a recurring theme in the research on JRNA and implementation science more generally and the authors suggest that early involvement of a variety of key stakeholders from frontline staff to agency or state-level policymakers is necessary in fostering organizational and staff support for these initiatives.

Beyond traditional sources of skepticism, the question of efficacy and skill have not been fully addressed in JRNA contexts. Some research on educational interventions suggests that teacher self-efficacy had an impact on their attitudes toward a new set of practices (Guskey, 1987). The fact that risk and needs assessment training includes some time on practicing interviewing skills also implies that the processes and procedures used in JRNA may not be innate and require some skill building. It is also likely that the level of skill and comfortability with the assessment will vary across users in each agency. For instance, the relationship between service time and orientation to evidence-based practice may in part reflect concerns about efficacy and skill among those who will be directly involved in implementation. Newer staff are likely to be exposed to the foundations of evidence-based practice in their education and early training and therefore may feel more comfortable with their implementation and use relative to existing practice (Satterfield et al., 2009). It is also the case, however, that openness to learning and using evidence-based practices can be cultivated socially (Nelson et al., 2006).

Several studies have considered attitudes toward evidence-based practices among practitioners, with a few focused specifically on risk and needs assessment practices. Hurducas and his colleagues (2014) carried out a systematic review of studies that looked at practitioner attitudes toward the use of violence risk assessments. Nine studies met their inclusion criteria. They categorized the surveys based on perceived quality, focusing especially on methodological indicators such as the inclusion of response rates and description of the survey tool. Though not fully covered due to the idiosyncrasies of individual studies, some studies showed traces of use/disuse depending on attitudes toward risk and needs assessment among staff. In those cases, users saw value in the tools because of their basis in evidence-based research but also thought that factors like time necessary for usage and lack of initial or ongoing training may present obstacles to full implementation. Most studies included individuals who seemed to have a clinical background in assessments and therefore may not be fully representative of the frontline staff in juvenile justice agencies who may have more skepticism about the evidence base, as well as backgrounds that are more varied with respect to carrying out assessments effectively.

Training and Engagement with Key Personnel

Those involved in the implementation of assessments should have a firm sense of staff attitudes and orientations toward the new approach. They also should take stock of the experiences and skills of their personnel to identify potential challenges (and supports) for implementation. For instance, interviewing skills are essential in the JRNA process (Bonta et al., 2001; Guy et al., 2014) and therefore a pre-assessment of the implementation context should investigate the degree to which relevant staff have those skills. Vincent, Guy, Gershenson, and McCabe (2012) describe a survey conducted in Louisiana prior to the implementation of new JRNA practices. This survey comprised questions about current practice and desired/potential changes. It was informative both for practices with respect to implementation broadly (e.g., what policies and practices should be put in place?) as well as for setting an agenda for staff training. Baird et al. (2013) suggest that the materials and training practices surrounding assessment tools are essential in ensuring it is reliably applied by staff members—especially given turnover and the presence of other day-to-day responsibilities.

Training is an essential element of the implementation of a new process or technology in the juvenile justice system. It offers the opportunity to socialize staff into the new way of doing things, promote needed skills, build practitioner self-efficacy, and introduce specific elements of the assessment tool and related policy and procedures to staff in the field. It also serves as an opportunity to seek out further feedback from those who will be using the tool and related procedures regularly (Vincent, Guy, Gershenson, & McCabe, 2012). JRNA training curricula vary, but usually comprise several key components: review of relevant policy and procedures; clear focus on the content of the assessment; information gathering and interviewing; scoring and classifying with the tool; and use of information from the tool.

As a case in point, the process for the Ohio Youth Assessment System (OYAS) tool consists of a series of steps across two days of training.[4] This includes an overview of the tool, practice of interview skills, and instruction on the manual and scoring procedures. Users also must be certified by passing a written test. That test generally consists of going through the data gathering with mock cases and an assessment of the degree to which the users' results correspond to the expectations outlined in the OYAS manual. Sites using the tool often mandate some booster training and re-certification over time, but it is not clear that is always adhered to (see Sullivan, Strange, et al., 2019).

Training must be delivered thoughtfully to ensure it is effective both in promoting buy-in *and* fidelity in use. As evident from the list of recommendations mentioned on p. 105, training practice requires a good deal of commitment from participants (users), trainers, supervisors, and implementing agencies. For example, the reticence of staff may not simply be about ideology or a belief that they "know better," but rather may also stem from questions about their own efficacy or skillset in working with this new approach. In this way, the training process should be a means of conveying specifics about the tool being implemented and also an opportunity to build up the needed capacity for its effective implementation, use, and sustainability. Since there is a fair amount of turnover in juvenile justice agencies, training and implementation will likely need to be tailored to a variety of skill and experience levels if they are to be effective in both conveying information specifically about the tool. Trainings should also offer an opportunity to enhance organizational capacity and motivation for the innovation being implemented (e.g., Taxman et al., 2014).

While mindful of how well all nuances can be covered in a training for busy practitioners, these procedures cover certain aspects of JRNA in more depth than others. In turn, it is not surprising that some elements of the JRNA logic model may be better mapped to the training that typically occurs. Usage of assessment information for case management emerged as a potential concern in Sullivan, Strange, and colleagues' (2019) surveys and interviews with juvenile justice personnel. This is relevant to both practical integration of information into the automated system used with the OYAS and the ability to then map that information to case planning, service matching, and case management. The initial OYAS training used as an example above can only spend a limited amount of time on case management during a two-day period. That is, however, a key aspect of operationalizing the assessment to match youths to appropriate services (see, e.g., Nelson & Vincent, 2018).

Organizationally, a training strategy must also account for attrition in staffing over time. Though relatively little is known about turnover across the juvenile justice system, some studies have suggested some cause for concern. Studying juvenile corrections turnover with a sample of 475 recent trainees, Minor et al. (2011) found that nearly one-quarter of staff had resigned within 12 months of completing a training academy (see also Mitchell et al., 2000). They studied several possible correlates of resignation and found that satisfaction in work, pay, and co-workers were positively related to organizational commitment. However, co-worker satisfaction was the only variable related to turnover. Although not turnover per se, in a survey study of juvenile corrections personnel, Mitchell and colleagues (2000) found that job satisfaction, staff support, and organizational communication had significant and moderate-sized relationships with intentions to leave the agency. Those tended to be more robust predictors than individual characteristics of the respondents. Turnover, of course, has problematic implications for juvenile justice agencies but can be especially impactful when engaging in wholesale system changes as is the case in JRNA. If time and effort is being added to staff members' tasks, then an effort must be made to identify and follow through on the elements of the process that are beneficial to them in doing their work.

Sustainability, Quality Assurance, and Continued Improvement

The implementation study by Sullivan, Strange, and colleagues (2019) found that the most common implementation practice across sites was a training on the assessment tool. While this is a necessary aspect of the implementation process as the new tool and practice must be introduced and mastered by those who will implement it, training alone is not enough to ensure that the process reaches its full potential. Among the overall interview sample, only about half of interviewees believed that other steps were taken to secure staff buy-in. Some other "second order" objectives were seemingly not attained based on practitioner responses. For example, in all three states respondents indicated that the use of the information gathered from the assessment process was not enough to support case management practices in the way that might be hoped for. Additionally, more than 60 percent of 168 interviewees reported that quality assurance or measures were not in place (42.9%) or they were unsure about whether they were (20.2%). Additionally, relatively few in that interview sample (28%), which comprised more personnel in management positions, reported that their agency uses the risk and needs assessment data as a planning tool.

Much of the insight and research around implementation comes from the early stages of adopting a new JRNA tool and process. This, however, only provides a snapshot of the early aspects of the process without considering much of what lies beyond that in terms of the evolution or enhancement of the process. It is important to consider the degree to which the risk and needs information was successfully converted into appropriate placements and treatment matching. This is another potential obstacle as it requires training on second-level uses of a JRNA tool for case management as well as the resources to appropriately place youths in line with the information drawn from the assessment. Without that, practitioners may be trained to collect information and generate risk scores, but not in using the information effectively to impact youth outcomes in a way that lends itself to sustainability over time.

One risk in the implementation and usage of JRNA tools and practices is the potential for goal displacement where administrative checkoffs take the place of a closer connection between the underlying logic model and case and agency outcomes. In asking about agency-level monitoring of JRNA practices, several interviewees mentioned that the administrative checks largely comprised determining whether the assessment was completed on their caseload as opposed to more formal consideration of whether the process led to the outcomes intended for given youths (e.g., percent of cases appropriately matched to services or supervision). In this way, it is important that bureaucratic goals be distinguished from implementation fidelity. That requires focusing on the degree to which services are matched to a youth's need profile as opposed to simply checking whether administrators recorded a score in a domain for which they show a need.

Sustainability and optimization also require a focus on continuous quality improvement over time. Completion of assessments, and then uploading the information into a designated system, is just one piece of having it used effectively for case- and agency-level decisions. Goal displacement or drift that leads to a loss of fidelity are potential challenges in the implementation of evidence-based programs generally (Chambers et al., 2013), but are especially salient in dealing with complex JRNA processes. It may be more straightforward to simply verify that assessments are being completed on schedule as opposed to considering whether the more difficult process of matching needs to interventions occurs. This can lead to service matching disparities and reinforcement of weighting toward risk in operationalizing assessment practices because the challenges of fully meeting the logic model of JRNA are quite challenging. In turn, risk may take immediate priority of assessing and addressing youth needs. Using OJJDP's Comprehensive Strategy as an example and a network-based approach to data gathering and analysis, Sridharan and Gillespie (2004) illustrate the need to maintain focus on goals among multiple stakeholders to sustain evidence-based practices.

There are also differences in the nature of the information gathered in risk and needs assessment that may create inherent patterns in the effectiveness of its usage in practice. The notion of risk—while it can be quite subjective—is relatively concrete in terms of how it might fit into case disposition or supervision options. It also involves a clearer "law and order," enforcement-driven perspective. Mapping domain-specific information to appropriate intervention may be more challenging without some degree of skill and training. For instance, in the OYAS, the substance use, mental health, and personality domain comprises of items that tap into each of those areas (see Lovins & Latessa, 2013). Therefore, that nonspecific information would have to be repackaged for use with treatment matching to align precisely with such recommendations.

Ongoing quality assurance practices can help ensure that there is continual focus on integrity in the use of the risk assessment tool to meet objectives for individual youths and the system. This should occur beyond the initial implementation phase and be maintained throughout the use of the tool in each juvenile justice system. Sullivan, Strange and colleagues' surveys and interviews found that there was general support for these tools, but that practitioners also saw places where more effort toward buy-in would have been beneficial and ongoing continuous quality improvement (CQI) practices would be welcome. Practitioner views in either realm might affect the likelihood of successful implementation so both must be considered in making effortful course corrections, but which also might prolong and enhance the fidelity of the assessment process.

There is relatively limited information on the degree to which implementation practices explicitly affect case outcomes within agencies. Still, given the general information on implementation of evidence-based practices and the complexity of the JRNA logic model it is likely that ineffective implementation would degrade outcomes for recidivism, youth development, fairness, and equity. For example, if youths are not effectively matched to services based on their specific needs, then one element of the underlying logic for the fully actualized JRNA process is diminished.

In addition to broader contextual influences, fidelity in implementation is also affected by granular factors such as the availability of programs and resources that are suitable for youths, which affect the ability to effectively manage cases in line with the logic of the assessment process. The effective operation of the overall JRNA process depends on identifying and responding effectively to those needs. This also offers some evidence that JRNA practices cannot solely be evaluated through predictive validity but rather that researchers and practitioners must also address implementation and usage to optimize JRNA to meet the full theory and logic laid out in Figure 3.1. The nature of the process that is being implemented brings with it several potential places where problems might emerge. Obtaining buy-in and effectively training juvenile justice personnel on the use of the assessment tool and process are early potential breaking points, but they are not the only ones. Initial buy-in and training are necessary, but not sufficient, to the effective use of an assessment process across a juvenile court caseload. Going a step further, those who offer services to youths must be aware of and properly use the assessment information to complete the process as intended. This could include passing off youths from courts to corrections agencies or possibly to private treatment providers or alternate services for justice-involved youths.

The small but growing research area focused on implementation and use of assessments in juvenile justice offers insight into the status of practice and some recommendations for future implementation, usage, and development. The ongoing work of those who study the implementation of policy, programs, and practices in various field settings can likewise contribute to the discussion of JRNA processes and related practices in the juvenile justice system. It is essential to have a holistic, but also detailed, understanding of the implementation environment going into the process and proceed accordingly. This should be part of an agency readiness assessment so that it is clear what type of implementation environment there is for JRNA. This will help to identify potential obstacles, pockets of support, and how the assessment may be contextualized alongside of other system and individual-level goals. Without assessments of agency readiness, those who seek to implement JRNA practices may be myopic in how they interact with staff around the process which will be a hindrance in promoting buy-in and building up the general and specific capacity needed to implement the JRNA process to its fullest potential in that environment (Wandersman et al., 2008).

Collectively, existing studies help identify important components in effectively implementing JRNA and reveal tentative support for these practices among practitioners—especially juvenile justice personnel. At the same time, however, there are places where the support is more tenuous. This means that while the readiness to adopt these tools and practices provides a foundation for good implementation and sustainability, it cannot simply be viewed as a process that will be successful if left unattended. Still, there is also little formal research on implementation practices within the JRNA logic model, including information gathering and synthesis, decision making, and ensuring the fidelity of those specific decisions. Thus, it is helpful to consider JRNA implementation in the context of broader research and thinking about implementation of the evidence-based practices.

Key Lessons and Challenges of JRNA Implementation and Use

Taken together the limited research and commentary on implementing JRNA and the more extensive body of work on implementation science offer some ideas about how to maximize the implementation process for strong practice and—presumably—quality outcomes relative to the JRNA logic model. When considered more holistically it is clear that there are several elements beyond simply training juvenile justice personnel to initial competence that must be considered when evaluating the effectiveness of the logic model that guides JRNA practices. These can be complicated in terms of how they manifest in juvenile justice processing and decision-making. For instance, interviews conducted with juvenile justice personnel who used the OYAS indicate that some might rely on greater (or lesser) collateral information in reaching scores within domains and on the overall system (e.g., record checking or focusing on interviews with youths and their parents only, Sullivan, Strange et al., 2019). This variability has implications for effective initial training and later follow-up coaching and boosters. Slight differences in how individuals work within the system can accumulate and have a considerable impact on the

implementation process and case outcomes. These findings also illustrate the
need for close attention to both big picture and grounded details in considering
the implementation and sustainability of JRNA.

Building on multiple studies, Vincent and colleagues (2018) identified
implementation drivers in JRNA based on research from several different sites and two distinct teams. Their recommendations about implementation respect the multi-faceted nature of the innovation being
introduced into the system. Those conclusions are summarized in Figure
4.3. In general, there are several core ideas driving the recommendations. Most importantly, implementation is a distributed process and
therefore various stakeholders must have a real voice in moving those
tools into practice. The JRNA tool and accompanying processes must
be phased in and allow for feedback from those key stakeholders about
how the process is working. Comprehensive and intensive training is
essential and should be geared toward usage by those in the field (i.e.,
linked to their day-to-day practice). It should be ongoing and reinforced by supervisory oversight and support, policy and procedure, and
information management capacity within the agencies implementing the
JRNA processes.

These general principles also come up in an independent set of case studies. Hussemann and Liberman's (2017) work on implementation of the
Juvenile Justice Reform and Reinvestment Initiative (JJRRI) focuses
broadly on the totality of the JRNA logic described on p. 28 and in the
logic model described earlier in this book (see also, Lipsey et al., 2017). As

General Recommendations for JRNA Implementation

> • *Promote positive staff perceptions about the reliability, credibility, and applicability of the
> instrument to the needs of their local jurisdictions.*
>
> • *Engage staff and other stakeholders in the initial strategic planning, goal setting, and problem
> solving to ensure early buy-in.*
>
> • *Adhere to a pilot period that focuses on training of staff and other stakeholders and allows for
> course correction if needed.*
>
> • *Provide ongoing supervisory support and training.*
>
> • *Develop standardized operating procedures and written policies in state and local agencies and
> the ability to share information across multiple stakeholders.*
>
> • *Create a strong data infrastructure, including both user-friendly technological systems to support
> data collection and staff data expertise.*

Figure 4.3 General Recommendations for JRNA Implementation
Source: Adapted from Vincent et al., 2018

described earlier, the development of disposition and service matrices is pertinent to the overall logic model driving JRNA. Their process evaluation across three demonstration sites identified several factors that affect implementation of a decision-making system that draws on risk and needs assessment. Among those factors are data and informational infrastructure to support change and sustainability of new practices; availability of resources; alignment of agency referral requirements and information from the assessment; funding training to ensure appropriate services are delivered to youths; buy-in from judges, attorneys, and service providers outside of juvenile justice; accounting for and building on pre-existing evidence-based initiatives and organizational orientation to evidence-based practice; need for close collaboration among areas of government and various youth-serving agencies and inclusion of an array of stakeholders in the planning and implementation process; and challenges linking these new initiatives to existing operations (Hussemann & Liberman, 2017).

Their case studies also illustrate that—even with supports in place—implementation of the process highlighted in Figure 4.1 and in Chapter 3 is challenging and multi-faceted, requiring concerted work over an extended time. Delaware was able to implement the PACT tool in community settings and residential facilities and rigorously study it, but there were still challenges with matching youths to necessary services and creating a data infrastructure for continuous improvement and sustainability (Husseman & Liberman, 2017). The Milwaukee site experienced challenges in the consistent use of the assessment tool and handling the information drawn from it. This in turn created difficulties in determining the effectiveness of a dispositional matrix that relies on the integration of those assessment data with the decision-making process.

Taken together, the broad suggestions offered by Vincent and colleagues (2018) and the implications from Husseman and Liberman (2017) integrate a great deal of insight from existing studies of JRNA and more general conclusions from the large and continuously growing area of implementation science. Vincent, Guy, and Grisso (2012) developed a comprehensive guidebook for implementation of risk assessment in juvenile justice settings based on several studies of the process of agencies adopting and using these tools to assess youths and make decisions about their cases. This includes studies of implementation in probation settings especially, but which have applicability across the system and different actors. Acknowledging the limited work in this area, Vincent and colleagues also utilized expert and advisory panel meetings in developing the guidebook. The framework and the process shown in Figure 4.4 offers some sense of how juvenile justice agencies might proceed in steps of planning, adopting, implementing, and sustaining JRNA practices.

The implication of the review and analysis to this point is that—if implemented properly—JRNA can alter the way in which system personnel

1. Develop Implementation Environment	• Develop strong awareness of the implementation context through formal assessment followed by planning, outreach, and involvement of appropriate stakeholders to promote readiness
2. Establish buy-in	• Work with stakeholders and staff (broadly) to ensure clear understanding of the objectives of the process, solicit feedback, and build an inclusive implementation process that can be sustained
3. Select and prepare tool	• Find or develop an assessment that fits the context and objectives of the system in which it will be implemented. Also applicable to making strategic modifications for quality improvement when a tool has already been adopted
4. Develop policy and procedured documents	• Implementation of JRNA should be accompanied by a series of support documents that bridge policy, practice, and the specific tool(s) being used and which are sustainable
5. Training	• Training should motivate the change, understand and respond to practitioner concerns, build knowledge of the tool and policy and procedure around it, and help in building necessary skills. Should also be boosters
6. Pilot Testing	• Identify sites or individuals within sites as early adopters and introduce the tool and accompanying processes to offer an early assessment and generate feedback
7. Full Implementation	• Ability to conduct assessment process reliably, effectively utilize information for placement and treatment decisions, and generally utilize the assessment in routine case-level practice and agency decision-making
8. Sustainability Practices	• Data gathering, ongoing training, and appropriate modification based on information about the JRNA process

Figure 4.4 Implementation Sequence in JRNA
Source: Adapted from Vincent, Guy, and Grisso, 2012

reach conclusions about justice-involved youths. These alterations can remove potentially detrimental attributions that historically informed how youths' cases were viewed, disposed of, and treated (see, e.g., Bridges & Steen, 1998; Curtis & Reese, 1994; Harris, 2009). One main objective of JRNA is to more systematically review and extract information about cases that can reduce gaps in how each youth is looked at relative to others. For example, in establishing the value of evaluating race/ethnicity and gender disparities in predictive validity, Schwalbe and colleagues (2006, p. 306) state, "these instruments are intended to reduce, in part, individual discretionary biases that are often associated with court decision-making and case dispositions." Theoretically, appropriate JRNA implementation should also lead to more efficient and effective decisions about case disposition, supervision, and appropriate intervention. Bonta and colleagues (2001, p. 237), suggest that the JRNA process can "open the door for more effective case management." That, however, is not fully determined just by conducting assessments as there are several obstacles to effective case management fully coming to fruition.

Chapter Summary

As in other scenarios in juvenile justice, identifying evidence-based practices like JRNA is only one small portion of effectively utilizing them in the field

(Sullivan, 2019). JRNA is being implemented in a complex juvenile justice eco-system, but that is just the start. The shift in information gathering and decision making affects fundamental premises of traditional agency operations—as well as typical human decision-making heuristics. Implementation effectiveness very clearly will lag if appropriate buy-in and staff capacity is not built and fostered broadly in the implementation environment. It will also suffer if the entire logic model of JRNA is not in place because of resource constraints or a lack of impetus from those within or surrounding the agency that wishes to implement these practices. Furthermore, inconsistent or incomplete implementation may promote false promise in JRNA or create more inconsistency and ineffectiveness in decision making (Sullivan, Strange, et al., 2019; Young et al., 2006).

The unique circumstances of implementing a structured decision-making process in the juvenile justice system require some consideration of broader principles in implementation science as well as an understanding of specific factors that can influence success in juvenile justice—and more specifically risk and needs assessment in juvenile justice. This chapter highlighted a number of those general and specific concerns, which we return to in making recommendations in Chapter 7. The complex implementation framework of juvenile justice also means that the individual and agency practice components assessed in this chapter are only one piece of the overall eco-system in which JRNA occurs. The steady increase in the adoption and use of risk and needs assessment in juvenile (and criminal) justice that has frequently focused on risk-centered, justice-based outcomes means that in most cases these processes have already been implemented to some extent and therefore the implications of analysis such as that carried out here must be informed by the fact that some operationalization of these ideas involves revision of current practice as opposed to implementation of entirely new systems. In that way, it is important that we reflect on the use of these tools both from a theoretical and pragmatic stance given the degree to which they are now prominent in juvenile justice practice.

The use of risk assessment has also spurred broader legal and social concerns about whether and how this information is used. This means that the relevant points of analysis in thinking about JRNA do not stop with implementation, usage, and outcomes within the juvenile justice system. Rather they extend out into broader questions about the implications of assessment—both those discussed here and others that may rely more heavily on emerging data processing and analysis technologies—for how juvenile justice and other regulatory systems deal with youths under the law and implications for individual and social welfare. Chapter 5 takes up those themes to offer a broader sense of where JRNA might fit into contemporary discussions of law and public policy. This effectively expands the lens with which we view risk and needs assessment with juveniles to consider broader questions of policy, law, and fairness that warrant attention in analyzing the relevant research findings and the practices that follow.

Notes

1 Implementation science offers numerous frameworks for these processes (see Nilsen, 2015). The Aarons et al. (2011) model provides a useful organizing structure for the discussion here and parallels one of the main sources of insight on implementing JRNA specifically by Vincent, Guy, and Grisso (2012). The Wandersman et al. (2008) framework helps to detail some actions and linkages among different components in the implementation process.
2 See www.azcourts.gov/jjsd/Automation/AZYAS
3 This finding is based on analysis of data from the Sullivan, Strange et al. (2019) implementation and use study focused on the satisfaction with the automated system used to input and track OYAS information and overall satisfaction with the assessment itself.
4 See www.uc.edu/content/dam/uc/corrections/docs/Training%20Overviews/ OYAS%20-%20Overview.pdf

References

Aarons, G.A., Hurlburt, M., & Horwitz, S.M. (2011). Advancing a conceptual model of evidence-based practice implementation in public service sectors. *Administration and Policy in Mental Health and Mental Health Services Research*, 38(1), 4–23. doi:10.1007/s10488-010-0327-7.

Backer, T.E. (1995). Assessing and enhancing readiness for change: Implications for technology transfer. *NIDA Research Monograph*, 155, 21–41. PMID: 8594459.

Baird, C., Healy, T., Johnson, K., Bogie, A., Dankert, E.W., & Scharenbroch, C. (2013). *A comparison of risk assessment instruments in juvenile justice*. Madison, WI: National Council on Crime and Delinquency. www.ojp.gov/pdffiles1/ojjdp/grants/ 244477.pdf.

Barnoski, R. (2004). *Washington State juvenile court assessment manual, version 2.1.* Olympia, WA: Washington State Institute for Public Policy.

Bernard, T.J., & Kurlychek, M.C. (2010). *The cycle of juvenile justice*. New York: Oxford University Press.

Bonta, J., Bogue, B., Crowley, M., & Motiuk, L. (2001). Implementing offender classification systems: Lessons learned. In G.A. Bernfeld, D.P. Farrington, & A.W. Leschied (Eds.), *Offender rehabilitation in practice: Implementing and evaluating effective programs* (pp. 227–245). Chichester, UK: Wiley.

Bray, T.M., Sample, L.L., & Kempf-Leonard, K. (2005). "Justice by geography": Racial disparity and juvenile courts. In D. Hawkins & K. Kempf-Leonard (Eds.), *Our children, their children (pp. 270–299)*. Chicago: University of Chicago Press.

Bridges, G.S., & Steen, S. (1998). Racial disparities in official assessments of juvenile offenders: Attributional stereotypes as mediating mechanisms. *American Sociological Review*, 63(4), 554–570. doi:10.2307/2657267.

Carroll, C., Patterson, M., Wood, S., Booth, A., Rick, J., & Balain, S. (2007). A conceptual framework for implementation fidelity. *Implementation Science*, 2(1), 1–9. doi:10.1186/1748-5908-2-40.

Chambers, D.A., Glasgow, R.E., & Stange, K.C. (2013). The dynamic sustainability framework: Addressing the paradox of sustainment amid ongoing change. *Implementation Science*, 8(1), 1–11. doi:10.1186/1748-5908-8-117.

Chung, G.H., Choi, J.N., & Du, J. (2017). Tired of innovations? Learned helplessness and fatigue in the context of continuous streams of innovation implementation. *Journal of Organizational Behavior*, 38(7), 1130–1148. doi:10.1002/job.2191.

Crime and Justice Institute (2017). *Implementing comprehensive juvenile justice system improvement in Hawaii*. Boston, MA: Crime and Justice Institute. www.crj.org/assets/2018/06/HI-Brief-v8-10-17-17_UPDATED_8-pages_FINAL_FINAL_FINAL_WEB.pdf

Curtis Jr, R.L., & Reese, W.A. (1994). Framed attributions and shaped accounts: A study of dispositional process in juvenile justice. *Criminal Justice Review*, 19(2), 244–270. doi:10.1177/073401689401900205.

Dembo, R., & Brown, R. (1994). The Hillsborough County juvenile assessment center. *Journal of Child & Adolescent Substance Abuse*, 3(2), 25–44. doi:10.1177/0032885598078004006.

Durlak, J.A., & DuPre, E.P. (2008). Implementation matters: A review of research on the influence of implementation on program outcomes and the factors affecting implementation. *American Journal of Community Psychology*, 41(3–4), 327–350. doi:10.1007/s10464-008-9165-0.

Exworthy, M., Berney, L., & Powell, M. (2002). 'How great expectations in Westminster may be dashed locally': The local implementation of national policy on health inequalities. *Policy & Politics*, 30(1), 79–96.

Feld, B.C. (1992). Justice by geography: urban, suburban, and rural variations in juvenile justice administration. *Journal of Criminal Law and Criminology*, 82, 156–210. doi:0091-4169/91/8201-0156.

Fixsen, D.L., Blase, K.A., Naoom, S.F., & Wallace, F. (2009). Core implementation components. *Research on Social Work Practice*, 19, 531–540. doi:10.1177/1049731509335549.

Fixsen, D., Blase, K., Naoom, S., & Duda, M. (2013). *Implementation drivers: Assessing best practices*. Chapel Hill, NC: University of North Carolina at Chapel Hill.

Gies, R. (2015). *Changing the footprint of Ohio's juvenile justice system*. Presentation given to University of Cincinnati School of Criminal Justice, Cincinnati, OH.

Greenhalgh, T., Robert, G., Macfarlane, F., Bate, P., & Kyriakidou, O. (2004). Diffusion of innovations in service organizations: Systematic review and recommendations. *The Milbank Quarterly*, 82(4), 581–629. doi:10.1111/j.0887-378X.2004.00325.x.

Guskey, T.R. (1987). Context variables that affect measures of teacher efficacy. *The Journal of Educational Research*, 81(1), 41–47.

Guy, L.S., Nelson, R.J., Fusco-Morin, S.L., & Vincent, G.M. (2014). What do juvenile probation officers think of using the SAVRY and YLS/CMI for case management, and do they use the instruments properly? *International Journal of Forensic Mental Health*, 13(3), 227–241. doi:10.1080/14999013.2014.939789.

Harris, A. (2009). Attributions and institutional processing: How focal concerns guide decision-making in the juvenile court. *Race and Social Problems*, 1(4), 243–256. doi:10.1007/s12552-12009-9020-9024.

Hawken, A. (2016). All implementation is local. *Criminology & Public Policy*, 15, 1229–1239.

Howell, J.M. (2005). The right stuff: Identifying and developing effective champions of innovation. *Academy of Management Perspectives,* 19(2), 108–119. doi:10.5465/ ame.2005.16965104.

Hurducas, C.C., Singh, J.P., de Ruiter, C., & Petrila, J. (2014). Violence risk assessment tools: A systematic review of surveys. *International Journal of Forensic Mental Health,* 13(3), 181–192.

Hussemann, J., & Liberman, A. (2017). *Implementing evidence-based juvenile justice reforms.* Washington, DC: Urban Institute.

Kelly, D., & Amburgey, T.L. (1991). Organizational inertia and momentum: A dynamic model of strategic change. *Academy of Management Journal,* 34(3), 591–612. doi:10.5465/256407.

Krisberg, B., Litsky, P., & Schwartz, I. (1984). Youth in confinement: Justice by geography. *Journal of Research in Crime and Delinquency,* 21(2), 153–181. doi:10.1177/0022427884021002005.

Laub, J.H. (2016) Life course research and the shaping of public policy. In M. Shanahan, J. Mortimer, & M. Kirkpatrick Johnson (Eds.), *Handbook of the life course.* Handbooks of Sociology and Social Research (pp. 623–637). Cham: Springer. doi:10.1007/978-3-319-20880-0_27.

Lee, S.J., Altschul, I., & Mowbray, C.T. (2008). Using planned adaptation to implement evidence-based programs with new populations. *American Journal of Community Psychology,* 41(3–4), 290–303. doi:10.1007/s10464-008-9160-5.

Lipsey, M.W., Conly, C.H., Chapman, G., & Bilchik, S. (2017). *Juvenile Justice System Improvement: Implementing an Evidence-Based Decision-Making Platform.* Washington, DC: Office of Juvenile Justice and Delinquency Prevention. www. ojp.gov/pdffiles1/ojjdp/grants/250443.pdf.

Lipsky, M. (1980). *Street Level Bureaucracy: Dilemmas of the Individual in Public Services.* New York, NY: The Russell Sage Foundation.

Lovins, B., & Latessa, E. (2013). Creation and validation of the Ohio Youth Assessment System (OYAS) and strategies for successful implementation. *Justice Research and Policy,* 15(1), 67–93.

McCafferty, J.T. (2016). The importance of counties: Examining the predictive validity of a state juvenile risk assessment instrument. *Journal of Offender Rehabilitation,* 55(6), 377–395. doi:10.1080/10509674.2016.1194944.

Mears, D. (2012). The front end of the juvenile court: Intake and informal versus formal processing. In D.M. Bishop, & B.C. Feld (Eds.), *The Oxford handbook of juvenile crime and juvenile justice* (pp. 1–35). New York: Oxford University Press.

Mears, D.P., Shollenberger, T.L., Willison, J.B., Owens, C.E., & Butts, J.A. (2010). Practitioner views of priorities, policies, and practices in juvenile justice. *Crime & Delinquency,* 56(4), 535–563. doi:10.1177/0011128708324664.

Meehl, P.E. (1954). *Clinical versus statistical prediction: A theoretical analysis and a review of the evidence.* Minneapolis, MN: University of Minnesota Press.

Miller, J., & Lin, J. (2007). Applying a generic juvenile risk assessment instrument to a local context: Some practical and theoretical lessons. *Crime & Delinquency,* 53(4), 552–580.

Miller, J., & Trocchio, S. (2016). Risk/need assessment tools and the criminal justice bureaucrat: Reconceptualizing the frontline practitioner. In F. Taxman (Ed.), *Handbook on risk and need assessment* (pp. 394–421). New York: Routledge.

Minor, K.I., Wells, J.B., Angel, E., & Matz, A.K. (2011). Predictors of early job turnover among juvenile correctional facility staff. *Criminal Justice Review*, 36(1), 58–75.

Mitchell, O., Mackenzie, D.L., Styve, G.J., & Gover, A.R. (2000). The impact of individual, organizational, and environmental attributes on voluntary turnover among juvenile correctional staff members. *Justice Quarterly*, 17(2), 333–357.

Nelson, R.J., & Vincent, G.M. (2018). Matching services to criminogenic needs following comprehensive risk assessment implementation in juvenile probation. *Criminal Justice and Behavior*, 45(8), 1136–1153.

Nelson, T.D., Steele, R.G., & Mize, J.A. (2006). Practitioner attitudes toward evidence-based practice: Themes and challenges. *Administration and Policy in Mental Health and Mental Health Services Research*, 33(3), 398–409. doi:10.1007/s10488-006-0044-4.

Nilsen, P. (2015). Making sense of implementation theories, models and frameworks. *Implementation Science*, 10, 53. doi:10.1186/s13012-13015-0242-0.

Office of Juvenile Justice and Delinquency Prevention (2016). *Juvenile drug treatment court guidelines*. Washington, DC: Office of Justice Programs, OJJDP. https://ojjdp.ojp.gov/programs/juvenile-drug-treatment-court-guidelines.

Pawson, R., & Tilley, N. (1997). *Realistic evaluation*. Thousand Oaks, CA: Sage Publications.

Rogers, E.M. (2010). *Diffusion of innovations*. New York: Simon and Schuster.

Satterfield, J.M., Spring, B., Brownson, R.C., Mullen, E.J., Newhouse, R.P., Walker, B.B., & Whitlock, E.P. (2009). Toward a transdisciplinary model of evidence-based practice. *The Milbank Quarterly*, 87(2), 368–390.

Scaccia, J.P., Cook, B.S., Lamont, A., Wandersman, A., Castellow, J., Katz, J., & Beidas, R.S. (2015). A practical implementation science heuristic for organizational readiness: R= MC2. *Journal of Community Psychology*, 43(4), 484–501. doi:10.1002/jcop.21698.

Schwalbe, C.S., Fraser, M.W., Day, S.H., & Cooley, V. (2006). Classifying juvenile offenders according to risk of recidivism: Predictive validity, race/ethnicity, and gender. *Criminal Justice and Behavior*, 33(3), 305–324. doi:10.1177/0093854806286451.

Shook, J.J., & Sarri, R.C. (2007). Structured decision making in juvenile justice: Judges' and probation officers' perceptions and use. *Children and Youth Services Review*, 29(10), 1335–1351. doi:10.1016/j.childyouth.2007.05.008.

Sridharan, S., & Gillespie, D. (2004). Sustaining problem-solving capacity in collaborative networks. *Criminology & Public Policy*, 3(2), 221–250. doi:10.1111/j.1745-9133.2004.tb00038.x.

Sullivan, C.J. (2019) *Taking juvenile justice seriously: Developmental insights and system challenges*. Philadelphia, PA: Temple University Press.

Sullivan, C.J., Park, I., & Holmes, B. (2019). *A micro and macro-level assessment of juvenile justice placement reform in Ohio*. Submitted to Office of Justice Programs, Office of Juvenile Justice and Delinquency Prevention. www.ojp.gov/pdffiles1/ojjdp/grants/254494.pdf.

Sullivan, C.J., Strange, C., Sullivan, C., Newsome, J., Lugo, M., Mueller, D., Petkus, A., Holmes, B., Lonergan, H., & McCafferty, J. (2019). *Multi-method study on risk assessment implementation and youth outcomes in the juvenile justice system*. Submitted to Office of Justice Programs, Office of Juvenile Justice and Delinquency Prevention. www.ojp.gov/pdffiles1/ojjdp/grants/252927.pdf.

Sydow, J., Schreyögg, G., & Koch, J. (2009). Organizational path dependence: Opening the black box. *Academy of Management Review*, 34(4), 689–709. doi:10.5465/amr.34.4.zok689.

Taxman, F.S., Henderson, C., Young, D., & Farrell, J. (2014). The impact of training interventions on organizational readiness to support innovations in juvenile justice offices. *Administration and Policy in Mental Health and Mental Health Services Research*, 41(2), 177–188. doi:10.1007/s10488-012-0445-5.

Viglione, J., Rudes, D., Nightingale, V., Watson, C., & Taxman, F. (2018). The many hats of juvenile probation officers: A latent class analysis of work-related activities. *Criminal Justice Review*, 43(2), 252–269. doi:10.1177/0734016817742688.

Vincent, G.M., Guy, L.S., Gershenson, B.G., & McCabe, P. (2012). Does risk assessment make a difference? Results of implementing the SAVRY in juvenile probation. *Behavioral Sciences & the Law*, 30(4), 384–405. doi:10.1002/bsl.2014.

Vincent, G.M., Guy, L.S., & Grisso, T. (2012). *Risk assessment in juvenile justice: A guidebook for implementation*. Implementation Science and Practice Advances Research Center Publications. Retrieved from https://escholarship.umassmed.edu/psych_cmhsr/573

Vincent, G.M., Guy, L.S., Perrault, R.T., & Gershenson, B. (2016). Risk assessment matters, but only when implemented well: A multisite study in juvenile probation. *Law and Human Behavior*, 40(6), 683–696. doi:10.1037/lhb0000214.

Vincent, G., Sullivan, C.J., Sullivan, C., Guy, L., Latessa, E., Tyson, J., and Adams, B. (2018). *Studying drivers of risk and needs assessment instrument implementation in juvenile justice*. Washington, DC: Office of Juvenile Justice and Delinquency Prevention. http://nysap.us/assets/publications/risk/Studying%20Drivers%20of% 20Risk%20and%20Needs%20Assessment%20Instrument%20Implementation% 20in%20Juvenile%20Justice.pdf.

Walker, S.C., Bumbarger, B.K., & Phillippi Jr, S.W. (2015). Achieving successful evidence-based practice implementation in juvenile justice: The importance of diagnostic and evaluative capacity. *Evaluation and Program Planning*, 52, 189–197. doi:10.1016/j.evalprogplan.2015.05.001.

Walters, W., Dembo, R., Beaulaurier, R., Cocozza, J., De La Rosa, M., Poythress, N., ... & Veysey, B.M. (2005). The Miami-Dade juvenile assessment center national demonstration project: An overview. *Journal of Offender Rehabilitation*, 41 (1), 1–37. doi:10.1300/J076v41n01_01.

Wandersman, A., Duffy, J., Flaspohler, P., Noonan, R., Lubell, K., Stillman, L., ... & Saul, J. (2008). Bridging the gap between prevention research and practice: The interactive systems framework for dissemination and implementation. *American Journal of Community Psychology*, 41(3–4), 171–181.

Ward, G., & Kupchik, A. (2009). Accountable to what? Professional orientations towards accountability-based juvenile justice. *Punishment & Society*, 11(1), 85–109. doi:10.1177/1462474508098134.

Ward, G., & Kupchik, A. (2010). What drives juvenile probation officers? Relating organizational contexts, status characteristics, and personal convictions to treatment and punishment orientations. *Crime & Delinquency*, 56(1), 35–69. doi:10.1177/0011128707307960.

Welsh, B.C., Sullivan, C.J., & Olds, D.L. (2010). When early crime prevention goes to scale: A new look at the evidence. *Prevention Science*, 11(2), 115–125.

Young, D., Moline, K., Farrell, J., & Bierie, D. (2006). Best implementation practices: Disseminating new assessment technologies in a juvenile justice agency. *Crime & Delinquency*, 52(1), 135–158.

Zajac, G., Lattimore, P.K., Dawes, D., & Winger, L. (2015). All implementation is local: Initial findings from the process evaluation of the honest opportunity probation with enforcement (HOPE) demonstration field experiment. *Federal Probation*, 79, 31–36.

Chapter 5

Doing Justice and Juvenile Risk and Needs Assessment

Analyzing research on implementation helps to establish an empirical basis for the development and use of JRNA tools but does not capture the full range of considerations and consequences for using these practices. When considering juvenile justice (and youths) it is also important to consider other dimensions of policy and practice that may affect the overall analysis of JRNA—or at least offer a wider lens from which to discuss its implications. This is an area where some broader issues of "doing justice" can be applied to JRNA in the sense that juvenile justice is a manifestation of the broader societal response to youth behavior via the legal system (Scott & Steinberg, 2009). With that, it is important to not only consider the impact of JRNA in terms of further involvement in the juvenile justice system and community safety, but also evaluate the net effect on youths and societal wellbeing. Bowker and Star (1999, p. 324) argue that classification systems, of which JRNA is one, have an "architecture" that is "simultaneously a moral and an informatic one." To this point—following the empirical literature—we have focused mostly on the informatics portion of JRNA by looking at what it means with respect to the technical aspects of doing juvenile justice.

A comprehensive examination of JRNA requires that we also look at overall benefits and costs in its use from the standpoint of youths, families, communities, the juvenile justice system, and society at large (Silver & Miller, 2002). This inherently raises questions regarding the moral or value-based aspects of juvenile justice decisions as a component in evaluating JRNA processes. Reflecting on its history, at least nominally, the juvenile justice system is an institution that both aims to "do justice" and protect community and government interests while also maintaining concern for the rehabilitation of the individual youth that comes before it (Bernard & Kurlychek, 2010; Scott & Steinberg, 2009; Tanenhaus, 2004). Thus, the broader objectives of the juvenile justice system are relevant when thinking about the effectiveness of JRNA now and in the future.

This chapter looks more deeply at the policy, social, and value-based questions that surround the use of JRNA. In doing so, it takes up several

DOI: 10.4324/9780367823122-5

points that touch on the foundations and execution of JRNA processes as they relate to societal and youth interests. We begin by briefly examining the political and legal foundations for the use of risk and needs assessment. Like other aspects of the legal response to delinquency, there is both overlap with adult criminal justice and some distinctions. Both are instructive and impactful when considering the implications of institutionalizing JRNA in processing cases of individual youths and in how the system generally operates. We then contemplate potential elements of risk and needs assessment that affect the benefits and costs to these youths—which include the inherent labeling that comes with scoring and classification, potential racial and gender inequity, development and change in youths and their risk and need profiles over time, how resource availability may affect the degree to which JRNA can meet its intended objectives, and whether these objectives are accomplished uniformly. Each of these issues may signal concerns about JRNA—regardless of basic empirical viability—that must be thoughtfully considered when utilizing JRNA in the field and considering it from a more holistic perspective.

Political and Legal Framework for Use of JRNA

An analysis of the broader context for JRNA requires tracing back its formulation as a solution to juvenile justice needs. Full consideration of the effects of JRNA requires attention to broader, structural issues in the history surrounding juvenile justice. The first adoption of assessment practices occurred early in the evolution of the juvenile court where "court clinics" were utilized to assess youths on relevant risk factors. Modern use of risk and needs assessments can be traced back to that point in the history of juvenile courts and correctional agencies, which Tanenhaus (2004, p. 111) refers to as the process of "medicalizing delinquency." Similarly, Bronner (1925) highlights the importance of applying scientific methods in understanding the multiple influences on delinquent behavior prior to court intervention. Healy (1915) describes several key factors and processes undertaken in his work at the juvenile court clinic in Chicago that bear strong resemblance to the procedures described in other sections of this book (see also Burgess, 1923; Laub, 2000). At the same time, Healy also acknowledged the clear variability among youths who he encountered in the clinic necessitating individual assessment and treatment planning (Tanenhaus, 2004).

JRNA approaches were imported into juvenile justice practice from the adult corrections system (Brogan et al., 2015; Singh et al., 2014). It is unclear, however, whether they translate optimally from one system to the other (Case & Haines, 2016). For example, the strong focus of the criminal justice system on fitting the punishment to the crime and the use of incapacitation as a form of deterrence means that a heavy emphasis on risk in the process of assessment and subsequent decision-making is potentially less problematic than it is when dealing with juveniles and the dual goals of punishment and rehabilitation. This is all relevant because the differing goals of juvenile justice policy and practice does affect the context within which JRNA is implemented and used. In turn, such differences can affect both the effectiveness of the process as well as its potential spillover effects on youths. It also reflects the original intent of using these practices in the juvenile justice system, which offers a sense of the value-base from which these policies and practices emanate. As suggested in earlier chapters, the empirical evidence base and other organizational improvements have led to a point where JRNA approaches are very common in juvenile justice and therefore can affect the many youths who become involved with the system, but we should look at potential concerns to fully evaluate the current state of JRNA practice and gather ideas for optimal use in the future. In this case, the service-to-need matching inherent in the RNR framework is even more crucial for juveniles but there may be challenges in operationalizing it effectively and equitably.

Potential Causes for Concern

Youths are very clearly impacted by the move to JRNA practices and are central targets of their use. They are therefore affected by the overall practice of JRNA and the degree to which it fully satisfies the logic and ideals of its adoption. Of course, the impact can be positive in terms of ensuring that all youths will be treated similarly to comparable peers (i.e., equity) and receive appropriate sanctions and interventions because of more precise delineation of their risks and needs (i.e., fairness). Appropriate sanctions and interventions, in turn, increase the likelihood of improved offender well-being after system involvement. However, some potential costs emerge when looking at these outcomes in greater depth. This interrogation of assumptions about the theory and logic of JRNA is essential in a well-rounded analysis of their contributions to juvenile justice and possible areas for improvement in the future. It also helps to sensitize key stakeholders to places where potential unintended consequences might occur in practice so that efforts can be made to try to reduce them.

Labeling and Locating Risk

While there is a recognition that broader societal forces are at play in the expression of delinquency, most of the diagnosis and intervention that stems from JRNA focuses on the youth and their immediate environment. This means that ultimately the classification inherent in JRNA will be attached to them in further decision-making by the system and any others who have knowledge of the assessment results (Etten & Petrone, 1994; Mankey et al.,

2006). This is no different than the early use of assessment in the juvenile court. For example, as the juvenile court evolved there was less impetus to consider the broader social context as a place of intervention and less clarity about the weight of structural forces in defining delinquency (Feld, 2017; Tanenhaus, 2004). Despite the recognition of a multicausal, multi-level system driving individual youths' delinquency, ultimately the product of the JRNA process will point toward the youth being assessed and their immediate environment. That immediate environment encompasses family, peer, and school risk factors, just as it did in the treatment of juveniles early in the juvenile court process (Tanenhaus, 2004). Whether this is meant to simplify the problem to ensure tractability in responding to it, it affects youths who are involved in the juvenile justice system in that the idea of "risk" is usually located in the youth and their immediate environment as opposed to in other factors such as community and institutional structures that may initiate causal processes that increase the likelihood of their juvenile justice involvement and lessen their ability to desist from delinquency.

Concerns about labeling have a long history in the juvenile justice process and in understanding societal responses to delinquency. Steen and colleagues (2005, p. 247) discuss the idea of "typification" as one that generates simplified classifications based on social and individual factors that juvenile justice officials perceive in individual cases. The very idea of diversion from the system is predicated on the fact that involvement can have unintended consequences for youths by making them more likely to continue their delinquent behavior (Bernburg, 2019; Mears, 2012; Schur, 1972; Schwalbe et al., 2012). This is confirmed in studies on the negative effects of juvenile justice contact (Gatti et al., 2009; Petrosino et al., 2014). Diversion affects juvenile justice systems in a fundamental way through their missions and decision-making procedures. For example, diversion provides a mechanism to filter out youths who are low risk, first time offenders. This filtering process removes youths from the system by providing them with a "second chance" to refrain from delinquent behavior and presumably allows those who remain to get more needed attention and resources, which links to the overall system within which the JRNA process is meant to operate and the philosophies of the RNR framework.

Labeling may work both through informal and formal processes to impact delinquency and further involvement in juvenile justice. Informal aspects of labeling and their internalization would come from the process of individual reflected appraisals of those around the youth like peers, family, and other members of the community (Brownfield & Thompson, 2005; Matsueda, 1992). The more formal perspective on labeling is based predominantly on interactions with institutions like schools, child welfare, and juvenile justice (Bernburg et al., 2006; Lee et al. 2015; Sweeten, 2006). Lee and colleagues (2015), for example, found that involvement in the legal system as a juvenile led to a process of social exclusion that reduced access to education and employment, which in turn impacted adult criminal behavior. Sweeten (2006) also found evidence of a labeling and exclusion effect where those—especially youths with lower initial risk—who had their education interrupted by an arrest in high school were less likely to graduate.

Schwalbe and Vincent (2016, p. 182) point out that some critics have argued that risk assessment:

> further entrenches labelling processes that undermine the rehabilitative purposes of juvenile justice system interventions. The institutionalization of the language of risk (e.g., "high risk") creates reasonable resistance among justice-involved adolescents and adults against the label, and also creates further roadblocks to their eventual desistance from crime as labels become adopted internally and also by the justice system itself.

Take, for example, the use of different terms in juvenile justice compared to the adult criminal justice system. Rephrasing "sentence" to "disposition" or "prison" to "residential placement" was intended to protect youths and the rehabilitative ideals of the juvenile justice system from the negative labels applied in the criminal justice system. It is possible that JRNA might re-introduce some of the stigma attached to juvenile justice involvement, triggering a series of collateral consequences that lessen the likelihood that some youths will take a different course in the future.

This means that, in juvenile justice, a broader assessment of JRNA in relation to labeling requires that evaluating the degree to which such processes can effectively assess risk across the spectrum of cases. In turn, the results of JRNA should not unduly affect the life chances of youths who are identified with a given score or risk level. It also requires consideration of the degree to which the system can use the JRNA process to effectively divert youths from more extensive involvement in the system. So, in other words, are labels like "high risk" applied judiciously such that the youth's chances of successfully leaving the supervision of the juvenile court or corrections and redirecting their life offset the potential consequences of the label? Conversely, does the assessment process sufficiently identify "low risk" youths such that they can be effectively removed from the oversight of the system thus limiting the level of social control imposed on them as well as potential exposure to other criminogenic aspects of justice involvement (e.g., official record, self-identification as a delinquent). These objectives in assessment systems mean to shift the way in which cases flow into the system and the decisions made from that point forward (e.g., Crime and Justice Institute, 2017; Lipsey et al., 2017; Sullivan et al., 2019). The impact of the label, or even worse, an inaccurate label, becomes even more important when considering the moderate levels of predictive accuracy discussed in previous chapters of this book.

Although the intent of the assessment system is to develop statistical groupings to simplify decision-making (Gottfredson, 1987), a full accounting of equity requires attention to the individual cases of youths who are assessed in terms of whether justice is carried out (Silver & Miller, 2002). This means considering how individual youths whose risk and needs do not align with the "average" in the group fare in terms of system decisions and later outcomes. It is also useful to consider the degree to which "narratives" about youths emerge and whether those are balanced and fully capture them as an individual. In JRNA, this often pertains to whether the assessment is holistic in nature so that it accounts for the individual and environmental risks of the youth while also accounting for the strengths and protective factors that offer a fuller picture of potential leverage points for effective intervention. It is easier to allow for the risk-based narrative if other important information is excluded from the process or deprioritized.

At a minimum, without being held in check, the typologies that emerge from JRNA processes are apt to interact with broader structural factors, system resources, and the socio-political climate of juvenile justice to affect how individual cases are handled (O'Malley, 1992; Robinson, 2016). In turn, this affects the balance of risk and reward in the use of those classifications. So, for example, in thinking about Bernard and Kurlychek's (2010) views of a juvenile justice policy that oscillates with the political climate, one could clearly see that a youth at a "moderate" level of risk and need might be treated differently depending on whether the policy climate trends more toward treatment or punishment. For example, in the zero-tolerance era in school delinquency, a youth who is judged to present any risk may be more subject to exclusionary discipline and juvenile justice processing than they were prior to that point where such an attribution might have been handled within the educational setting (Curran, 2016; Kupchik, 2010).

Decades of research suggest that labels applied to youths because of juvenile justice or some other form of intervention (e.g., child welfare, school discipline) can lead to negative outcomes for youths including low self-esteem, negative self-labeling, further delinquent behavior, and unjust treatment by actors at later stages of the system (Cuevas et al., 2017; Kroska et al., 2017; Liberman et al., 2014). It is imperative to understand how or under what circumstances JRNA results may increase the chances of these consequences. Researchers, system decision-makers, and other key stakeholders typically must balance between the usefulness of risk classifications in terms of equitable decision-making and appropriate matching of needs and interventions with avoiding potential consequences of the application of an additional label on youths. It is likely that this balance will vary both within and across system decision-makers. For example, prosecutors' access and use of JRNA results might be controversial given the role that they play in juvenile cases—especially with respect to communities of color (Henning, 2013). In that way, JRNA results can work against youths who fall within higher risk categories by using these results to frame an argument for guilt or culpability. Thus, in addition to considering how JRNA policies and practices help juveniles throughout the court process (i.e., equity, targeted intervention), it is also important to consider how certain policies and practices (e.g., sharing JRNA results across stakeholders) may work to disadvantage them as well.

Balancing Risks with Strengths

Considering strengths within the JRNA process is especially salient as assessment is limited in its scope and how it sees the youth and their immediate environment. The practice of JRNA may inherently become too deficit-based when we consider the objectives and principles of the juvenile justice system relative to what is known about risk assessment practices and effective intervention. Adichie (2009) highlights the danger of a "single story" and the "flatten[ing]" that occurs when we only know or focus on one story about a person or group. The lack of focus on strengths can have deleterious consequences, especially for youths, and therefore has been argued as a deficit in the contemporary juvenile justice system. There is often an imbalance in what is assessed and how that is used which, in turn, hinders a more holistic focus on a strength-based or positive youth development approach (Barton & Butts, 2008). There is also an inherent element of reductionism since youth behavior is dynamic and multicausal (National Research Council, 2013) and counting or grouping does not fully account for an underlying developmental narrative which involves the relative strength of risks, needs, *and* assets as well as the complex interactions among these various influences on a youth's behavior and development.

Case and Haines (2016) argue that youth justice systems have been contaminated by an emphasis on various types of risks posed by youths (e.g., early onset of offending, criminal history) which has institutionalized the actuarial practices of JRNA. This means that youth assets are infrequently integrated into the decision-making process and later case management. This process frequently places a strong influence on the youth and the immediate microsystem (like families) in assessing risk. A paradigm, like RNR, directs the attention of the system's efforts to factors that are assumed to cause delinquent behavior (see Robinson, 2016). This links to the perspective that the interests of those in the middle and upper class continue to be dominant decision-makers in the juvenile justice system. As a result, decisions about its direction are still typically made by policymakers and system personnel who are outside of the identity and culture groups of the youth being served (Bernard & Kurlychek, 2010). For example, Hawkins and Kempf-Leonard (2005) suggest that there continues to be a divide between how middle and upper-class adults would want their children punished and treated (i.e., with some flexibility and leniency) relative to how the juvenile justice system works for youths and families who come predominantly from different races and classes.

This, of course, can affect attributions that are made in explaining and problematizing delinquent behavior in children from particular groups. In a comprehensive review, Miller (1995) considered differences in parents' and nonparents' attributions about children's behavior. He indicates that those with different vantage points may give distinct reasons for youth behavior. Miller found a positivity bias when parents evaluate the behavior or disposition of their children relative to others. He also reviews the literature comparing parent and teachers' assessments and attributions about academic performance. While both groups may have some inclination to rate youths positively, Miller suggests that the inclination is apt to be stronger for parents. Research in the area did suggest some discordance between the raters where parents may make slightly different attributions about their children compared to other observers. In turn, Morrissey-Kane and Prinz (1999) report that parental attributions about children's behavior have implications for treatment engagement and expected outcomes for youths. Coupled with the risk emphasis and racial disparities in juvenile justice processes, there is a likelihood that this bias may be heightened—with important contextual influences disregarded— for youths who are members of racial and ethnic minority groups. These youths face structural disadvantages to greater degrees than White children (Lowery & Smith, 2020; Rodriguez, 2013; Sampson & Laub, 1993), but those would not be acknowledged to a great degree in JRNA.

With this lack of focus on broader structural influences, it is essential to know the degree to which individual strengths are being incorporated into the assessment process itself and—if so—what weight those are given in subsequent decisions about a youth's case. In systems where strengths are not formally assessed it is essential that researchers and practitioners consider whether identified strengths are used in developing case management or intervention plans for youths. Jones and colleagues (2016) argued that traditionally the RNR model has focused on youths' deficits and that while there may be some attention to strengths in the services and programming that youths receive, formal assessment of strengths has been limited to date in juvenile justice. Their study focused on 464 youths on community supervision in one province in Canada. Findings showed that the strengths measured in the Youth Assessment and Screening Instrument (YASI) were related to youth recidivism and mitigated the impact of high risk status for youths. Singh and colleagues (2014) went a step further finding that effective use of strengths in the process of moving from assessment to intervention helped to reduce the level of externalizing behaviors among 120 justice-involved adolescents.

This line of research suggests that there is value in including strengths in the formal assessment processes in juvenile justice settings. Beyond empirical justifications lies the importance of being true to the developmental mission of the juvenile justice system. Gathering individual strengths is useful in fashioning the best response to particular cases and it also aligns well with the mission of the juvenile justice system and general fairness in developing the full story about the youth and their case before making decisions that can affect their development. Without that the juvenile justice system may be trading bureaucratic expedience for the fairest (and most empirically sound) practice. Jones and colleagues (2016) allude to the fact that incorporation of strengths to a greater degree can facilitate more active participation of the youth (and their family) in the case.

Elements of the juvenile justice system are posed as attempts to "help" the youth stay out of trouble and improve in the future (Scott & Steinberg, 2009; Sullivan, 2019), but a focus only on deficits has the potential to push them away from active engagement with the process which can preclude the youth and the system from attaining those goals. For instance, self-efficacy, empowerment, and motivations to change are consistently found to be important mediators for treatment adherence and positive treatment outcomes (Burleson & Kaminer, 2005; Norcross et al., 2011; Taddeo et al., 2008). In considering the foundational principles of JRNA, which rest on the notion that each youth is unique in their risk and needs, the lack of information regarding youths' strengths precludes accomplishing this goal. The ways in which different types and/or levels of strengths moderate the effects of the identified risks and needs on delinquent behavior can vary across youths.

Considering youths' strengths during reassessments helps to fully identify change. This is particularly important given the heavy reliance on static risk factors, which do not change as a function of intervention. Improvements in youth strengths are likely a key driver of desistance from delinquent behavior. Thus, to obtain a truly representative assessment of each youth's unique circumstances, accounting for risk, needs, and assets is necessary. The ways in which assets condition risks/needs will vary and is very important in considering risk level and intervention. As Rashid and Ostermann (2009, p. 490) indicate "deficit-oriented models of assessment, in our view, paint an incomplete picture of the client, reducing clarity, information, and completeness." Coupled with the possibility of labeling (and accompanying negative biases) and static risk assessment this closes off possibilities in helping youths to redirect their developmental trajectories.

Race and Ethnic Disparities

While the matter of labeling and JRNA has received limited attention, a frequently discussed concern relative to the application of risk and needs assessment is how race and ethnicity interact with risk assessment processes.

Feld (2017) argues that youths' experiences, including interactions with juvenile justice personnel, are affected by social structure and racial disparities. The standardized risk assessment process is meant to reduce racial stereotype-based attributions like the ones found in previous studies (e.g., Graham & Lowery, 2004). For example, Bridges and Steen (1998) studied probation officers' narrative reports for juvenile cases to identify potential attributions made about the origins of youths' delinquent behavior and assessment of future risk. They found that these characterizations tended to disadvantage racial minorities due to the framing of cases with respect to the role of individual pathology versus external constraints. The former attribution was predominant for minority youths while the latter was more likely to be viewed as a source of White youths' delinquency. Using a sample of 161 pre-disposition reports of youths, Steen and colleagues (2005) suggest that racial differences in the attributions that juvenile probation officers (JPOs) used to explain offending behavior were also conditioned by risk level, reflecting a degree of interaction and contingency among these perceptions and the decisions that emerge from them.

Case disposition and risk assessment data from roughly 12,000 cases processed in a large county's juvenile court in Ohio were used to investigate the potential relationship between race (coded Black and White for this analysis) and risk scores independently and interactively with detention (16.1 percent of cases) and referral to secure confinement in a state facility (0.5 percent of cases).[1] Black youths had 22 percent greater odds of detention and about 130 percent greater odds of secure placement relative to their White peers. The OYAS risk score was statistically significant in both cases as well with 4 percent greater odds of secure confinement and 1 percent greater odds of detention for each one-point increase on the OYAS risk score. When looked at interactively, the odds ratio for the interaction of race and risk score with detention status was 1.05 which means that the effect of a point increase on the risk score was roughly 5 percent greater for Black youths compared to those who were White. Though it was not statistically significant, the interaction term was similarly sized (OR = 1.06) for the same relationship in the statistical model for placement in a secure residential facility.[2]

Items pertaining to juvenile justice history, school, family, or community risk may disproportionately inflate the scores of youths of color. Influences driving these differences could include targeted enforcement in high crime neighborhoods or disadvantaged schools for juvenile justice history and school risk. Family socioeconomic status (SES) and, in turn, parental supervision may also be correlated with race in ways that affect the results of risk assessments. The basic tenet of the differential offending perspective is that youths from minority groups have higher levels and more cumulative risk factors than their White counterparts, which in turn leads to more offending behavior, more serious delinquency, and increased likelihood of recidivism

(Feld, 2009; Kempf-Leonard, 2007; Pope & Snyder, 2003). Essentially, this perspective suggests that differences in risk level and reoffending behavior are the result of true differences in risk, need, and reoffending.

Extending this perspective to JRNA, the assessment process is a mechanism to measure and account for these varying degrees of risk across racial and ethnic subgroups. As Vincent and Viljoen (2020) and Skeem and Lowenkamp (2016) point out, group differences in the proportion of youths that fall into each risk category do not necessarily imply that JRNA processes are biased. Instead, the higher rates of risk to reoffend among some groups reflect higher rates or more diverse risk factors for reoffending (i.e., differential risk). Based on this argument, accounting for risk level in group comparisons of reoffending behavior should reduce or eliminate any observed differences in reoffending behavior. However, most JRNA studies to date find that controlling for risk level does not eliminate differences in recidivism across race and ethnicity (e.g., Baglivio & Jackowski, 2013; Campbell et al., 2018).

According to Bishop and Leiber (2011), factors that appear to connote differential offending can also reflect the ways in which minority youths are socially situated. Critics argue that these assessments frequently rely on factors that are highly correlated with race, which may be out of the control of individual youths and their families and, instead, tied to monitoring and enforcement practices of the justice system (Eckhouse et al., 2019; van Eijk, 2017). For example, Sullivan et al. (2016) found that DMC at the front end of the system is sometimes perceived to be a byproduct of the patterns of differential enforcement in predominantly Black and Hispanic neighborhoods. Unequal or biased surveillance practices can introduce systematic error into the most strongly weighted criterion for risk classification—prior history of justice involvement (Baird et al., 2013). The reliance on prior arrests or convictions in risk assessments assumes that youths who engage in those behaviors are arrested or adjudicated at the same rates, regardless of race/ethnicity (Eckhouse et al., 2019). However, substantial evidence suggests that youths of color are more likely to get arrested and adjudicated compared to their White peers for the same or similar offenses (Guevara et al., 2006; Peck & Jennings, 2016; Pope & Feyerherm, 1990). These differences can inflate risk classifications for certain groups of youths (i.e., minoritized youths).

As a result, the static risk factors included on juvenile risk assessments, which center around historical factors such as prior arrests or age of onset, have been the topic of debate. It is argued that minority youths are often placed at a disadvantage in system decisions due to higher static risk scores, which will follow youths throughout the juvenile justice system as they cannot be changed in a downward direction (Baird et al., 2013; Schwalbe et al., 2006). Based on these arguments, the assessment process may lead to higher rates of false positives (i.e., group considered high risk more than other groups) among youths from racial and ethnic minority groups due to inflated static risk factors that are the result of biased enforcement practices.

This discussion is especially relevant within the context of modern risk and needs assessments, as one of the stated goals of JRNA is to curtail racially coded judgments about youths and their cases by systematizing the information gathering and decision-making process (e.g., Cabaniss et al., 2007; Chapman et al., 2006). In theory, JRNA tools are meant to flatten differentials in attributions based on race or ethnicity because, ideally, alike cases will get similar scores, placements, and treatments, regardless of their racial or ethnic identity. Standardized tools are meant to formalize the structure of assessment and classification to minimize any subjectivity or biases (Vincent & Viljoen, 2020). However, the possibility of residual disproportionality remains and may be overlooked due to the empirically grounded nature of the risk assessment tool. Given targeted police patrol and enforcement patterns and interactions with youths of color (Kakar, 2006; Rios, 2011; Sullivan et al., 2016), it is highly probable that there will be some degree of inequity across different race groups that is embedded in items that are meant to be appropriate for the purposes of assessment and identifying appropriate case dispositions. This is especially salient in considering the tools that rely entirely on individual and social history items to derive a risk score (e.g., PACT).

To highlight this point, Figure 5.1 lists the items included on the OYAS Diversion tool to estimate risk, which affects the important early decision of diversion or formally processing a given youth (Mears, 2012). These items are historical in nature and often can be influenced by structural factors such as selective enforcement practices. The "current charge" item, for example, may be affected by discretionary decisions related to the youth's race. The first contact with the juvenile justice system may also be related to enforcement practices as opposed to behavioral differences from one youth to another. Leiber and Fox (2005) therefore suggest that factors related to differential involvement in the juvenile justice system may be "racially tainted" and at least partly attributable to "interrelationships among racial stereotyping, decision making, and case outcomes" (p. 490).

Select Items on OYAS Diversion Tool

1. Prior Offenses (0=No, 1=Yes)
2. Current Charge (0=Status, 1=Misdemeanor, 2=Felony)
3. 1ˢᵗ Contact with the Juvenile Justice System (0=16 or Older, 1=15 or Younger)
4. Prior Probation (0=No, 1=Yes)
5. Family Member Arrested (0=No, 1=Yes)
6. Parents Have Difficult Time Supervising Youth (0=No, 1=Yes)

Figure 5.1 Select Items on OYAS Diversion Tool
Source: Latessa et al., 2009

Similarly, whether a youth was on probation previously involves some type of discretionary decision that may also be related to item #6, "parents have a difficult time supervising youth." These items are commonly used, often dominating the early-stage screening and assessment tools in juvenile justice. Florida's CAT (e.g., Community Assessment Tool Pre-Screen) contains far more items than the OYAS diversion tool, but one major section focuses on age of first juvenile justice referral and the nature of prior referrals (and their outcomes).

Beyond the fact that race may be associated with certain juvenile justice record items, there are possibilities that (1) certain types of items (e.g., family, community) can lead to negative attributions of youths of color based on subjective aspects of the assessment process where juvenile justice personnel make decisions in information gathering and scoring. (2) Certain items and domains will work differently across race and ethnicity subgroups. Again, having a family member arrested is not only out of the youth's control but also may be linked to the potentially racialized nature of juvenile justice decisions (Feld, 1999; 2017; Ward, 2012). SES and employment factors may also affect the degree to which typical, middle-class perspectives on supervision might represent the lives of these youths. These effects will not necessarily show up if researchers and practitioners are focused too heavily on predictive validity as the sole measure to assess the performance of tools.

Looking at differences in risk scoring across race in a more focused way by considering dynamic, youth-centered needs, Lee and Sullivan (2020) studied OYAS records for roughly 4,331 youths across two midwestern states. The sample was 63 percent White and 37 percent from other races, predominantly Black. There were significant differences in the overall average OYAS score (a nearly four-point difference of 7.13 to 10.93), which translates to more than a half standard deviation difference across the groups in terms of the youths' assessment results. Further analysis showed that greater variations in certain domain scores is leading to the racial disparity in overall risk classification, with the largest differences in domains related to the youth's social support and values, which can vary inherently across race and ethnicities. For example, in the *Values, Beliefs, and Attitudes* domain there is a "pro-criminal sentiments" item, which is based on the interviewer's impressions of youths' responses that might justify or support delinquency. Depending on how the assessor approaches the information gathering process this could be very subjective.

These disparities matter from the standpoint of how youths score and their risk classification but it is also important to consider how that process affects subsequent supervision intensity or resource allocation. Taking the first of those, juvenile justice history is a domain that affects the level and length of supervision to which a youth will be subjected by the system, particularly in jurisdictions that rely on disposition matrices and graduated sanctions models based on the results of risk assessment processes (Caudill et al., 2013; Schwalbe & Maschi, 2009). For example, FDJJ PACT data shows that, compared to White and Hispanic youths placed on probation, Black youths placed on probation, on average, scored significantly higher on the criminal history domain (Black youths: mean = 9.79, standard deviation = 4.11; Hispanic youths: mean = 7.98, standard deviation = 3.47; White youths: mean = 8.32, standard deviation = 3.46; $p < .001$), but significantly lower on the social history domain (Black youths: mean = 5.51, standard deviation = 2.84; Hispanic youths: mean = 5.74, standard deviation = 2.99; White youths: mean = 6.33, standard deviation = 3.24; $p < .001$).[3] This has implications for the degree to which youths on probation will be watched and opportunities for minor technical violations that will lead to deeper penetration into the juvenile justice system. If this domain and the overall risk level is partly dependent on these previous disproportionate contacts, then it is likely that a youth's race will impact these decisions in a way that might not be readily apparent because it is more subtle. The use of JRNA to make decisions about release readiness is another example of the ways in which selective enforcement and the incorporation of static factors into estimates of risk can disadvantage minority youths. The nature of static risk items, such as prior criminal history or parental criminal history, means that these items do not change over time. Therefore, risk scores that are weighted heavily toward such historical items will remain high, regardless of intervention and rehabilitation progress.

Similarly, these disparities might also impact the degree to which youths receive appropriate services based on the results of an assessment. So, for example, Black and Latino/a youths may be scored differently on certain family-based items. Rodriguez and colleagues (2009, p. 198) found that juvenile court actors' decision-making was linked to "attributions about good and bad families, as well as their assessments of whether the family can provide care, supervision, and control over the youth within the community." In turn, differential scores and attributions may subject youths of color to more intensive family-based interventions like Functional Family Therapy (FFT) and Multisystemic Therapy (MST) than White youths who are more suited to the items included in the assessment. These programs have been found effective in evaluations (Schaeffer & Borduin, 2005; Timmons-Mitchell et al., 2006), but this does not obviate questions about cultural sensitivity in family-focused justice programming (Chapman & Schoenwald, 2011; Foster et al., 2009; Ryan et al., 2013). Without well-calibrated interventions, these intensive programs may also expand the juvenile justice system's net and the duration of involvement of youths and their families in the juvenile justice system than if their risk and needs scores warrant more diversionary actions (Grattet et al., 2011; Long & Sullivan, 2017).

Despite these outstanding questions, structured risk and needs assessments are viewed as a potential solution to issues of disparity by race and ethnicity in juvenile justice practice (Vincent & Viljoen, 2020). Juvenile court interviewees in an Ohio study conducted by Sullivan and colleagues (2016) mentioned structured risk assessment and accompanying evidence-based practices as one element of the state and their court's efforts to reduce racial and ethnic disparities in decision-making. Considered differently, Ward (2012) reports in his book, *The Black Child-Savers*, that it is difficult to understand the origins of structured decision-making in the juvenile justice system without paying attention to race and racism in its history. For example, he finds that identifying appropriate resources for Black youths was a low priority in the juvenile court's mission to identify alternatives to adult institutions for youths who were adjudicated as delinquent. In a more contemporary sense, this differential availability of resources might have a disparate impact on youths of color and in turn may affect their likelihood of being able to escape any label applied within the juvenile justice system through engagement with effective programming.

Despite the intent to limit discretion and promote systematic and equitable decisions, Vincent and Viljoen (2020) suggest that it is important to bear in mind that human judgment is still necessary to make effective decisions in the context of structured assessments. This human judgment is a benefit of the JRNA process within juvenile justice because it allows practitioners to consider the "totality of the youth's circumstances" based on systematic information gathering. This is a potential point of concern given that human judgment, or discretion, can also lead to biases to infiltrate the assessment process, particularly in scoring and decision-making. Consequently, it is important to blend understanding of the context and process of JRNA and juvenile justice with the information gleaned from the assessment.

The process of conducting the risk and needs assessment with a youth and family interview may be affected by race and ethnicity as well. Graham and Lowery (2004) studied the effects of racial priming in a sample that included probation officers—who frequently conduct such assessments—and found that those in the experimental group (i.e., with the racial priming) had significantly higher assessment of the youth's culpability and expectation for their later recidivism. Differentials in disclosure could also come into play here and hurt impressions of youths from racial and ethnic minority groups. Youths from groups that have been disproportionately involved in the justice system may have more fear and mistrust of this process. Fine and colleagues (2017), for example, found that youths from racial and ethnic minority groups had more negative perceptions of the justice system after being arrested for the first time. This could negatively impact the outcome of the risk assessment process through any related negative interactions, especially those in interviews conducted by intake officers, probation officers, and other assessors where perceived truthfulness and respectful demeanor may be at a premium.

Case and Haines (2016, p. 68) note that risk assessment and the factors that it identifies are subject to "partiality" in that it typically weighs toward factors in the youth and their close social environment like family and peers, or what Bronfenbrenner (1979) would call the microsystem, as opposed to studying broader structural influences that may be tied up with racial disadvantages (i.e., macrosystem). To be fully and fairly responsive, JRNA and the juvenile justice system must be cognizant of the risks inherent in the outer parts of the ecological model, promote change in these parts of the system, and recognize the degree to which these structural factors might affect the youths who encounter the system. The Steen et al. (2005) analysis of probation officers' assessments also considered the appropriate response of the court to youths at given levels of risk and did identify differences in what might be necessary (e.g., how factors like race may affect judgments about character and motivation that then influence decisions). Given the goal of fairness and the desire to treat similarly situated youths the same via risk and needs assessment, it is essential to consider the actual use of JRNA from as many angles as possible to avoid unintentionally disadvantaging certain groups of youths who encounter the juvenile justice system.

Gender Disparities

As with race, the perception of juvenile justice actors—including the assessment of girls' truthfulness and reasons for their behavior—can affect the decisions made about them (Gaarder et al., 2004). Though trends in juvenile delinquency and juvenile justice involvement in the early 2000s have largely been positive, some disparities between girls and boys for certain offenses have also been noted. In particular, the higher rate of system contact for minor delinquent or status offenses, as well as substantially larger increases in the rate of arrest for some violent offenses (e.g., assault), among girls has been the topic of study in recent years (e.g., Chesney-Lind & Shelden, 2013; Tracy et al., 2009; Zahn et al., 2008). This line of research considers whether these dissimilar trends among boys and girls are more attributable to the behavior of the justice system than girls themselves (see, e.g., Feld, 2009, Steffensmeier & Schwartz, 2009). Generally, the research concludes that shifts in prevalence in the juvenile justice system is more attributable to the operations of the system itself as opposed to major society-wide changes in girls' behavior. Gelsthorpe and Sharpe (2006) suggest that the interventionist nature of the juvenile court has been more frequently applied to girls than boys in recent decades. According to Feld (2009) and Javdani and colleagues (2011) this often occurs through the re-labeling or bootstrapping of girls' lower-level offenses to maintain juvenile justice control.

There are two competing perspectives about the treatment of girls involved in the justice system. The chivalry hypothesis posits that girls are treated with more leniency because system decision-makers view female offenders as less dangerous or culpable than male offenders (Belknap, 2007). This perspective is supported by research that finds boys are treated more harshly than girls for similar offenses (Bishop & Frazier, 1992; Horowitz, & Pottieger, 1991). The paternalistic perspective suggests that girls receive harsher treatment than boys because of the belief that girls need protection and guidance (Chesney-Lind, 1977; Guevara et al., 2006). Paternalism is supported by the recent increases in harsher treatment of girls (but not boys) for status offenses and other minor delinquent behaviors (MacDonald & Chesney-Lind, 2001). Since changes in girls' involvement in the justice system have occurred during the time that JRNA practices have come to dominate the juvenile justice landscape, it is worth examining the degree to which gender interacts with JRNA processes. Selective enforcement, chivalry, and paternalism should also be considered in terms of potential gender disparity in information gathering and scoring. For instance, the greater likelihood of girls being arrested for minor delinquent or status offenses could increase their scores on items related to criminal history and age of onset. It is also possible that chivalry or paternalism occurs during administration of the instrument according to assessors' beliefs about girls involved in the system. Prior research offers evidence that system decision-makers tend to attribute girls' delinquency to external circumstances and perceive them as less dangerous than their male peers (Mallicoat, 2007; Bloom et al., 2002).

Miller and Mullins (2009, p. 31) note that gender "orders social life and social institutions in fundamental ways." It is therefore easy to anticipate that there may be gendered effects of risk and needs assessment, and subsequent placement, when considering domains and types of items (Pusch & Holtfreter, 2018; Schwalbe, 2008). Most JRNA instruments have been constructed and validated on full samples of juvenile offenders which are comprised mostly of boys (Emeka & Sorenson, 2009; Hubbard & Matthews, 2008). This means that the risk and need factors that are more influential or unique to girls' delinquency may not be included on the assessment instrument or may not be weighted accurately for them. Trauma and abuse are risk factors that have been found to be much higher among delinquent girls, compared to delinquent boys (Funk, 1999; Salisbury et al., 2009). Other scholars have noted differences in the importance of social relationships (Hubbard & Pratt, 2002; Farrington & Painter, 2004) and the higher prevalence of depression and anxiety among delinquent girls (e.g., Cauffman, 2004; Teplin et al., 2005). Although not evoked to necessarily ensure parity, there are still expectations that the assessment process will lead to equitable placement and appropriate assessments across gender groups (Bloom et al. 2002; Goodkind, 2005). However, if differences in the type of risk/needs, as well as the ways in which these risk factors lead to delinquency, are not accounted for in formal assessments of risk and needs, there is a chance that the goals of structured decision-making may not be fully achieved for girls. Ensuring equity in assessment practices and case-level decisions also requires that those practitioners responsible for assessing and making decisions about programming for girls focus on their unique needs (Anderson et al., 2019; Anderson & Walerych, 2019).

Achieving the goals of the JRNA process also entails using gender-responsive services that meet the potentially unique needs of justice-involved girls (e.g., trauma-informed treatment), again getting into the need to have resources available to the juvenile justice system (Kempf-Leonard, 2012). As is the case with race, the empirical examination must move beyond solely focusing on the relationship between the assessment results and recidivism and consider other questions. Given the perspectives described on p. 131, it is also important to understand the effects of the label produced by the JRNA process on girls' treatment throughout the system. For example, could chivalry or paternalism also be applied to girls who score high risk? Based on research that suggests that girls are more likely to experience self-labeling and internalize negative reactions to their behavior (Koita & Triplett, 1998; McGrath, 2014; Zhang, 1997), girls and boys may react differently to the labels produced during the JRNA process.

Development, Change, and Dynamic Assessment

As the National Research Council (2013) argued in its report on moving to a more developmental juvenile justice system, we must be mindful of the fact that juvenile delinquency can be attributed to multiple factors and that it is changing over time. This must be accounted for in the assessment of cases in juvenile justice. Gina Vincent and colleagues (2012) highlighted the fact that developmentally responsive JRNA inherently must be dynamic in nature. The broader objectives of juvenile justice and general disposition to youthfulness and adolescence under the law require some focus on growth, development, and change (see National Research Council, 2013; Scott & Steinberg, 2009; Sullivan, 2019). In turn, this means that the use of JRNA should meet that objective in how it is applied to youths involved with the juvenile justice system. If an assessment is static or the youth is only re-assessed when they encounter the juvenile justice system again, then there may be some unfairness in applying an initial label via assessment but not affording the youth a full opportunity to work on that area and demonstrate progress that shows up in their assessment and later decision-making about their case (e.g., continuation of probation supervision, successful completion of treatment).

Figure 5.2 considers the relative properties of static and dynamic approaches to assessment and summarizes their possible implications for youths who would be assessed and monitored in each of those respective systems. This helps to illustrate that JRNA operationalization impacts youths because the degree to which the initial score, or label, is fixed would change

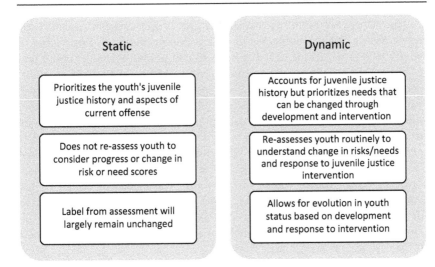

Figure 5.2 Comparison of Properties of Static and Dynamic Approaches

depending on whether that dynamic assessment process is adhered to in their case. With juveniles, the ability to inform and assess change is essential. Importantly, as noted in Chapter 4, the operationalization of the JRNA process in terms of the use of different types of placements and interventions will impact the degree to which the youth can achieve and demonstrate change that modifies the attached score or label. This in turn is dependent on other structural and system-level factors that can impact equity and fairness in how JRNA works in practice.

Resources, Placements, and Level of Control

The overall logic and theory of JRNA requires that the three-step process is equitable *and* that the subsequent aspects of that process do not lead to disparities and assign labels without the potential for change. A focus on the entirety of the process is essential in thinking about the equitable use of JRNA. With that, system resources (whether captured in funding, time, space, or programming), supervision, and placement options will inherently affect how JRNA information is used to the benefit or detriment of youths who are involved in the justice system. The question that requires a good deal of elaboration is how these differential placement options and labels affect case decisions, supervision, and level of control, and later developmental outcomes for youths. With the greater permeation of JRNA into juvenile justice practices and the view that this information can be used for case management practices, the strength of classification in decision-making is likely to continue to grow.

The degree of resource availability (or lack thereof) can affect the application of JRNA practice and policy along three lines. First, a lack of ability to respond to identified risk/needs comprehensively—coupled with a desire to ensure that assessment information is used in decision-making—may create a "default" to a risk focus as opposed to effectively balancing both risks and needs. So, the information may be used in supervision decisions but not really applied to inform intervention and treatment. Does this mean that youths at different risk levels should be given an arbitrary dosage of CBT? Should the same sanction or treatment be mandated for all low risk cases? Or, is their individualized matching only targeting factors where intervention is available (instead of those considered "criminogenic")? The ways that the information is used for decision-making obviously has a lot to do with its total effectiveness and fairness and can reduce the potential benefit of JRNA relative to the costs if the system is not cognizant of them.

Second, reflecting on the notions of labeling and balancing static and dynamic assessment on p. 117, it is also possible that resource deficits lead to scenarios where youths are identified at a particular risk and need level but do not receive the necessary intervention—or what they receive is not optimal to facilitate their development and change. Looking at this from within the assessment, Baird (2009), for example, considers the possible linkage between risk assessment and subsequent oversight of the youth's case at an item or domain level. Specifically, he observes that the items in a risk assessment—even if they have not themselves been shown to be associated with recidivism—are labeled as criminogenic risk factors. In turn, the expectation is that addressing them will impact a youth's risk and later outcomes. He notes that this may lead to inappropriate and wasteful interventions. Additionally, depending on the nature of the item, its label, and the type of intervention, youths may be exposed to the juvenile justice system in more depth as a result, in turn increasing their likelihood of recidivism.

The assessment process and resources available for subsequent treatment can also interact with other potential sources of inequity. In a study of youths released from residential facilities, McCafferty and colleagues (2017) found that (1) *Family and Living Arrangements* and (2) *Education and Employment* domains of the OYAS were not significantly associated with return to custody for a new offense, a common measure of recidivism in JRNA studies. Additionally, the levels of risk/need on these domains (especially on *Education and Employment*) as well as their strength of relationship with returns to custody and item-level fit differed across race and ethnicity. Despite these patterns, however, it is easy to see how scores from those domains might be used to classify needs of a given youth, offer (or not) treatment in that area, and assess recidivism based on those decisions. This could, however, be inefficient, inequitable, and ineffective if we are not focused on broader questions around possible differences in resource availability in JRNA and the availability of appropriate treatment modalities.

Third, resource availability also has an impact on the potential for increased—or at least continued—"justice by geography" in the juvenile justice system. Butts and Singer (2013) identify the degree to which the operation of the juvenile justice system is dependent on the resources available at various stages of the juvenile justice process and surrounding networks of service providers. This means that even within a system that is meant to be standardized across jurisdictions, important variation emerges (Sarri et al., 2001; Weiner et al., 2011). For example, research suggests that available services for youths and their families in rural versus urban areas vary in several important ways including funding for "brand name" or other model interventions (e.g., MST, FFT), the education and qualifications of the frontline service providers, the number and types of programs available, travel times, and the availability of public transportation (e.g., Pullen & Oser, 2014).

While within-jurisdiction or case-to-case variability is arguably more problematic from the standpoint of equity, this is also a matter of some concern when systems are adopted at a state level with the same policies and regulations in place but local differences in decision-making emerge (Bray et al., 2005; Feld, 1991; Sullivan et al., 2019). It inherently cuts into the fairness and equity with which JRNA processes are applied. While developers and champions do not believe that application will be uniform across place, there is a general expectation that the three-step JRNA process will help to level out decision-making processes. Therefore, the degree to which this occurs in different places must be a focus of research as to whether the full logic of JRNA is being implemented effectively within and across jurisdictions. As noted, this might include assessment of race and gender but also should look more closely at the degree to which there is resource-driven disparity across systems in how well JRNA works in practice. As with the other concerns outlined here, this also has links to the notion of balance of strengths and risks, as a system with limited treatment resources may in some way be implicitly forced to be weighted toward risk management when it conceives of and executes JRNA practices.

Chapter Summary

There are clear advantages to the use of systematic assessment practices in juvenile justice. However, the disadvantages are not as extensively understood. The analysis in this chapter identifies several questions in JRNA practice that move beyond merely linking assessment to recidivism outcomes or implementation. These broader, value-based questions might not be as easily resolved with empirical data, though such analysis is relevant to the discussion in identifying possible benefits and assessing how well the

JRNA practices work. These questions warrant more attention in the next generation of analyses of JRNA as they are relevant to the JRNA logic model and can be implemented and used as intended with minimal downsides for youths who are involved in the juvenile justice system. Such questions also clearly align with values of equity and fairness in the operations of the juvenile justice system.

Assessment processes have unique standing due to their grounding in evidence-based practice. It is therefore important to consider and use them responsibly to ensure that they fit the aims of juvenile justice. There is always some attribution and stereotyping that carries forward when individual practitioners make judgments about cases (e.g., Emerson, 1969 reports on that in his work). Therefore, it is important to acknowledge that a scientific veneer lends more credence, perhaps giving the public, legislators, practitioners, and researchers more reason to expect that the in-theory benefits of JRNA will be achieved in practice than is the case. For example, Silver and Miller (2002, p. 138) identify use of actuarial risk assessment for prediction as a demarcation point between "traditional" and "advanced" societies. Grove and Meehl (1996, p. 315) review actuarial methods and assert that "the dazzling achievements of Western post-Galilean science are attributable not to our having any better brains than Aristotle or Aquinas, but to the scientific method of accumulating objective knowledge." Still, these advances do not obviate all concerns. In juvenile justice, Hawkins and Kempf-Leonard (2005, pp. 442–443) note:

> We must provide a framework in which competent decisions can be made. This framework should be structured to encourage consistency and accountability of decision makers, but it should not be devoid of the power to deliberate effectively. Too often when procedures are standardized or mandated in an effort to be neutral on race, sex, class, or age the unintended consequences of the reforms actually exacerbate existing inequities, create new problems, and institutionalize both. This happens because the social dimensions that interact with demographic traits are not considered.

This in turn necessitates a look at the structure in which standardized JRNA practices operate to fully understand their implications for youths involved in the justice system. It also requires attention to the potential problems associated with creating a "black-box" around the ways in which JRNA practices affect decision-making by focusing mainly on outcomes of the process (Steen et al., 2005).

As seen in previous chapters, a complex logic model underlies these practices and it can be difficult to attain fidelity in practice. The juvenile justice system is in part informed by societal values about youths that affect how it wishes to respond to delinquency. Therefore, it is important to expand the focus beyond just (or mainly) empirical concerns. More specifically, it is essential to fully consider the degree to which now ubiquitous risk and needs assessment practices offer additional value beyond previous approaches across a variety of areas mentioned in this chapter and previous ones. It is also important that an effort is made to continuously improve the quality of the JRNA process so that assessment practices are used effectively and fairly or at least there is continuous progress toward that goal.

Despite predictive validity and its potential invariance among youth subgroups, numerous big picture and day-to-day questions must be asked when thinking about how to use these tools as effectively and fairly as possible. In turn, this analysis signals that juvenile justice agencies must be balanced in how JRNA is used, attentive to what the assessment process means for each youth and cultivate the resources necessary to effectively respond to their risks/needs. These practices will inevitably increase the benefits of JRNA relative to the potential costs discussed (discussion begins on p. 117). This returns to the questions of the values and objectives of the juvenile justice system in the first place because without concerted focus on the obligations underlying the use of JRNA practices, it is easy to generate the properties of an unfunded mandate where a policy and practice is introduced without any increase or adjustment in resource distribution to effectively carry it out otherwise (Ross, 2018; St. George, 1995). Likewise, researchers can and should consider these broader questions in assessing the widespread adoption and use of JRNA with an eye toward improving practices that have now almost fully permeated juvenile justice. This means taking on some of the value-based questions that are inherent in all juvenile justice practice and getting beyond the question of whether these tools are fairer than what preceded them and moving toward optimization across a spectrum of possible outcomes. It also means not oversimplifying or "dumb[ing] down" the complex, multilevel, and multi-developmental systems etiology of delinquency to fit it neatly into a checklist (Case & Haines, 2016, p. 68), but rather use JRNA as a tool toward better and fairer practice.

Clearly, simplifying and making more systematic decisions is a laudable goal in juvenile justice practice but it is important to ensure that the challenges of JRNA are dealt with appropriately (Schwalbe & Vincent, 2016). Without full realization of the key objectives of JRNA, there is a real risk in applying sticky labels to youths while the systems lack the ability to address their needs in a manner that gives them a real chance to change. The high stakes in applying "risk" and "need" labels to youths emphasizes the critical role of continuous quality improvement and the importance of moving beyond mere risk management. This is especially salient given the impact of structural factors related to race, economics, and politics that affect the practice of juvenile justice.

The final two chapters of the book describe ways in which the research and practice of JRNA can more comprehensively account for the various objectives and stakeholders embedded in its logic in the future. With that the analysis in the book up to this point can offer some insight into what JRNA stakeholders and researchers should look for as we move forward in the next wave of use of these tools. This requires a focus on research related to JRNA but also means emphasizing the long-term implications for youth wellbeing and the fundamental mission of the juvenile justice system.

Notes

1 Analysis was conducted with multivariate logistic regression models, including number of offenses in case, whether there was a felony charge, age of first arrest, youth's current age, youth's sex.
2 The differences in these findings are likely due to the difficulty of detecting interaction terms given the nature of the data utilized here (see, e.g., McClelland & Judd, 1993).
3 These data are from the Full-Screen PACT assessment conducted closest to the referral date. Similar results were observed using data from the PACT Pre-Screen which includes lower risk youths who do not meet criteria for the full assessment. Results are based on Bonferroni's pairwise comparison of means test.

References

Adichie, C.N. (2009). *The danger of a single story*. TEDGlobal. Available: www.ted. com/talks/chimamanda_ngozi_adichie_the_danger_of_a_single_story

Anderson, V.R., & Walerych, B.M. (2019). Contextualizing the nature of trauma in the juvenile justice trajectories of girls. *Journal of Prevention & Intervention in the Community*, 47(2), 138–153. doi:10.1080/10852352.2019.1582141.

Anderson, V.R., Hoskins, K.M., & Rubino, L.L. (2019). Defining gender-responsive services in a juvenile court setting. *Women & Criminal Justice*, 29(6), 338–354. doi:10.1080/08974454.2019.1588836.

Baglivio, M.T., & Jackowski, K. (2013). Examining the validity of a juvenile offending risk assessment instrument across gender and race/ethnicity. *Youth Violence and Juvenile Justice*, 11(1), 26–43.

Baird, C. (2009). *A question of evidence: A critique of risk assessment models used in the justice system*. Madison, WI: National Council on Crime and Delinquency. www. evidentchange.org/sites/default/files/publication_pdf/special-report-evidence.pdf

Baird, C., Healy, T., Johnson, K., Bogie, A., Dankert, E.W., & Scharenbroch, C. (2013). *A comparison of risk assessment instruments in juvenile justice*. Madison, WI: National Council on Crime and Delinquency.

Barton, W.H., & Butts, J.A. (2008). *Building on strength: Positive youth development in juvenile justice programs*. Chicago, IL: Chapin Hall Center for Children at the University of Chicago. https://jeffreybutts.files.wordpress.com/2008/08/building. pdf.

Belknap, J. (2007). *The invisible woman: gender, crime, and justice* (3rd Ed.). Belmont, CA: Thompson Wadsworth.

Bernard, T.J., & Kurlychek, M.C. (2010). *The cycle of juvenile justice*. New York: Oxford University Press.

Bernburg, J.G. (2019). Labeling theory. In M.D. Krohn, N. Hendrix, G. Penly Hall, & A.J. Lizotte (Eds.), *Handbook on crime and deviance* (pp. 179–196). New York: Springer.

Bernburg, J.G., Krohn, M.D., & Rivera, C.J. (2006). Official labeling, criminal embeddedness, and subsequent delinquency: A longitudinal test of labeling theory. *Journal of Research in Crime and Delinquency*, 43(1), 67–88. doi:10.1177/0022427805280068.

Bishop, D.M., & Frazier, C.E. (1992). Gender bias in juvenile justice processing: Implications of the JJDP Act. *Journal Criminal Law & Criminology*, 82, 1162–1186. doi:0091-4169/92/8204-1162.

Bishop, D., & Leiber, M. (2011). Race, ethnicity, and juvenile justice: Racial and ethnic differences in delinquency and justice system responses. In D. Bishop & B. Feld (Eds.), *Juvenile justice* (pp. 445–484). New York, NY: Oxford University Press.

Bloom, B., Owen, B., Deschenes, E.P., & Rosenbaum, J. (2002). Moving toward justice for female juvenile offenders in the new millennium: Modeling gender-specific policies and programs. *Journal of Contemporary Criminal Justice*, 18(1), 37–56. doi:10.1177/1043986202018001004.

Bowker, G.C., & Star, S.L. (1999). *Sorting things out: Classification and its consequences.* Cambridge, MA: MIT Press.

Bray, T.M., Sample, L.L., & Kempf, K. Leonard. (2005). "Justice by geography": Racial disparity and juvenile courts. In D.F. Hawkins & K. Kempf-Leonard (Eds.), *Our children, their children* (pp. 270–299). Chicago: University of Chicago Press.

Bridges, G.S., & Steen, S. (1998). Racial disparities in official assessments of juvenile offenders: Attributional stereotypes as mediating mechanisms. *American Sociological Review*, 63(4), 554–570. doi:10.2307/2657267.

Brogan, L., Haney-Caron, E., NeMoyer, A., & DeMatteo, D. (2015). Applying the risk-needs-responsivity (RNR) model to juvenile justice. *Criminal Justice Review*, 40(3), 277–302. doi:10.1177/0734016814567312.

Bronfenbrenner, U. (1979). *The ecology of human development: Experiments by nature and design.* Cambridge, MA: Harvard University Press.

Bronner, A. (1925). The contribution of science to a program for treatment of juvenile delinquency. In J. Addams (Ed.), *The child, the clinic, and the court: A group of papers* (pp. 75–92). New York: New Republic.

Brownfield, D., & Thompson, K. (2005). Self-concept and delinquency: The effects of reflected appraisals by parent and peers. *Western Criminology Review*, 6(1), 22–29.

Burgess, E.W. (1923). The study of the delinquent as a person. *American Journal of Sociology*, 28(6), 657–680.

Burleson, J.A., & Kaminer, Y. (2005). Self-efficacy as a predictor of treatment outcome in adolescent substance use disorders. *Addictive Behaviors*, 30(9), 1751–1764. doi:10.1016/j.addbeh.2005.07.006.

Butts, J., & Singer, S. (2013). Current practice in the juvenile justice system. In Richard J. Bonnie, Robert L. Johnson, Betty M. Chemers, & Julie A. Schuck (Eds.), *Reforming juvenile justice: A developmental approach* (pp. 49–88). Washington, DC: National Research Council of the National Academies.

Cabaniss, E.R., Frabutt, J.M., Kendrick, M.H., & Arbuckle, M.B. (2007). Reducing disproportionate minority contact in the juvenile justice system: Promising practices. *Aggression and Violent Behavior*, 12(4), 393–401. doi:10.1016/j.avb. 2006.09.004.

Campbell, C., Papp, J., Barnes, A., Onifade, E., & Anderson, V. (2018). Risk assessment and juvenile justice: An interaction between risk, race, and gender. *Criminology & Public Policy*, 17(3), 525–545.

Case, S., & Haines, K. (2016). Taking the risk out of youth justice. In C. Trotter, G. McIver, & F. McNeill (Eds.), *Beyond the risk paradigm in criminal justice* (pp. 61–75). London: Palgrave.

Caudill, J.W., Morris, R.G., Sayed, S.E., Yun, M., & DeLisi, M. (2013). Pathways through the juvenile justice system: Predictors of formal disposition. *Youth Violence and Juvenile Justice*, 11(3), 183–195. doi:10.1177/1541204012472211.

Cauffman, E. (2004). A statewide screening of mental health symptoms among juvenile offenders in detention. *Journal of the American Academy of Child & Adolescent Psychiatry*, 43(4), 430–439. doi:10.1097/00004583-200404000-00009.

Chapman, J.E., & Schoenwald, S.K. (2011). Ethnic similarity, therapist adherence, and long-term multisystemic therapy outcomes. *Journal of Emotional and Behavioral Disorders*, 19(1), 3–16. doi:10.1177/1063426610376773.

Chapman, J.F., Desai, R.A., Falzer, P.R., & Borum, R. (2006). Violence risk and race in a sample of youth in juvenile detention: The potential to reduce disproportionate minority confinement. *Youth Violence and Juvenile Justice*, 4(2), 170–184. doi:10.1177/1541204006286316.

Chesney-Lind, M. (1977). Judicial paternalism and the female status offender: Training women to know their place. *Crime & Delinquency*, 23(2), 121–130. doi:10.1177/001112877702300203.

Chesney-Lind, M., & Shelden, R.G. (2013). *Girls, delinquency, and juvenile justice*. Hoboken, NJ: John Wiley & Sons.

Crime and Justice Institute (2017). *Implementing comprehensive juvenile justice system improvement in Hawaii*. Boston, MA: Crime and Justice Institute.

Cuevas, C., Wolff, K.T., & Baglivio, M.T. (2017). Self-efficacy, aspirations, and residential placement outcomes: Why belief in a prosocial self matters. *Journal of Criminal Justice*, 52, 1–11. doi:10.1016/j.jcrimjus.2017.06.006.

Curran, F.C. (2016). Estimating the effect of state zero tolerance laws on exclusionary discipline, racial discipline gaps, and student behavior. *Educational Evaluation and Policy Analysis*, 38(4), 647–668. doi:10.3102/0162373716652728.

Eckhouse, L., Lum, K., Conti-Cook, C., & Ciccolini, J. (2019). Layers of bias: A unified approach for understanding problems with risk assessment. *Criminal Justice and Behavior*, 46(2), 185–209. doi:10.1177/0093854818811379.

Emeka, T.Q., & Sorensen, J.R. (2009). Female juvenile risk: Is there a need for gendered assessment instruments? *Youth Violence and Juvenile Justice*, 7(4), 313–330.

Emerson, R.M. (1969). *Judging delinquents*. New Brunswick, NJ: Transaction Publishers.

Etten, T.J., & Petrone, R.F. (1994). Sharing data and information in juvenile justice: Legal, ethical, and practical considerations. *Juvenile and Family Court Journal*, 45(3), 65–90. doi:10.1111/j.1755-6988.1994.tb01473.x.

Farrington, D.P., & Painter, K.A. (2004). *Gender differences in offending: Implications for risk-focused prevention*. London: Home Office.

Fine, A., Cavanagh, C., Donley, S., Frick, P.J., Steinberg, L., & Cauffman, E. (2017). Is the effect of justice system attitudes on recidivism stable after youths' first arrest? race and legal socialization among first-time youth offenders. *Law and Human Behavior*, 41(2), 146–158. doi:10.1037/lhb0000229.

Feld, B.C. (1991). Justice by geography: Urban, suburban, and rural variations in juvenile justice administration. *Journal of Criminal Law and Criminology*, 82(1), 156–210. doi:10.2307/1143795.

Feld, B.C. (1999). *Bad kids: Race and the transformation of the juvenile court.* New York: Oxford University Press.

Feld, B.C. (2009). Violent girls or relabeled status offenders? An alternative interpretation of the data. *Crime & Delinquency*, 55(2), 241–265. doi:10.1177/0011128708330629.

Feld, B.C. (2017). *The evolution of the juvenile court: Race, politics, and the criminalizing of juvenile justice.* New York: NYU Press.

Foster, S.L., Cunningham, P.B., Warner, S.E., McCoy, D.M., Barr, T.S., & Henggeler, S.W. (2009). Therapist behavior as a predictor of Black and White caregiver responsiveness in multisystemic therapy. *Journal of Family Psychology*, 23(5), 626–635. doi:10.1037/a0016228.

Funk, S.J. (1999). Risk assessment for juveniles on probation: A focus on gender. *Criminal Justice and Behavior*, 26(1), 44–68.

Gaarder, E., Rodriguez, N., & Zatz, M.S. (2004). Criers, liars, and manipulators: Probation officers' views of girls. *Justice Quarterly*, 21(3), 547–578. doi:10.1080/07418820400095901.

Gatti, U., Tremblay, R.E., & Vitaro, F. (2009). Iatrogenic effect of juvenile justice. *Journal of Child Psychology and Psychiatry*, 50(8), 991–998. doi:10.1111/j.1469-7610.2008.02057.x.

Gelsthorpe, L., & Sharpe, G. (2006). Gender, youth crime and justice. *Youth Crime and Justice*, 47–61. www.ojp.gov/ncjrs/virtual-library/abstracts/gender-youth-crime-and-justice-youth-crime-and-justice-p-47-61-2006

Goodkind, S. (2005). Gender-specific services in the juvenile justice system: A critical examination. *Affilia*, 20(1), 52–70. doi:10.1177/0886109904272061.

Gottfredson, D.M. (1987). Prediction and classification in criminal justice decision making. *Crime and Justice*, 9, 1–20. doi:10.1086/449130.

Graham, S., & Lowery, B.S. (2004). Priming unconscious racial stereotypes about adolescent offenders. *Law and Human Behavior*, 28(5), 483–504. doi:10.1023/B:LAHU.0000046430.65485.1f.

Grattet, R., Lin, J., & Petersilia, J. (2011). Supervision regimes, risk, and official reactions to parolee deviance. *Criminology*, 49(2), 371–399. doi:10.1111/j.1745-9125.2011.00229.x.

Grove, W.M., & Meehl, P.E. (1996). Comparative efficiency of informal (subjective, impressionistic) and formal (mechanical, algorithmic) prediction. *Psychology, Public Policy and Law*, 2, 293–323. doi:10.1037/1076-8971.2.2.293.

Guevara, L., Herz, D., & Spohn, C. (2006). Gender and juvenile justice decision making: What role does race play? *Feminist Criminology*, 1(4), 258–282. doi:10.1177/1557085106292778.

Hawkins, D.F., & Kempf-Leonard, K. (Eds.). (2005). *Our children, their children: Confronting racial and ethnic differences in American juvenile justice.* Chicago: University of Chicago Press.

Healy, W. (1915). *The individual delinquent. A textbook of diagnosis and prognosis for all concerned in understanding offenders.* Boston: Little Brown & Co.

Henning, K. (2013). Criminalizing normal adolescent behavior in communities of color: The role of prosecutors in juvenile justice reform. *Cornell Law Review*, 98 (2), 383–461. doi:2128857.

Horowitz, R., & Pottieger, A.E. (1991). Gender bias in juvenile justice handling of seriously crime- involved youths. *Journal of Research in Crime and Delinquency*, 28 (1), 75–100. doi:10.1177/0022427891028001005.

Hubbard, D.J., & Pratt, T.C. (2002). A meta-analysis of the predictors of delinquency among girls. *Journal of Offender Rehabilitation*, 34(3), 1–13.

Hubbard, D.J., & Matthews, B. (2008). Reconciling the differences between the "gender- responsive" and the "what works" literatures to improve services for girls. *Crime & Delinquency*, 54(2), 225–258. doi:10.1177/0011128706296733.

Javdani, S., Sadeh, N., & Verona, E. (2011). Gendered social forces: A review of the impact of institutionalized factors on women and girls' criminal justice trajectories. *Psychology, Public Policy, and Law*, 17(2), 161–211. doi:10.1037/a0021957.

Jones, N.J., Brown, S.L., Robinson, D., & Frey, D. (2016). Validity of the youth assessment and screening instrument: A juvenile justice tool incorporating risks, needs, and strengths. *Law and Human Behavior*, 40(2), 182–194. doi:10.1037/lhb0000170.

Kakar, S. (2006). Understanding the causes of disproportionate minority contact: Results of focus group discussions. *Journal of Criminal Justice*, 34(4), 369–381. doi:10.1016/j.jcrimjus.2006.05.003.

Kempf-Leonard, K. (2007). Minority youths and juvenile justice: Disproportionate minority contact after nearly 20 years of reform efforts. *Youth Violence and Juvenile Justice*, 5(1), 71–87.

Kempf-Leonard, K. (2012). The conundrum of girls and juvenile justice processing. In B.C. Feld & D. Bishop (Eds.), *The Oxford handbook of juvenile crime and juvenile justice*. (pp. 485–525). New York: Oxford University Press.

Koita, K., & Triplett, R.A. (1998). An examination of gender and race effects on the parental appraisal process: a reanalysis of Matsueda's model of the self. *Criminal Justice and Behavior*, 25(3), 382–400. doi:10.1177/0093854898025003006.

Kroska, A., Lee, J.D., & Carr, N.T. (2017). Juvenile delinquency and self-sentiments: Exploring a labeling theory proposition. *Social Science Quarterly*, 98(1), 73–88. doi:10.1111/ssqu.12307.

Kupchik, A. (2010). *Homeroom security: School discipline in an age of fear*. New York: NYU Press.

Latessa, E., Lovins, B., & Ostrowski, K. (2009). *The Ohio youth assessment system: Final report*. Cincinnati, OH: University of Cincinnati, Center for Criminal Justice Research.

Laub, J.H. (2000). A century of delinquency research and delinquency theory. In M. K. Rosenheim, F.E. Zimring, D.S. Tanenhaus, & B. Dohrn (Eds.), *A century of juvenile justice* (pp. 179–205). Chicago: University of Chicago Press.

Lee, J.S., Courtney, M.E., Harachi, T.W., & Tajima, E.A. (2015). Labeling and the effect of adolescent legal system involvement on adult outcomes for foster youth aging out of care. *American Journal of Orthopsychiatry*, 85(5), 441–451. doi:10.1037/ort0000090.

Lee, P., & Sullivan, C.J. (2020). *Assessing racial disparity in juvenile risk and needs classification*. Unpublished poster prepared for University of Cincinnati Undergraduate Scholarship Showcase.

Leiber, M.J., & Fox, K. (2005). Race and the impact of detention on juvenile justice decision making. *Crime & Delinquency*, 51, 470–497. doi:10.1177/0011128705275976.

Liberman, A.M., Kirk, D.S., & Kim, K. (2014). Labeling effects of first juvenile arrests: Secondary deviance and secondary sanctioning. *Criminology*, 52(3), 345–370. doi:10.1111/1745-9125.12039.

Lipsey, M.W., Conly, C.H., Chapman, G., & Bilchik, S. (2017). *Juvenile justice system improvement: Implementing an evidence-based decision-making platform.* Washington, DC: Office of Juvenile Justice and Delinquency Prevention. www.ojp.gov/pdffiles1/ojjdp/grants/250443.pdf

Long, J., & Sullivan, C.J. (2017). Learning more from evaluation of justice interventions: Further consideration of theoretical mechanisms in juvenile drug courts. *Crime & Delinquency*, 63(9), 1091–1115. doi:10.1177/0011128716629757.

Lowery, P.G., & Smith, J.C. (2020). The impact of concentrated affluence and disadvantage on the pre-adjudication detention decision: A status characteristics approach. *Crime & Delinquency*, 66(6–7), 915–948. doi:10.1177/0011128720907581.

MacDonald, J.M., & Chesney-Lind, M. (2001). Gender bias and juvenile justice revisited: A multiyear analysis. *Crime & Delinquency*, 47(2), 173–195. doi:10.1177/0011128701047002002.

Mallicoat, S.L. (2007). Gendered justice: Attributional differences between males and females in the juvenile courts. *Feminist Criminology*, 2(1), 4–30. https://doi.org/10.1177/1557085106296349.

Mankey, J., Baca, P., Rondenell, S., Webb, M., & McHugh, D. (2006). *Guidelines for juvenile information sharing.* Washington, DC: Office of Juvenile Justice and Delinquency Prevention. www.promoteprevent.org/sites/www.promoteprevent.org/files/resources/215786_0.pdf

Matsueda, R.L. (1992). Reflected appraisals, parental labeling, and delinquency: Specifying a symbolic interactionist theory. *American Journal of Sociology*, 97(6), 1577–1611.

McCafferty, J., Newsome, J., & Sullivan, C.J. (2017). *Study of Arizona youth assessment system (AZYAS)-Residential.* Cincinnati, OH: University of Cincinnati Center for Criminal Justice Research.

McClelland, G.H., & Judd, C.M. (1993). Statistical difficulties of detecting interactions and moderator effects. *Psychological Bulletin*, 114(2), 376–390.

McGrath, A.J. (2014). The subjective impact of contact with the criminal justice system: The role of gender and stigmatization. *Crime & Delinquency*, 60(6), 884–908. doi:10.1177/0011128710389589.

Mears, D. (2012). The front end of the juvenile court: Intake and informal versus formal processing. In D.M. Bishop & B.C. Feld (Eds.), *The Oxford handbook of juvenile crime and juvenile justice* (pp. 1–35). New York: Oxford University Press.

Miller, J., & Mullins, C.W. (2009). Feminist theories of girls' delinquency. In M. Zahn (Ed.), *The delinquent girl* (pp. 30–49). Philadelphia, PA: Temple University Press.

Miller, S.A. (1995). Parents' attributions for their children's behavior. *Child Development*, 66(6), 1557–1584. doi:10.2307/1131897.

Morrissey-Kane, E., & Prinz, R.J. (1999). Engagement in child and adolescent treatment: The role of parental cognitions and attributions. *Clinical Child and Family Psychology Review*, 2(3), 183–198. doi:10.1023/A:1021807106455.

National Research Council (2013). *Reforming juvenile justice: A developmental approach.* Washington, DC: National Academies Press.

Norcross, J.C., Krebs, P.M., & Prochaska, J.O. (2011). Stages of change. *Journal of Clinical Psychology,* 67(2), 143–154. doi:10.1002/jclp.20758.

O'Malley, P. (1992). Risk, power and crime prevention. *Economy and Society,* 21(3), 252–275. doi:10.1080/03085149200000013.

Peck, J.H., & Jennings, W.G. (2016). A critical examination of "being Black" in the juvenile justice system. *Law & Human Behavior,* 40(3), 219–232.

Petrosino, A., Turpin-Petrosino, C., & Guckenburg, S. (2014). The impact of juvenile system processing on delinquency. In D.P. Farrington & J. Murray (Eds.), *Labeling theory: Empirical tests advances in criminological theory* (Volume 18, pp. 113–147). New Brunswick, NJ: Transaction.

Pope, C.E., & Feyerherm, W.H. (1990). Minority status and juvenile justice processing: An assessment of the research literature (Part I). *Criminal Justice Abstracts,* 22(2), 327–335.

Pope, C.E., & Snyder, H.N. (2003). *Race as a factor in juvenile arrests.* Washington, DC: US Department of Justice, Office of Justice Programs, Office of Juvenile Justice and Delinquency Prevention.

Pullen, E., & Oser, C. (2014). Barriers to substance abuse treatment in rural and urban communities: Counselor perspectives. *Substance Use & Misuse,* 49(7), 891–901.

Pusch, N., & Holtfreter, K. (2018). Gender and risk assessment in juvenile offenders: A meta- analysis. *Criminal Justice & Behavior,* 45(1), 56–81. doi:10.1177/0093854817721720.

Rashid, T., & Ostermann, R.F. (2009). Strength-based assessment in clinical practice. *Journal of Clinical Psychology,* 65(5), 488–498. doi:10.1002/jclp.20595.

Rios, V.M. (2011). *Punished: Policing the lives of Black and Latino boys.* New York: NYU Press.

Robinson, G. (2016) The rise of the risk paradigm in criminal justice. In C. Trotter, G. McIvor, & F. McNeill (Eds.), *Beyond the risk paradigm in criminal justice* (pp. 9–23). London: Palgrave.

Rodriguez, N. (2013). Concentrated disadvantage and the incarceration of youth: Examining how context affects juvenile justice. *Journal of Research in Crime and Delinquency,* 50(2), 189–215. doi:10.1177/0022427811425538.

Rodriguez, N., Smith, H., & Zatz, M.S. (2009). "Youth is enmeshed in a highly dysfunctional family system": Exploring the relationship among dysfunctional families, parental incarceration, and juvenile court decision making. *Criminology,* 47(1), 177–208.

Ross, J.M. (2018). Unfunded mandates and fiscal structure: Empirical evidence from a synthetic control model. *Public Administration Review,* 78(1), 92–103. doi:10.1111/puar.12867.

Ryan, S.R., Cunningham, P.B., Foster, S.L., Brennan, P.A., Brock, R.L., & Whitmore, E. (2013). Predictors of therapist adherence and emotional bond in multisystemic therapy: Testing ethnicity as a moderator. *Journal of Child and Family Studies,* 22(1), 122–136. doi:10.1007/s10826-012-9638-5.

Salisbury, E.J., Van Voorhis, P., & Spiropoulos, G.V. (2009). The predictive validity of a gender-responsive needs assessment: An exploratory study. *Crime & Delinquency,* 55(4), 550–585.

Sampson, R. J., & Laub, J. H. (1993). Structural variations in juvenile court processing: Inequality, the underclass, and social control. *Law and Society Review*, 285–311. doi:10.2307/3053938.

Sarri, R., Shook, J.J., Ward, G., Creekmore, M., Albertson, C., Goodkind, S., & Soh, J.C. (2001). *Decision making in the juvenile justice system: A comparative study of four states*. Ann Arbor, MI: Institute for Social Research.

Schaeffer, C.M., & Borduin, C.M. (2005). Long-term follow-up to a randomized clinical trial of multisystemic therapy with serious and violent juvenile offenders. *Journal of Consulting and Clinical Psychology*, 73(3), 445–453.

Schur, E. (1972). *Radical nonintervention*. Berkeley, CA: University of California Press.

Schwalbe, C.S. (2008). A meta-analysis of juvenile justice risk assessment instruments: Predictive validity by gender. *Criminal Justice and Behavior*, 35(11), 1367–1381. doi:10.1177/0093854808324377.

Schwalbe, C.S., & Maschi, T. (2009). Investigating probation strategies with juvenile offenders: The influence of officers' attitudes and youth characteristics. *Law and Human Behavior*, 33(5), 357–367. doi:10.1007/s10979-008-9158-4.

Schwalbe, C., & Vincent, G. (2016). Putting risk in its place. In C. Trotter, G. McIvor, & F. McNeill (Eds)., *Beyond the risk paradigm in criminal justice* (pp. 181–199). London, UK: Palgrave.

Schwalbe, C.S., Fraser, M.W., Day, S.H., & Cooley, V. (2006). Classifying juvenile offenders according to risk of recidivism: Predictive validity, race/ethnicity, and gender. *Criminal Justice & Behavior*, 33(3), 305–324.

Schwalbe, C.S., Gearing, R.E., MacKenzie, M.J., Brewer, K.B., & Ibrahim, R. (2012). A meta-analysis of experimental studies of diversion programs for juvenile offenders. *Clinical Psychology Review*, 32(1), 26–33. doi:10.1016/j.cpr.2011.10.002.

Scott, E.S., & Steinberg, L.D. (2009). *Rethinking juvenile justice*. Cambridge, MA: Harvard University Press.

Silver, E., & Miller, L.L. (2002). A cautionary note on the use of actuarial risk assessment tools for social control. *Crime & Delinquency*, 48(1), 138–161.

Singh, J.P., Desmarais, S.L., Sellers, B.G., Hylton, T., Tirotti, M., & Van Dorn, R. A. (2014). From risk assessment to risk management: Matching interventions to adolescent offenders' strengths and vulnerabilities. *Children and Youth Services Review*, 47, 1–9. doi:10.1016/j.childyouth.2013.09.015.

Skeem, J.L., & Lowenkamp, C.T. (2016). Risk, race, and recidivism: Predictive bias and disparate impact. *Criminology*, 54(4), 680–712.

St. George, J.R. (1995). Unfunded mandates: Balancing state and national needs. *The Brookings Review*, 13(2), 12–16.

Steen, S., Bond, C.E., Bridges, G.S., & Kubrin, C.E. (2005). Explaining assessments of future risk. In D. Hawkins & K. Kempf-Leonard (Eds.), *Our children, their children: Confronting racial and ethnic differences in American juvenile justice* (pp. 245–269). Chicago: University of Chicago Press.

Steffensmeier, D.J., & Schwartz, J. (2009). Trends in girls' delinquency and the gender gap: Statistical assessment of diverse sources. In M. Zahn (Ed.), *The delinquent girl* (pp. 50–83). Philadelphia, PA: Temple University Press.

Sullivan, C.J. (2019). *Taking juvenile justice seriously: Developmental insights and system challenges*. Philadelphia, PA: Temple University Press.

Sullivan, C.J., Blair, L., Latessa, E., & Sullivan, C.C. (2016). Juvenile drug courts and recidivism: Results from a multisite outcome study. *Justice Quarterly*, 33(2), 291–318. doi:10.1080/07418825.2014.908937.

Sullivan, C.J., Park, I., & Holmes, B., (2019). *A micro and macro-level assessment of juvenile justice placement reform in Ohio*. Submitted to Office of Justice Programs, Office of Juvenile Justice and Delinquency Prevention. www.ojp.gov/pdffiles1/ojjdp/grants/254494.pdf.

Sweeten, G. (2006). Who will graduate? Disruption of high school education by arrest and court involvement. *Justice Quarterly*, 23(4), 462–480. doi:10.1080/07418820600985313.

Taddeo, D., Egedy, M., & Frappier, J.Y. (2008). Adherence to treatment in adolescents. *Paediatrics & Child Health*, 13(1), 19–24. doi:10.1093/pch/13.1.19.

Tanenhaus, D. (2004). *Juvenile justice in the making*. New York: Oxford University Press.

Teplin, L.A., Abram, K.M., McClelland, G.M., Washburn, J.J., & Pikus, A.K. (2005). Detecting mental disorder in juvenile detainees: Who receives services. *American Journal of Public Health*, 95(10), 1773–1780. doi:10.2105/AJPH.2005.067819.

Timmons-Mitchell, J., Bender, M.B., Kishna, M.A., & Mitchell, C.C. (2006). An independent effectiveness trial of multisystemic therapy with juvenile justice youth. *Journal of Clinical Child & Adolescent Psychology*, 35(2), 227–236. doi:10.1207/s15374424jccp3502_6.

Tracy, P.E., Kempf-Leonard, K., & Abramoske-James, S. (2009). Gender differences in delinquency and juvenile justice processing: Evidence from national data. *Crime & Delinquency*, 55(2), 171–215. doi:10.1177/0011128708330628.

van Eijk, G. (2017). Socioeconomic marginality in sentencing: The built-in bias in risk assessment tools and the reproduction of social inequality. *Punishment & Society*, 19(4), 463–481. doi:10.1177/1462474516666282.

Vincent, G.M., & Viljoen, J.L. (2020). Racist algorithms or systemic problems? Risk assessments and racial disparities. *Criminal Justice and Behavior*, Online First, doi:0093854820954501.

Vincent, G.M., Guy, L.S., & Grisso, T. (2012). *Risk assessment in juvenile justice: A guidebook for implementation*. Washington, DC: MacArthur Foundation.

Ward, G.K. (2012). *The black child-savers: Racial democracy and juvenile justice*. Chicago: University of Chicago Press.

Weiner, D.A., Leon, S.C., & Stiehl, M.J. (2011). Demographic, clinical, and geographic predictors of placement disruption among foster care youth receiving wraparound services. *Journal of Child and Family Studies*, 20(6), 758–770. doi:10.1007/s10826-011-9469-9.

Zahn, M.A., Brumbaugh, S., Steffensmeier, D., Feld, B.C., Morash, M., Chesney-Lind, M., Miller, J., Payne, A.A., Gottfredson, D.C., & Kruttschnitt, C. (2008). *Violence by teenage girls: Trends and context*. Washington, DC: US Department of Justice, Office of Justice Programs, Office of Juvenile Justice and Delinquency Prevention, 6–7. www.ojp.gov/pdffiles1/ojjdp/218905.pdf.

Zhang, L. (1997). Informal reactions and delinquency. *Criminal Justice and Behavior*, 24(1), 129–150. doi:10.1177/0093854897024001008.

Chapter 6

Returning to Underlying Theory and Principles

To this point in the book, we have articulated the strengths and positive applications of JRNA relative to its objectives. We have also noted some places where improvements could be made in the future. One risk with any evidence-based practice is that once it is used widely, the original intent and underlying foundations that first led to its use fade away. This can lead to shortcomings or contradictions in the evidence-base that are nonfatal, but nevertheless hinder optimal use of the practice. This chapter considers where structured assessment fits into existing frameworks for juvenile justice decisions and identifies places where current practice and research could be reconsidered to set a stronger and continuous improvement-based foundation for the future use of risk and needs assessment processes in justice settings.

Theoretical Origins and Foundations

The future use of JRNA practices should be mindful of the original goals of assessment practices as the early intent of these diagnostic tools was to better anchor assessment practices within robust research findings about risk factors for delinquency and to enhance equity and fairness in system decisions. This can also relate to the current rationales that frequently justify JRNA practices, such as risk, needs, and responsivity. However, these early intentions are rarely integrated into empirical tests of JRNA.

Clinical and Statistical Judgment

The origins of structured assessment come from formalized processes meant to draw subjectivity out of clinical diagnosis procedures. This use of "statistical" as opposed to "clinical" judgment (and related prediction) was the focus of work by Paul Meehl (Grove, 2005). Coupled with the early diagnostic approaches used to classify, treat, and study youths in the juvenile court (e.g., Glueck & Glueck, 1934; Healy & Bronner, 1936), this grounds the systematic assessment process firmly in the tradition of measurement and assessment in clinical

DOI: 10.4324/9780367823122-6

psychology (Laub, 2000; Sullivan et al., 2012).[1]Meehl (1954, p. 3) describes the fundamental problems with systematic assessment, which are "predict[ing] how a person is going to behave" and determining "in what manner should we go about this prediction?"

Although Meehl and colleagues ultimately came down firmly behind the idea of actuarial assessment and decision-making, they also offered several conditions under which these practices should be used (see also Grove & Meehl, 1996). Meehl (1954, p. 39), for example, asserted that "if a given variable does not, in fact, make any difference[in prediction], the clinician should not be using it." He then goes on to suggest that weighted scoring systems can capture a given item's contribution to predicting the outcome. In expanding the objectives for JRNA practice to areas like case management, it is important to return to these first principles for guidance on how to proceed going forward. As a case in point, inclusion/exclusion of items based on their predictive relevance and weighted scoring are not used in most cases (see also Baird, 2009; Baird et al., 2013). So, while JRNA does have a practical objective that cannot be ignored (i.e., systematic assessment), it is also important to recognize that the foundations of the approach rest in psychometric measurement that requires certain assumptions and checks on evidence to ensure it is being optimized for use by juvenile justice personnel and researchers.

Risk, Needs, and Responsivity (RNR) Framework

As discussed in Chapter 3, the RNR framework identifies three key elements for correctional effectiveness: estimating an offender's risk to reoffend and matching sanction restrictiveness to the level of risk (i.e., risk), assessing offenders' intervention needs based on criminogenic risk factors and matching intervention services to the identified areas of need (i.e., need), and considering an offender's individual characteristics that carry the potential to influence treatment effectiveness (i.e., responsivity). The overarching assumption of the RNR framework is that individualized approaches to offender rehabilitation that address criminogenic risk factors are the most effective of possible approaches (Andrews & Bonta, 2010). This perspective aligns well with the founding principles of the juvenile justice system which emphasize targeted and individualized rehabilitation efforts that account for the developmental status of children and adolescents. It also fits with the purpose of systematic assessment as a foundation for directing the appropriate allocation of resources to individual youths and caseloads.

Despite the growing body of research that acknowledges the RNR principles, little research has adequately addressed all three RNR principles in juvenile justice settings. Instead, JRNA research has focused very heavily on determining how well the overall risk score predicts recidivism and has neglected to consider the needs and responsivity components of the framework within these studies. Studies that examine the relationship between need/service matching and recidivism do not typically consider the risk/sanction match or responsivity components. Responsivity has received the least amount of empirical attention—although its applicability to the ways in which unique developmental characteristics among youths can influence juvenile justice system outcomes cannot be ignored (Brogan et al., 2015). The tendency to study the effectiveness of each RNR principle in silos, without considering how all three components work together, has led to some unanswered questions about how well the RNR framework operates across different youth circumstances. Nelson and Vincent (2018) and other juvenile justice scholars (e.g., Peterson-Badali et al., 2015; Shook & Sarri, 2007; Vieira et al., 2009) suggest that the RNR model, although pervasive in discussion of intervention with adults and juveniles, may be challenging to implement in settings involving youths.

It is often assumed that risk and needs gradually increase at the same rate (Basanta et al., 2018). This means that the general expectation is that high risk youths will also be high need and, therefore, restrictive sanctions and intensive intervention go hand in hand. Similarly, it is often assumed that low risk youths will be low need, and therefore, diversion from the system and minor or no treatment services are most appropriate. What is not clear is how well the RNR framework, or the JRNA process more specifically, works for youths that score as "low risk, high need" or "high risk, low need." This also leads to dilemmas in how the juvenile justice system responds to individual cases as the direction of resources for needs may be out of alignment with that for risk when one considers RNR (Sullivan, 2019). For instance, existing research suggests that girls are disproportionately referred to the juvenile justice system for minor offenses, but show higher rates of mental health symptoms, suicidal ideation, and histories of trauma (Zahn et al., 2009; Huizinga et al., 2013). These findings, together, suggest the possibility for girls to be scored "low" risk but "high" on needs factors such as mental health. As this likely scenario suggests, accomplishing both risk/sanction and need/service matching may prove to be a challenge for youths with atypical risk and need characteristics. If intensive intervention services are reserved for high risk offenders, it is unclear whether "low risk, high-need" youths are receiving appropriate services, given the assumption that intensive services should be reserved for the higher risk offenders. There are also financial repercussions for youths and families. Higher risk youths with the same needs may have cost-free access to intensive services through the restrictive sanction (i.e., youths sent to a residential facility can receive intensive mental health services through the program while in custody) while the only community-based intensive services available to low risk youths require service fees. This could create disparity in the availability of effective rehabilitation services for youths that is contingent on financial status and risk level.

Ratings of "high risk, low-need" are also likely to be found among youths with a history of system involvement or other historical factors. According to the selective enforcement arguments described on p. 126, this scenario is likely to occur given the documented evidence of selection bias in enforcement practices (e.g., Peck & Jennings, 2016). The critical question is what happens if the JRNA process fails to identify areas of "high need" that are amenable to treatment but results in a score of high(er) risk to reoffend. The focus on rehabilitation in the juvenile justice system, combined with the recommendation of restrictive sanctioning (due to the high risk estimate), does not suggest that no or low intensity treatment services for high risk youths is ideal. However, the results of the JRNA suggest that intensive treatment services are not necessary. Providing unnecessary intervention has been shown to cause iatrogenic effects—including increased behavioral problems, negative peer associations, and unnecessary financial costs and resources (Cécile & Born, 2009; Dishion et al., 2001; Gatti et al., 2009). Both likely scenarios present major challenges to accomplishing the most optimal risk/sanction and need/service matching. They also offer a place where the RNR framework might require further consideration when applied to youths' different combinations of risk and need levels.

The scope of thinking about use of JRNA in decision-making and subsequent sanctions and treatment might also be expanded. Several scholars have discussed the concept of loose coupling and how it relates to effective and fair juvenile justice outcomes (Alarid et al., 2011; Ericson & Eckberg, 2015; Hagan et al., 1979; Singer, 1997). Loose coupling was originally developed by organizational scholars to highlight the low levels of interdependency within organizations (Weick, 1976). The theory of loose coupling emphasizes the need to simultaneously consider the interdependence and indeterminacy in the interactions among organizations within a broader network or system (Beekun & Glick, 2001; Orton & Weick, 1990). In their application of loose coupling to juvenile justice decision-making, Bishop et al., (2010, p. 216), describe a juvenile justice system where "...multiple agencies involved in decision making are independent, governed by different rules and mandates, and oriented toward goals and objectives that are frequently different from and sometimes incompatible with the priorities of other organizational units."

Loose coupling can be applied to the JRNA process in ways that may also influence the utility of the RNR framework in juvenile justice settings. For example, there are multiple "users" of the JRNA results. Agency managers use data to accomplish the goals of resource allocation; judges use JRNA data to make case-processing decisions; probation officers use the JRNA results to make treatment referrals; and treatment providers may use the JRNA results to develop treatment plans and treatment goals, as well as intensity and frequency of treatment services. This can lead to a disconnect between the scores that are derived through the information gathering process, how this information is used during judicial decision-making, and the delivery of intervention services. In particular, the intervention phase of the system (i.e., needs/services matching) involves participation and decisions from multiple agencies with diverse values and experiences. Once a youth's needs are identified and judicial recommendations for intervention are made, the actual delivery of the intervention is most often accomplished by community-based treatment providers that are working outside of the formal justice system. As a result, the goals or recommendations of the justice system may not be fully realized during treatment services given treatment providers' focus on rehabilitation, harm reduction, and strength-based intervention. For example, a youth was scored high need on substance use due to the information provided to the assessor (e.g., prior history of marijuana use), a positive drug test, and a possession of marijuana charge. Based on these assessment results, the judge mandates the youth to an intensive, community-based substance abuse program delivered by a countywide agency that provides behavioral health interventions to children and adults. Yet, when the youth begins the community-based substance use program, the provider quickly realizes that the offender is not using frequently and is not a viable candidate for intensive substance abuse services. These conflicting perspectives lead to a situation where the treatment provider does not follow the recommendations of the judge, which were based on the JRNA results.

Other scholars have criticized the RNR model for its lack of theoretical scope and applicability to practice (Basanta et al., 2018; Ward & Brown, 2004; Ward & Stewart, 2003; Ward et al., 2007). These criticisms center around the framework's failure to consider additional, noncriminogenic risk factors and focusing too narrowly on risk and need while discounting responsivity and other resiliency factors. For example, Ward et al. (2007, p. 210) argue that focusing solely on criminogenic needs "…is a necessary but not sufficient condition for treatment." Critics of the RNR model point to a lack of emphasis on factors that have been empirically shown to influence treatment effectiveness including therapeutic alliance, resiliency factors, and other noncriminogenic characteristics that align with the responsivity element but are rarely examined or considered in studies of RNR. Accordingly, Ward and colleagues have argued that the RNR framework leads to a "one size fits all approach" relying on risk profiles and failing to consider "its own principle of responsivity" which is central to adapting intervention decisions to the unique needs of justice-involved youths.

All these concerns become especially important when considering how the RNR framework works within the developmental context of juvenile justice (Basanta et al., 2018; National Research Council, 2013; Scott & Steinberg, 2009; Sullivan, 2019). In particular, the notion of JRNA processes leading to a "one size fits all" approach to rehabilitation or the lack of clear policies/protocols to address responsivity factors does not align with the founding principles of the juvenile justice system which center around individualized treatment tailored to the unique circumstances of each youthful offender. Considering the ways in which dynamic needs interact with each other and with other, noncriminogenic characteristics such as individual characteristics (i.e., responsivity), treatment readiness, and the therapeutic environment, is a critical piece to confirming the utility of the RNR model in rehabilitating adolescent offenders. More specifically, confirmation that the implementation of the JRNA process within juvenile justice settings does not result in universal intervention decisions that are not in the best interests of the child is needed. To accomplish this, both general and specific responsivity factors must be considered. The general responsivity principle is concerned with matching the style and mode of intervention to the learning styles of the clients, whereas specific responsivity is concerned with matching the noncriminogenic characteristics of the offender, such as personality and treatment motivation, to the intervention program. Understanding the role of specific responsivity factors, or characteristics that may mediate or moderate the relationship between criminogenic needs and treatment outcomes, is central to any assessment of how well the RNR framework works in practice. Such tests of the RNR model will provide valuable information regarding whether the decision-making procedures should consider the unique criminogenic *and* noncriminogenic circumstances of youthful offenders (Brogan et al., 2015).

New developments in sanction and treatment matrices can reduce this "one size fits all" dynamic if they are appropriately used (Vincent et al., 2012). These matrices should be informed and closely checked against the types of interventions available in a particular jurisdiction. This requires clear service inventories and mapping relative to youth needs and consideration of any service barriers (e.g., Fountain & Mahmoudi, 2020; Maschi et al., 2008). It also requires consideration of the overall relevance of a set of available services to the juvenile justice population at hand (Bernstein et al., 2015) and identifying gaps in those services (Silvestro, 2005). The Florida Department of Juvenile Justice's map based on their 2017 Service Continuum Analysis is an especially good example of such an approach (Weber et al., 2018).[2] Once that step is completed, the matrix should be directive but not totally prescriptive in the sense that there should be room for necessary discretion based on the responsivity factors just mentioned (e.g., mental health needs, cultural competency). Variation within risk-level groupings also must be kept in mind to avoid applying sanctions or treatment that is misaligned to the case—especially when considering domain area scores relative to the available treatment (Sullivan, 2019).

Measurement and Methodology

Measurement and statistical principles are at the core of the JRNA process via its reliance on the prioritization of actuarial guidance over clinical judgment. The basic assumption of the risk assessment process is that a variety of youth characteristics can be directly measured and then used to make accurate conclusions about broader constructs such as risk and need by utilizing classifications to group and then predict the likelihood of reoffending (Gottfredson, 1987). Risk to reoffend is impossible to measure because it is not directly observable, therefore, it is a latent construct that can only be captured with observed items that, together, are expected to represent the construct (Jöreskog, 1993; MacCallum & Austin, 2000). The actual items scored on the assessment instrument are the observed items used to represent risk and need. These items are assumed to covary in ways that represent distinct latent subfactors, which are the risk/need domains. In turn, these risk domains covary in ways that reflect a unidimensional latent construct, "risk to reoffend." Figure 6.1 provides an illustration of the internal structure of a risk and needs assessment instrument.

The measurement model depicted in the figure represents a fictional risk assessment instrument with 12 items that are measured through information gathering (Step 1 of the JRNA process). These 12 items are assumed to represent four risk domains. Since these domains are not directly measured, they are unobserved latent factors. These four risk domains are assumed to represent a higher-order latent construct representative of likelihood to reoffend. Most often, this higher-order construct is a categorial latent factor that corresponds to risk classification such as low risk, moderate risk, and high risk.

Given the *a priori* assumptions about the covariation among the observed risk items and the latent risk domains, the internal structure of a risk assessment instrument can be compared to a measurement model in factor analyses and/or mixture modeling techniques (see Bollen, 2002; Muthén, 2001). In basic terms, the objective is to test whether the data fit the hypothesized measurement model, which is often based on theory or previous empirical evidence (Brown, 2015; Long, 1983). When applied to the

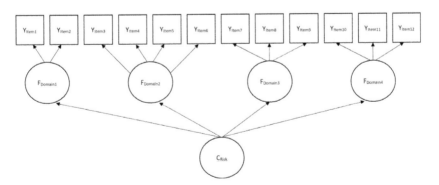

Figure 6.1 Generic JRNA Measurement Model

internal structure of a risk assessment instrument, the inclusion of individual items is based on extant theory and research that supports the expectation that the covariation among the observed items is due to a common (unobserved, first-order latent construct) domain of risk, and that these risk domains covary in ways that reflect an offender's overall risk to reoffend (which is an unobserved, second-order latent construct).

Very little research has been devoted to testing elements of validity other than predictive validity (Hilterman et al., 2016; Lee, 2013). For example, the internal structure of juvenile risk assessment instruments has not received a great deal of attention but carries important implications about what exactly is being measured. An instrument has face validity when it appears, superficially, to be measuring the intended constructs. Given the reliance on risk items that have been shown to be robust predictors of delinquent behavior, face validity is not much of a concern. Construct validity, however, is a stricter measure of validity that includes different elements of measurement (e.g., criterion-validity, content validity) and warrants empirical attention.

The paucity of research that examines construct validity can be partly attributed to a priori assumptions about the covariation among the risk items, risk domains, and overall risk to offend. Although direct tests of the factor structure of juvenile risk assessment instruments are rare, decades of theoretical and empirical work suggest that the data should fit the expected structure. Several questions about the measurement model are embedded in the risk assessment process, however. Some questions are related to the items and domains used to measure risk (content validity), and their true relationship to reoffending (criterion validity) while other questions are about consistency in the measurement model across groups of offenders (measurement invariance). The commonality among these concerns is whether the measurement model embedded in the risk assessment process is valid and reliable.

Moving to a real-world example, we considered the measurement structure for a sample of 459 disposition stage cases from 11 counties in one midwestern state that uses the Ohio Youth Assessment System (OYAS) tool. This empirical example focuses on the measurement structure of the OYAS. As noted above, this element is often neglected, but quite important because it can convey whether fundamental assumptions about youths' risk of reoffending hold in each sample. This can also give a sense of which domains might be effective in driving decision-making and which ones may not. Table 6.1 summarizes the results of a confirmatory factor analysis (CFA) for the same OYAS tool and sample just described.

The overall model fit is statistically significant, which is generally undesirable in a CFA context. The CFI and RMSEA statistics meet their respective thresholds for good fit, but the SRMR is above the standard cutoff of .05 (Hu & Bentler, 1999). This suggests that the different domains do not all fit as well with an underlying, latent risk level for youths as might be anticipated in theory. This is confirmed by the factor loadings across the

Table 6.1 Summary of Measurement Analysis (CFA) for OYAS Disposition Tool

Model Fit Indices	Estimate
Model Fit Chi Square (df)	46.6 (14)*
Comparative Fit Index (CFI)	**.93**
Std. Root Mean Square Residual (SRMR)	.07
Root Mean Square Error Approximation (RMSEA)	**.05**
Domain Factor Loadings	
Juvenile Justice History	.23
Family-Living Arrangement	**.62**
Peer	**.47**
Education-Employment	.35
Prosocial Skills	**.64**
Substance Abuse, MH, Personality	**.56**
Values, Attitudes, and Beliefs	**.65**

Notes: * p < .05; Weighted Least Squares Estimation for Dichotomous Indicators; standardized Factor Loadings of .40 or greater are generally viewed as acceptable; bolded values fall above or below standard cutoffs for good fit at the model or domain level.

seven OYAS domains where five exceed conventional criteria but two (Juvenile Justice History, Education-Employment) do not. This suggests that those two domains are behaving somewhat differently than the others in terms of their relationship to "risk" among this sample of youths.

The second stage of this measurement analysis is summarized in Table 6.2. This reflects the multi-tiered process of measuring and assessing risk in youths where the overall risk score comprises of a set of domains, which in turn are themselves made up of individual items that are scored. Analytically, this translates into the "second order" factor structure shown in Figure 6.1. The analysis shown in Table 6.2 illustrates that the expected factor structure does not hold that well in this case.[3] First, none of the conventional thresholds for Model Fit are met for this model in this sample of OYAS disposition cases. Second, although six of the domain level factor loadings meet conventional cutoffs of > .40, the juvenile justice history domain still falls below that range (.35)—suggesting that it somehow differs in its contribution to the overall risk score for these youths. Additionally, five of the seven domains have individual items that fall below that criterion for factor loadings, suggesting that the domain organization is not effectively capturing interrelationships among the items. This, in turn, affects how well the overall OYAS score captures risk and the degree to which the domains may be effective ways of understanding youths' supervision and treatment needs. A brief review of some important considerations regarding the psychometric properties of juvenile risk assessment instruments is provided in the following sections.

Table 6.2 Fit Statistics for Second-Order CFA with OYAS Disposition Items

Model Fit Indices	*Estimate*
Model Fit Chi Square (df)	1006.88 (422)*
Comparative Fit Index (CFI)	.81
Std. Root Mean Square Residual (SRMR)	.11
Root Mean Square Error Approximation (RMSEA)	.06
Domain Factor Loadings	Item Factor Loadings
Juvenile Justice History (2 items)	.53–.77
Family-Living Arrangement (6 items)	.12–.83
Peer (6 items)	.26–.80
Education-Employment (3 items)	.37–.45
Prosocial Skills (3 items)	.65–.98
Substance Abuse, MH, Personality (6 items)	.32–.66
Values, Attitudes, and Beliefs (5 items)	.23–.71

Note: * p < .05.

Items versus Domains

Measurement quality also considers the role of risk domains, or the first-order latent constructs, in measuring risk and need. Most existing studies rely on domain scores to measure predictive and incremental validity, as well as service/need matching (e.g., Baglivio et al., 2018; Luong & Wormith, 2011; Nelson & Vincent, 2018; Peterson-Badali et al., 2015). The implications for relying on domain scores versus individual items are not straightforward. There are clear statistical advantages to relying on domain scores, primarily data reduction and parsimony. There are also overt consequences, both from a statistical and an intervention standpoint. Statistically, relying on risk domains, or subscales, to assess predictive validity or psychometric properties will lose effect within each of the observed items. That is, the use of subscales in factor analysis, without considering the effects of the individual items on the factor structure, does not consider that the associations between the items could result in different internal structures with subscales that indicate different needs across groups (Hilterman et al., 2016). Failing to consider the relationship between each item and risk to reoffend can also distort an accurate understanding of an offender's needs in a particular area. This, in turn, can impact whether youths are directed toward appropriate treatment.

For example, if $F_{domain3}$ (in Figure 6.1) represents the family functioning domain, what happens when youths lack parental attachment but not parental monitoring or involvement (i.e., a youth scores high risk on one item but low risk on two items)? By considering the domain score (e.g., average across all three items), instead of each item individually, important information could get lost. Using the family domain score, the youth would mostly likely score "in the middle" for family needs, although the offender and their family are likely to benefit from a family-focused intervention to strengthen parental attachment. Thus, from a decision-making standpoint, does relying on risk domains to capture risk and needs lose important information that targets the unique circumstances of adolescent offenders?

Data from 460 adjudicated offenders placed on probation in three parishes in Louisiana showed that, compared to youths placed on probation who did not recidivate, juvenile probationers who recidivated were rated significantly higher on all three SAVRY risk domains which include a historical risk domain (no reoffending: mean = 4.75, s.d. = 3.42; one or more re-arrests: mean = 5.94, s.d. = 5.94, $t(454) = -3.63$, $p < .001$), social/contextual risk domain (no reoffending: mean = 3.06, s.d. = 2.42; one or more re-arrests: mean = 3.92, s.d. = 2.60, $t(457) = -3.57$, $p < .001$), and individual risk domain (no reoffending: mean = 4.38, s.d. = 3.52; one or more re-arrests: mean = 6.19, s.d. = 4.12, $t(458) = -4.98$, $p < .001$) (see Soderstrom et al., 2020). A closer look at differences in individual SAVRY items among this same sample showed that six out of the ten historical risk items, four out of six social/contextual risk items, and seven out of eight individual-risk items were significantly different (t, $p < .05$) across youths that reoffended and those that did not reoffend. This means that 30 percent of the individual SAVRY items were not related to recidivism although, when considered as a group, all three risk domains were related to recidivism.

The second issue related to the items included on a JRNA instrument is what Baird (2009, p. 3) referred to as the risk assessment "conundrum" which centers around the value of risk items, or domains, that are not statistically related to recidivism. These authors argue that the inclusion of items that are not related to recidivism likely reduces the predictive validity of the overall instrument and introduces "noise" into accurate classifications because "…many risk assessment models label the needs as criminogenic, implying a claim about causality that generally far exceeds what can legitimately be concluded from the assessment data." Based on these arguments, definitions of "risk," "need," and "criminogenic need" must be considered in analyses of measurement quality. Items that may be highly representative of a treatment need, such as substance use, may not necessarily be a cause of reoffending. A characteristic, such as drug use, could be a cause of delinquent behavior for one youth (i.e., criminogenic need) and a consequence of delinquent behavior for another youth (i.e., multi-problem behavior).

The problem identified by Baird (2009) is highlighted using 459 cases assessed with the OYAS to consider the relationship between domain summary scores and new juvenile court referrals. A typical approach to studying a tool would focus heavily on its overall predictive validity. That process is summarized in Table 6.3. The overall score suggests that the area

Table 6.3 Summary of Predictive Validity Analysis for OYAS Disposition Tool

	AUC (CI)
Overall Score-Bivariate	.56 (.50–.61)
Overall Score-Multivariate	.56 (.51–.61)
Domain Scores	*OR (CI)*
Juvenile Justice History	1.06 (.87–1.29)
Family-Living Arrangement	1.11 (.98–1.27)
Peer	**1.13 (1.00–1.28)**
Education-Employment	1.20 (.99–1.44)
Prosocial Skills	1.17 (.98–1.39)
Substance Abuse, MH, Personality	**1.19 (1.01–1.40)**
Values, Attitudes, and Beliefs	**1.19 (1.00–1.43)**

Notes: AUC = Area Under the Curve statistic; CI = 95% Bootstrapped Confidence Interval (1,000 replications); OR = Odds Ratio; Multivariate models include controls for Age, Sex, Non-White Race, Violent or Sex Offense; Bolded Values are statistically significant at p < .05.

under the curve (AUC = .56) statistic reflects prediction of a new juvenile justice referral better than chance alone. Clearly, however, the domains varied in their predictive value relative to that overall score. *Peer risk* and needs, *substance abuse, mental health and personality*, and *values, attitudes, and beliefs* were the only statistically significant predictors based on a test that considers the size of the estimates relative to their standard errors. Those standard errors, in part, reflect the variance in the domain scores and new referrals to juvenile court, which suggests that the predictive value of the domains is somewhat different—even though their Odds Ratios are mostly similar (with the exception of *juvenile justice history*).

This is potentially problematic from the standpoint of how well sets of items and domains individually contribute to the predicting recidivism and characterizing risk (Baird et al., 2013). Given such predictive validity findings in domains (and individual items), some scholars have called for the separation of risk and needs assessment to reduce such "noise" (Douglas & Kropp, 2002; Heilbrun, 1997; Baird et al., 2013). For example, Gottfredson and Moriarty (2006, p. 192) argue that "…predicting who will or will not behave criminally is risk assessment, whereas using predictive methods to attempt a reduction in criminality through assignment to differential treatments is needs assessment." Thus, assessment items that are related to treatment success or failure, or change in needs over time, but are not related to recidivism, should not be accounted for in estimations of risk. This argument focuses on a clear dichotomy in assessment with different criterion variables (Gottfredson & Moriarty, 2006). Risk assessment should target public safety and estimate risk based only on those items that are statistically related to reoffending outcomes. Needs assessment should target crimino-genic needs with criterion variables related to treatment outcomes.

This simultaneously raises questions as to the fit of the RNR framework in juvenile justice as risk/sanction and need/services matching can become more complicated in the context of the juvenile justice system's desire to address both public safety and individual youth development. Certain interventions may be designed for youths who are low-to-moderate risk but have high needs that may generate further problems if they go unaddressed, which at least somewhat veers away from the RNR promotion of reserving limited resources for the highest risk cases (Sullivan, 2019). There is also the question of whether a "risk" orientation is the best framework for intervening with youths and the degree to which RNR effectively prioritizes such an approach (Case & Haines, 2016). To that end there may be less risk weighted perspectives from which to consider youth assessment in juvenile justice and related contexts (Schwalbe, 2008; Shlonsky & Wagner, 2005).

Risk Reduction

Risk assessment is also used as a tool to measure risk reduction or change in risk classification over time (Baird et al., 2013). This function of risk assessment is also tied to measurement and statistics in obvious ways. Static risk factors, which are often most strongly correlated with risk classification, are historical in nature and not amenable to change (Bonta, 2002). Dynamic risk factors, on the other hand, are the items on the instrument that are meant to serve as targets of change because they are characteristics that are amenable to intervention efforts.

There are two overarching questions regarding the use of risk assessment instruments to measure change appropriately. The first question is related to the repeated measurement of the same items (Douglas & Skeem, 2005; Serin et al., 2013). Repeated assessment of historical items should produce similar risk scores because they do not change. As a result, considering changes in risk scores, that include historical items, will not produce valid measures of change because the score of the historical items will remain the same across each assessment point. The second question is related to the expectation of change in dynamic risk factors, without accounting for treatment availability or treatment engagement (Skeem & Monahan, 2011). As outlined in the three-step JRNA process, as well as the RNR framework (see Andrews et al., 1990; Bonta, 2002), risk reduction is contingent on service/need matching. Therefore, the availability of services to address offenders' dynamic needs is paramount to the appropriate measurement of change. Dynamic risk factors that cannot be targeted due to unavailable services will not change. The combination of repeated assessment of his-torical risk factors that cannot be changed and the assessment of dynamic risk factors that were not targets of intervention could lead to inaccurate, or biased, estimates of risk reduction in ways that should not be held "against" the youths' rate of risk reduction. Future research should consider how strongly assessments of risk reduction are driven by historical risk factors and/or dynamic needs that are unable to be addressed through intervention and whether there are other methods to reflect improvements more accurately in risk and need factors during custody. Research also should look at samples of youths who reappear in the juvenile justice system as well as those who do not understand the implications of change in risk and needs over time. Again, this is in line with the developmental focus of the juvenile justice system.

Measurement Invariance

Another critical component to an instrument's internal structure is measurement invariance which occurs when the relationship between a latent construct and the observed items is equal across groups and over time (Floyd & Widaman, 1995; Widaman & Reise, 1997; Widaman et al., 2010). Essentially, this means that the JRNA measurement model (i.e., risk domains, risk to reoffend) is the same across independent groups of youths (e.g., based on race or gender) and in reassessment. When applied to risk assessment, measurement invariance is concerned with whether the internal structure, outlined in Figure 6.1, is the same across groups of youths (or time).[4] For instance, actuarial scoring procedures, where the scoring algorithm is the same for every youth, assume measurement invariance because the same formula to estimate risk is applied universally, regardless of group characteristics (e.g., race, gender).

However, it is possible that the items measured on the same instrument covary in ways that are unique to certain groups. This could be due to variation in the type of risk factors related to reoffending or to the strength of the relationships among specific risk factors and delinquent behavior (e.g., peers, trauma, mental health symptoms) across subgroups of youths (e.g., race, gender, developmental or age differences). In sum, these potential differences suggest that risk to reoffend may manifest differently for different groups' offenders. Only a small number of studies have examined differences in the measurement model of a juvenile risk assessment instrument across groups. Most of these studies have focused on gender differences and provide mixed results regarding measurement invariance (Lee, 2013; Sijtsema et al., 2015; Thompson & McGrath, 2012). For example, when testing invariance of the SAVRY, Hilterman et al. (2016) found that the measurement model was similar across boys and girls, but the strength of the factor loadings, or association between the items and the factors, was substantially different whereas Childs et al. (2016) failed to find any gender differences in the structure of the SAVRY across boys and girls.

Measurement invariance is an essential component of the psychometric properties of assessment instruments. The issue of measurement invariance becomes even more critical when considering the potential ramifications of imprecise measurement across groups and how it may contribute to biased decision-making and misimpressions about individual youths and demographic subgroups involved in the juvenile justice system. A lack of measurement invariance implies that risk and needs, as captured with the JRNA instrument, may be interpreted differently across groups which can lead to higher rates of inappropriate juvenile justice decisions. In fact, Lee (2013, p. 166) argued that, "the internal consistency and construct validity of instruments is a prerequisite to the study of predictive validity." Thus, until research confirms the internal consistency of the JRNA measurement model, predictive validity cannot be confirmed. The accuracy of findings regarding predictive validity rests on the assumption of strong measurement quality (i.e., accurate measurement model, measurement invariance). Unfortunately, however, tests of predictive validity are plentiful while tests of an instrument's internal structure and its invariance across groups of offenders are rare (Lee, 2013).

Tests of Predictive Validity

Although tests of JRNA predictive validity are common, significant variation in the strength of predictive ability has been found across studies, instruments, and the type of reoffending measured (e.g., violent reoffending versus general reoffending). This has led to debate concerning the most accurate statistical methods for evaluating an instrument's predictive validity. For example, significant weight is given to AUC values in studies of predictive validity. As described in earlier chapters of this book, AUC estimates are considered diagnostic tests that provide an estimation of accurate classification, above and beyond chance alone (Rice & Harris, 1995). Among studies involving juvenile risk assessment, a value over .65 is often considered to reflect a valid prediction (.50 represents chance prediction). The benefits of the AUC value are that it is a straightforward measure with agreed upon cutoff values for predictive validity that can be compared across studies and samples (Singh et al., 2013; Szmukler et al., 2012). However, there are some drawbacks to the reliance on AUC values as the only measure of predictive accuracy. These include a lack of information describing the "area under the curve" or the type of errors in prediction, the inability to account for additional legal or extralegal factors that may be influencing the risk-level-recidivism relationship, the requirement that recidivism is dichotomous which precludes an assessment of the frequency of reoffending or the time to recidivate, and the resistance to base rates of reoffending behavior (Gottfredson & Moriarty, 2006; Singh et al., 2013; Singh, 2013; Szmukler et al., 2012). Many of these drawbacks can be accounted for by using other, supplemental statistical techniques that could improve our understanding of the "why, how, and who" of inaccurate classification.

Discrimination quality is one important component of the psychometric properties of an assessment instrument that has not received much empirical attention (see Lee, 2013). There are two different forms of discrimination. The first examines the amount and direction of errors in prediction and studies how well categories of risk can distinguish between those that do and do not reoffend. Sensitivity and specificity indices are used to understand these error rates (Singh, 2013; Szmukler et al., 2012). Sensitivity is concerned with high risk offenders and represents the proportion of youths who were rated high risk and recidivated. This is also referred to as the true positive rate. Specificity is concerned with youths rated low risk and represents the proportion of youths rated low risk that did not reoffend. This is also referred to as the true negative rate. The false positive rate represents those youths rated high risk but who did not go on to reoffend. The false negative rate represents those youths rated low risk but did reoffend. Error rates are considered less frequently than AUC values, although they provide more detailed information about the direction and magnitude of the errors in classification. For example, a basic analysis of PACT and re-arrest data from the FDJJ (2007–2014) shows that 72 percent of juvenile probationers rated low risk did not reoffend within one year of probation completion (true negative). However, 28 percent of youths rated low risk did reoffend within one year of probation completion (false negative). Among high risk youths placed on probation, 49 percent did not reoffend (false positive) and 51 percent (true positive) did reoffend at least once within a year of probation completion. Similar rates were found using SAVRY risk ratings from three parishes in LA. Among youths rated low risk, 77 percent did not recidivate within one year of probation completion (true negative) and 23 percent did recidivate (false negative); among youths rated high risk, 60 percent did not recidivate (true positive) and 40 percent did recidivate at least once (false positive). In the three-state OYAS court disposition sample studied by Sullivan and colleagues (2019) (n = 2,859), 72 percent of youths assessed as low risk did not have a new referral during the follow-up period (true negative) while 18 percent of youths in that group were referred to the juvenile court again (false negative). Looking at the high risk group, 29 percent of youths were referred back into the juvenile justice system (also true positives), conversely, 71 percent of high risk cases did not have a new referral (false positives).

Although the usefulness of such analyses is certainly tempered by the fact that they are based on official recidivism measures, the information gleaned from them is a critical piece to a more comprehensive understanding of JRNA tools, including identifying and acknowledging the potential adverse effects of inaccurate classification. The implications of false positive versus false negative estimates are very different. False positives can lead to unnecessary labels, restrictions, intervention intensity, and costs associated with more restrictive and intensive services; false negatives can lead to increased threats to public safety and decreased access to effective intervention services. Sensitivity (i.e., true positive) and specificity (i.e., true negative) are connected to the AUC values through receiver operating curves (ROC) models, but it is not common for these measures to be discussed in the context of JRNA predictive validity and AUC estimations (see Baird et al., 2013 for a lengthier discussion on the use of AUC values). One major drawback to considering error rates is that only two groups are included in estimations of error, the low risk and high risk groups. As a result, valuable information about what is happening "in the middle" (i.e., moderate risk discrimination) is not obtained. This is an important limitation because a large proportion of youths score in the moderate to moderate-high risk categories and—despite that—case-processing decisions are made according to each risk classification. Furthermore, like AUC estimates, error rate calculations do not necessarily account for any additional legal or extralegal factors that may be driving these error rates.

The second component of discrimination involves comparing the probability of reoffending across each risk category, referred to as calibration (Skeem & Lowenkamp, 2016; DeMichele et al., 2020). Often, a regression-based approach is used to test the clarity in discrimination across risk categories for distinct probabilities of reoffending across groups, and evaluates whether these differences occur in a linear form where the probability of reoffending increases with a one-unit increase in risk classification. The categorical nature of risk classifications means that this type of discrimination analysis involves comparing the probability of reoffending across risk group—not just comparing all risk groups to the "low" or "high" risk group as in tests of error rates. Clear discrimination across the low risk and high risk groups is not surprising given that these groups represent the "lowest" and "highest" risk youths. However, it is important to understand how well the middle groups (e.g., moderate risk, moderate-high risk) discriminate from the low and high risk groups (Baird et al., 2013). It is possible that the moderate levels of predictive validity are driven by poor discrimination "in the middle." In this sense, confirmation of meaningful classifications across all risk levels is necessary to bolster confidence in the ways in which risk is classified. There are also potentially consequential differences in the sanctions and interventions that are recommended based on low versus moderate risk classifications and moderate risk versus high risk classifications. For example, using Florida's Disposition Matrix recommendations, a low risk youth charged with a minor offense may get diversion while a moderate risk youth charged with the same offense may get formally processed, adjudicated, and placed on probation.

There are also concerns about relying on group-level data to make conclusions about individual youths (Cooke & Michie, 2010; Eckhouse et al., 2019; Silver & Miller, 2002; Skeem & Monahan, 2011). A full evaluation of the risk assessment process therefore requires a consideration of this interdependence between the case and the group in decision-making. Indeed, a

Table 6.4 Bivariate Relationship Between OYAS Risk Score and New Juvenile Justice Referral

Grouping	b (se) Odds Ratio
Full Sample (n = 2,859)	.03 (.001)* 1.03
Low-Risk Level (n = 1,208)	.01 (.004)* 1.01
Moderate-Risk Level (n = 1,164)	−.01 (.005) .99
High-Risk Level (n = 487)	−.01 (.006) .99

Note: *p < .05.

founding principle of the juvenile justice system was to effectively target the unique needs of children and adolescents. Even when relying on extant research to make risk assessment guidelines, there will always be variation, or error, in the precision of those assessments. The question is whether the margins of error are too wide to make predictions meaningful (Hart et al., 2007). Most researchers contend that group data can be very useful for making predictions about individual behavior (Hanson & Howard, 2010; Skeem & Monahan, 2011), with the right provisions. One important provision is that variation (or error) is random—with different groups of youths experiencing similar levels of error in measurement quality and predictive accuracy. Nonrandom variation can lead to biased risk assessment processes, and in turn, biased decision-making practices.

These are versions of broader inferential problems encountered when applying aggregate results of individuals (e.g., ecologic fallacy; Silver & Miller, 2002) and the paradox where relationships may look different when considered across subgroups of a population relative to a sample average (i.e., Simpson or Lord's Paradox). This is especially important in risk and needs assessment as the population is frequently stratified into levels that are then used in decision-making processes. Table 6.4 provides an example of how these types of relationships work within the risk subgroups using data from a study of 2,859 disposition cases across three states. In particular, the overall average unstandardized coefficient for the OYAS risk and new referral relationship is .03 (p < .001) in this sample. However, when broken down across the three possible risk levels, the relationship is no longer statistically significant and changes sign for the moderate and high risk levels. This suggests that it is important to consider potential disaggregation when looking at the intricacies of how the risk and recidivism relationship may work slightly differently across subgroups of youths—or at the very least differ in strength.

According to Andrews et al. (1990), correctional effectiveness (i.e., reductions in reoffending) is enhanced when information gathering is systematic, sanctions are based on classifications of risk to reoffend, and rehabilitation services are targeted toward identified criminogenic needs. Thus, by design, juvenile risk assessment should increase consistency in the information used to make decisions, fairness, and equity in system experiences, and reduce group differences in system outcomes (Andrews & Dowden, 2007; Bonta & Andrews, 2017; Schwalbe et al., 2006). However, several factors have been introduced as potential mechanisms by which the assessment process may not accomplish the goal of fairness and equity in system outcomes (Hannah-Moffat, 2009; Harcourt, 2015; Hubbard & Matthews, 2008; Moore & Padavic, 2011).

Data and Measurement in JRNA Research

Many of the concerns about the state of JRNA research just described speak to the depth of analyses that have been carried out in prior studies of predictive validity. What is less often said is that these studies are almost exclusively based on administrative records and official reports. The nature of data typically used in these studies—in part due to what is available to researchers—also raises some questions about the existing body of research. This can be added to some of the other concerns about these studies (e.g., Baird, 2009; Singh et al., 2013). As shown in Sullivan et al. (2019), self-reports of new offenses and system contacts may differ from what is observed in system records. This potential lack of correspondence between self-report and official records has been identified in multiple studies of general population youths (Kirk, 2006) as well as those who are involved in the juvenile justice system (Piquero et al., 2014). In turn, these types of discrepancies may affect the strength of the association between the risk assessment information and recidivism outcomes (and others that researchers might aspire to use). More importantly, they unduly affect determinations of "success" and "failure" such that it becomes difficult to identify false positives and false negatives well. So, strengthening the body of evidence around JRNA will inherently involve expanding the pool of available data sources both to evaluate assessments in terms of their main purposes and to expand to other relevant outcomes (e.g., self-reported offending, other well-being indicators). Overall, it is crucial to focus as much on the data that goes into the process of studying JRNA as the procedures used to analyze those data.

JRNA and Decision-Making

Decision Theory

In addition to measurement and statistics and the basic theoretical frameworks underlying JRNA, theories about decision-making can also be applied to the three-step JRNA process to highlight the fact that its logic is dependent on human decision-making. Several theories have been developed to explain how human beings think and act in relation to the information available to help make decisions. At the heart of these theories is discretion—or the ways in which decision-makers use available information, the types of information used when scoring the assessment, and how the risk score is weighted when making case-processing decisions. Past research consistently finds that juvenile justice decisions vary by legal and extralegal factors and that subjectivity can infiltrate the decision-making process which results in disparity in system decisions for youths charged with the same offense (e.g., Leiber et al., 2009; Peck & Jennings, 2016).

In the case of JRNA, there is room for discretion to enter the process at each of the three steps. Juvenile justice personnel are trained in best practices for information gathering and scoring and research indicates that many assessment instruments possess moderate to good inter-rater reliability (Baird et al., 2013). However, not much is known about the reliability of juvenile assessment instruments in the field. Instead, most of what we know about reliability is carried out in "laboratory-like settings" where it may be more difficult for stereotypes to influence decisions (Vincent, Guys, Fusco, & Gershenson, 2012). In practice, information gathering and scoring is often accomplished by a single probation or intake officer which can lead to variability in the types of information gathered (e.g., collateral information), skills of the interviewer (e.g., motivational interviewing), and the interpretation of assessment items from both the probation officer and the youth/family. Unconscious stereotypes can also penetrate how information is gathered, interpreted, and how risk severity is scored. In one of the only studies to investigate juvenile probation officers' (JPO) perspectives of the risk assessment process, JPOs reported difficulties with ratings due to a lack of clarity in assessment protocols, only using the instrument to "back up" existing thoughts about risk level and recommendations about supervision and intervention, and beliefs that prior JPO experience and knowledge are more beneficial than JRNA practices (Guy et al., 2014). These findings suggest that variation in the use of assessment results across system actors does occur and some of this variation may be due to concordance between practitioner impressions of the youth and the assessment results (also see Sullivan et al., 2019; Viglione et al., 2015).

The role that JRNA results play in decisions about youth cases can also vary across decision-maker characteristics, individual circumstances, and the interaction of the two. There is very little research on the factors that lead decision-makers, such as judges, to use or not use risk assessment results during case-processing decisions (Eckhouse et al., 2019; Guy et al., 2014). It is likely that decision-makers also vary in their use of the risk assessment results and these variations are based on a combination of work-related factors (e.g., buy-in, case load) and whether scores align with beliefs or stereotypes about youths and case circumstances. To better conceptualize how biases may subvert the JRNA process, we rely on research and theory on discretion and decision-making in the juvenile justice system to consider how JRNA may or may not exacerbate disparities in system outcomes. These theories help identify ways in which JRNA may not fully live up to its promise of reducing subjectivity and disproportionality—though the JRNA process is likely more superior than just using fully subjective, clinical information.

Focal Concerns

The focal concerns perspective has been applied to disparities in sentencing in the adult criminal justice system, and more recently, juvenile court processing (Demuth & Steffensmeier, 2004; Holmes et al., 2020; Steffensmeier & Demuth, 2006; Ulmer & Johnson, 2004). According to this perspective, case decisions are based on three goals (or focal concerns): fair and just punishment, public safety, and eliminating negative system outcomes (Steffensmeier et al., 1998). To accomplish these goals, decision-makers often rely on a "perceptual shorthand," using both legal factors (e.g., current offense) and stereotypes related to extralegal factors, such as race/ethnicity or gender. In their application of the focal concerns perspective to juvenile justice decision-making, Bishop and colleagues (2010, p. 214) argue the first focal concern (fairness) requires information on the offense and the offender, the second focal concern (public safety) requires the accurate prediction of risk of reoffending, and the third focal concern (negative social consequences) requires an assessment of viable disposition outcomes. They further argued that the rehabilitation ideal of the juvenile justice system provides an additional opportunity where extralegal factors may disadvantage certain groups of youths (e.g., racial or ethnic minorities) depending on the stage examined. Decision-making stages that include various court actors with differing goals and values may translate into greater disparities across groups of juveniles (e.g., judicial disposition), where tightly-coupled stages with a sole court actor (e.g., judge at adjudication) will result in fewer disparities. According to Bishop et al. (2010, p. 215) "…justice officials apply perceptual shorthand based on racial stereotypes when assessing culpability and danger, so too, we suspect, are they likely to rely on stereotypes when assessing treatment needs."

On one hand, the systematization that juvenile risk assessment brings to the decision-making process clearly aligns with the three focal concerns outlined by Steffensmeier and colleagues (1998) and carries the potential to minimize perceptual shorthand in both sanction and treatment decisions. Based on these arguments, the assessment process should reduce or eliminate differences in case decisions through a systematic process for information gathering and decision-making that reduces subjectivity. On the other hand, it is possible that "perceptual shorthand" may also penetrate the JRNA process. According to Graham and Lowery (2004, p. 485), system actors often resort to unconscious stereotypes to manage information overload and make decisions more efficiently. Information overload can certainly become an issue during the information gathering process given the large number of items included on the assessment and range of collateral information expected to be collected. Accordingly, if a "perceptual shorthand" is also operating during the assessment process, estimates of risk and need may not align with the intended measurement model discussed above.

Attribution Theory

Attribution theory is based on concepts drawn from social psychological research that address how and why individuals use information to make assessments and decisions about other individuals (Heider, 1958; Fiske & Taylor, 1991; Mallicoat, 2007). When integrated into criminological research, attribution theory focuses on decision-makers' beliefs about what causes a person to engage in crime. Criminologists have posited that disparities in juvenile justice decisions are the result of unconscious stereotypes regarding the causes of, or attributions linked to, delinquent behavior (Bridges & Steen, 1998; Graham & Lowery, 2004; Rodriguez, 2007). This argument has been applied to racial and gender disparities in juvenile court outcomes (Bishop & Frazier, 1992; Mallicoat, 2007). For example, Bridges and Steen (1998) found that juvenile probation officers perceived delinquent behavior among White juveniles to be caused by external forces (e.g., environmental factors, delinquent peers, negative family situations) and delinquency among minority offenders to be caused by internal forces (e.g., personality, attitudes, lack of remorse). As a result, and paralleling earlier research, juveniles whose behavior was attributed to external factors were perceived to be less culpable for their delinquent behavior and therefore more amenable to treatment than juveniles with negative internal attributions (see also Emerson, 1969; Rotter, 1966). As such, unconscious racial stereotypes (or attributions) about the causes of one's behavior were stratified across racial lines and influenced decisions about how best to process youthful offenders. Similarly, Graham and Lowery (2004) found that decision-makers perceived Black youths to be more mature, and thus, more culpable for their behavior delinquency.

There is also evidence to suggest that decision-makers' attributions about delinquent girls can lead to differences in case outcomes for girls compared to boys for the same or similar offenses. As discussed in Chapter 5, the paternalism perspective posits that girls are treated more harshly than their male counterparts to "teach them a lesson" for engaging in behavior that is more characteristic of boys' behavior (Chesney-Lind, 1977). The chivalry hypothesis, on the other hand, suggests that girls are treated with leniency because of the perception that they are less culpable, less dangerous, and more amenable to treatment (Steffensmeier et al., 1993; Price & Sokoloff,

2004). Although somewhat contradictory, prior research supports both perspectives in that girls are found to receive harsher treatment for minor or status offenses and more lenient case-processing decisions for more serious or violent offenses (Ehrmann et al., 2019; Feld, 2009; Spivak et al., 2014). When applied to the juvenile risk assessment process, chivalry or paternalism may occur during assessment and scoring because of one's beliefs about girls' culpability.

The tenets of attribution theory carry important implications. For instance, differences in one's beliefs about the causes of delinquency may influence estimates of the severity (or risk level) of each risk factor (e.g., current living arrangements, attitudes/behaviors, current mental health status, aggression) that is identified, influencing the scoring of risk items or the weight given to each item when considering case outcomes and treatment needs. Correspondence among decision-makers' beliefs about the causes of delinquency and the results of the risk assessment may also influence the weight given to the assessment results during the decision-making process. This means that, although the same items are used to estimate risk to reoffend and make case decisions, practitioners' perceptions about each item and its relevance to the likelihood of reoffending can vary based on their beliefs about culpability and dangerousness (Guy et al., 2014). Since JRNA is used as a tool to identify, assess severity, and target criminogenic risk and needs (which essentially means identifying the causes of misbehavior), unconscious stereotypes about the causes of delinquency can influence whether the right needs are being targeted for intervention and appropriate levels of supervision. Both of which are key factors in system effectiveness.

Heuristics and Biases in Decision-Making

Meehl (1954, p. 45) pointed out that assessment processes are based on reaching a "conception" of a person, predicting aspects of the future from it, and then making decisions accordingly. With that, it is important to consider all the ways that such conceptions are reached and how juvenile justice personnel make decisions based on those conceptions. In considering the totality of decisions made in the JRNA process, it is useful to include some perspective on how justice actors are oriented to the decisions that they make, especially building on the work in attribution theories. Many of the frameworks on information processing and decision-making used in explaining justice decision-making to date have relied on a rational actor model of decision-making where the information from risk and needs assessment is integrated into juvenile justice processes to facilitate rational, more evidence-based decisions. Knowledge about situational decision-making processes has evolved in recent years such that it now more explicitly accounts for both cognition (i.e., information processing) and emotional effects on choices, which recognizes the limitations of a pure rational choice perspective (Manktelow, 2012). These perspectives on decision-making can inform our thinking about the three-step process of JRNA that we have considered in this book.

Generally, these theories rely more on bounded rationality and a more subjective view of decision-making. Herbert Simon (1972) framed bounded rationality in a manner applicable to the idea of pure rational decision-making where an actor performs a cost-benefit analysis based on complete information prior to making a choice. Instead, this view recognizes risk, uncertainty, complexity, and lack of full information about different options that is relevant to decision-making in JRNA.

Emotion and subjectivity likewise have been included in decision models that have been developed more recently. Kahneman (2003) labeled the two systems involved in decision-making as (1) Intuition and (2) Reasoning. He notes that, while ideally System 1 is monitored by System 2, this does not necessarily always happen in practice. In JRNA this means that the information from the assessment may not gain as much traction as is assumed relative to other types of attributions that might be made about a youth. Similarly, this perspective considers the relative "accessibility" of information that individuals use in making decisions based on the degree to which they can easily call it to mind in making decisions. This is a salient point in the context of the information that is available from an assessment where an overall risk level may be more immediately intuitive than a more complex set of need domain scores. To reinforce this point, in a study of two London courts, Dhami (2003) found that even with additional information about the case, judges tended to use relatively few, informationally limited, cues in making case decisions (e.g., previous bail orders).

An alternative decision-making framework seems warranted based on the variability in the juvenile justice population, such as differing motivations and points of emphasis of juvenile justice staff, often restricted placement options, uncertainty about youths' potential outcomes (even with JRNA information), and unevenness in use and other implementation challenges. This is especially true when considering the degree to which JRNA can improve decision-making toward better youth and system outcomes as well as in deciding how the JRNA process might be optimized toward those ends.

Although these perspectives on decision-making in the juvenile justice system provide valuable frameworks for considering how discretion may negatively impact one or more of the steps involved in the JRNA process, it is important to acknowledge the robust finding that relying on standardized assessment procedures, instead of unstructured clinical judgment, is far more effective in reducing differential treatment or disparate case outcomes (Ægisdóttier et al., 2006; Shlonsky & Wagner, 2005). Therefore, juvenile justice researchers and practitioners tend to believe that the benefits of a systematic process for making assessments about offender risk and needs and making decisions based on those assessments outweigh the potential consequences of the potential variability in practices used to gather information, score the assessment, and incorporate the results into case-processing decisions. This is especially true when JRNA instruments can be optimized locally and tested for measurement quality, predictive validity, and group differences in both measurement and prediction. Therefore, the next section provides some suggestions on the ways in which researchers and practitioners can work together to ensure that the JRNA process is effective, fair, and equitable at the local level.

Collaborative Researcher-Practitioner Partnerships

Community-based research is a term used to describe research projects that involve a collaborative partnership between researchers and practitioners. The foundation of this form of research is that all parties share two common goals: advancing knowledge and improving practice (Strand et al., 2003). Community-based research acknowledges the importance of understanding and valuing what those in the field are experiencing while also working collaboratively to ensure effectiveness and equality within a particular community or jurisdiction. Israel and colleagues (1998, p. 177) note that a fundamental element of community-based research is the emphasis on the participation and influence of nonacademic researchers in the process of creating knowledge. Research is conducted *with* active engagement and influence of community members in the research process. Such collaborative research partnerships help reduce the gap between research, practice, and theory that is all too common in criminal justice settings. Three important elements make this form of research unique: collaboration, multiple sources of knowledge, and social action (Strand et al., 2003). We consider how these elements, and collaborative research partnerships more broadly, can help advance knowledge and improve JRNA practices.

Collaboration

As described in Chapters 3 and 4, the implementation of JRNA offers agencies much more than a prediction of a given outcome for each youth (i.e., reoffending), there are broader agency impacts including resource allocation, financial costs, fairness and equity in system decisions, and measures of intervention effectiveness. Many of these longer-term outcomes (see logic model in Chapter 3) are not easily measured and tracked over time, which is like tests of measurement and prediction. Researchers or employees with the statistical skills necessary to carry out these tests are not typically embedded in juvenile justice agencies. Therefore, working collaboratively with researchers is essential to ensuring that JRNA is working optimally in each local agency.

Collaborative partnerships can provide benefits to all parties involved in the JRNA process and potentially deal with some of the limitations identified at multiple points in the book (e.g., implementation challenges, overly restrictive evidence-base). Agencies will benefit through validation of the psychometric properties (e.g., internal consistency, predictive validity) of the instrument among the local population and continual quality assurance through longitudinal studies of longer-term agency-level impacts. Researchers benefit through access to assessment data to test theory related to JRNA including RNR and decision theories as well as to contribute to the broader knowledge base regarding the costs and benefits of the implementation of JRNA. In this way, collaborative research partnerships ensure theoretically and empirically informed JRNA practices at the local level and that practice-informed theory is used to expand the body of research on JRNA.

Multiple Sources of Knowledge

JRNA involves multiple stakeholders/organizations (see logic model for example). Each stakeholder has a different role in the three-step process. This includes: (1) youth and family as the stakeholders that are being assessed, (2) frontline workers who are administering the assessments, (3) "users" of the information such as system decision-makers, agency managers, and treatment providers, and (4) researchers who examine the implementation process, outcomes, and theoretical implications of the experiences in the local community and disseminate this information to the other stakeholder groups. As a result, collaboration and co-learning is vital to JRNA effectiveness because each stakeholder brings a unique set of JRNA experiences (Israel et al., 1998). For example, youth and family members' experiences with the JRNA process is much different than the frontline personnel administering the assessment. Similarly, users of the assessment results may have very different experiences regarding the utility of the results depending on the nature of their work. Judges' experiences with using the tool to make decisions may be quite different from agency managers using the aggregate results to make decisions about resource allocation and intervention needs.

These varied stakeholders coupled with the array of research questions that must be answered require a research agenda that incorporates diverse perspectives about the effectiveness, implementation, use, and equity of these tools. Collaborative partnerships strengthen the quality of research by incorporating local knowledge and theory based on the different experiences of those involved in the JRNA process (Israel et al., 1998). Community-based research relies on the knowledge that each party brings to the research process—experiential (or local) knowledge of those involved in the JRNA process (i.e., youths/families, "users") and the specialized knowledge and skills of the researchers evaluating the process (Strand et al., 2003).

Social Action

The lack of community-based research partnerships in criminal justice (and other disciplines) can lead to a "...sterile evidence base from more artificial rather than practice-based circumstances" (Green, 2008, p. 23). A defining feature of community-based research is the acceleration of change(s) at the local level to improve the quality of the practice and to ensure justice for all stakeholders involved. There are two types of products that result from community-based research: dissemination of findings (standard outcome of any research study) and actions taken to facilitate change in policy or practice.

Considering the distinction between efficacy and effectiveness is one way to exemplify the distinction between the two products. Efficacy studies involve rigorous research designs, high quality program implementation in laboratory-like settings, and researcher control over confounding factors (Flay et al., 2005, p. 153). Collaborative partnerships are rare in efficacy studies; most often the community or juvenile justice agency serves as the laboratory for researchers and findings are disseminated to practitioners and other researchers simultaneously with little input or local knowledge integrated. The goal of most efficacy studies is knowledge generation and confirmation of an evidence-base for the program or policy under investigation. Effectiveness studies focus on important contextual factors such as the quality of implementation and program outcomes under existing local conditions (Flay et al., 2005, p. 153). Often, once a program is found to be efficacious, it is named an evidence-based practice (Howell et al., 2014). However, it is likely that what works in controlled research settings or in one jurisdiction (i.e., efficacy, evidence-based practice) may not work in others due to several factors present in the external environment. Therefore, studies of effectiveness within the local environment where the practice will be carried out are critical to ensuring that the policy or program being implemented is meeting its objectives in a fair and consistent manner and to identifying areas in need of reform.

When applied to JRNA, an efficacy study may involve the administration of the assessment by highly trained researchers, using a comparison group that did not receive the assessment, and administering the assessment under optimal conditions such as in a private office or other location. A study of effectiveness, by contrast, may involve the frontline personnel administering the assessment after a short training, but have no comparison group because all cases are assessed, and administration in the field with other family members in proximity. As this example illustrates, tests of implementation and quality assurance of JRNA practices will likely vary across controlled settings (i.e., efficacy) and in the field (i.e., effectiveness). Understanding how well JRNA accomplishes its goals in each jurisdiction requires local evaluation in that jurisdiction, which can be more easily accomplished through researcher-practitioner partnerships than through research that does not incorporate those ideas. This is also consistent with the best practices for engaging and fostering stakeholder buy-in that were discussed in Chapter 4.

In summary, community-based research studies are ideal for agencies that are implementing, reforming, or interested in continuous quality assurance of JRNA practices. Extending the discussions in earlier sections of this chapter, evaluation of JRNA practices at the local level are essential to ensuring the JRNA process is operating as intended. This means monitoring the psychometric properties of the instrument among the local population of justice-involved youths, routine testing of predictive validity, concordance among the assessment results and case-processing and intervention decisions, and implementation quality. This also involves testing the invariance of the psychometric properties, predictive validity, and concordance in decisions across subgroups of delinquent youths.

In other words, it requires application of the expanded view of research on JRNA but also acknowledges that collaborative research partnerships can expedite answers to some essential questions by transferring the theoretical and empirical tasks that are not easily accomplished by agency personnel to the research partner. Stakeholders whose day-to-day responsibilities involve working with youths and families can maintain active participation in these research endeavors through communication, feedback loops that integrate multiple sources of knowledge and experiences, and necessary changes to practice or policy that promote JRNA effectiveness and fairness within the local environment. This type of practice-informed research can also help to drive quality implementation of JRNA (Vincent, Guy, & Grisso, 2012).

Chapter Summary

This chapter described important theoretical and methodological frameworks to highlight the need for more research on the accuracy and utility of the JRNA process. As discussed, several remaining questions about the psychometric properties of JRNA instruments, the degree to which discretion enters the three-step JRNA process through conscious or unconscious biases, and whether the full RNR framework can adequately explain all of the processes that lead to desistance from delinquent behavior. We argue that an effective approach to answering these questions is through collaborative research partnerships that integrate guiding theoretical frameworks, multiple sources of knowledge, and empirical assessment of the quality of the JRNA process and measures that carries the potential to lead to actionable steps to improve the JRNA process.

Chapter 7 builds on the points made here and more clearly lays the groundwork for the "next generation" of research and practice by outlining key areas that will facilitate the continuous improvement of juvenile risk and needs assessment—relative to current trends in juvenile justice. It uses the analysis of the current state of JRNA research and practice to set a possible course for the future focused on continuous quality improvement that draws on the foundational logic of systematic assessment, advances to this point, and the areas that require work to ensure effective, efficient, and equitable risk and needs assessment and related usage for justice-involved youths.

Notes

1 Burgess (1928) also conducted an important early risk assessment study with parole cases.
2 See www.djj.state.fl.us/research/reports/reports-and-data/static-research-reports/service-continuum-analysis/service-continuum-analysis-2017
3 Full list of OYAS items included in this analysis can be found in the book's web page at Routledge.
4 Though we use group-based measurement invariance for discussion and demonstration here, the same principles and logic are easily transferred across time points.

References

Ægisdóttier, S., White, M.J., Spengler, P.M., Maugherman, A.S., Anderson, L.A., Cook, R.S., Nichols, C.N., Lampropoulos, G.K., Walker, B.S., Cohen, G., & Rush, J.D. (2006). The meta-analysis of clinical judgment project: Fifty-six years of accumulated research on clinical versus statistical prediction. *Counseling Psychologist*, 34, 341–382. doi:10.1177/0011000005285875.

Alarid, L.F., Sims, B.A., & Ruiz, J. (2011). Juvenile probation and police partnerships as loosely coupled systems: A qualitative analysis. *Youth Violence and Juvenile Justice*, 9(1), 79–95. doi:10.1177/1541204010374298.

Andrews, D.A., & Bonta, J. (2010). Rehabilitating criminal justice policy and practice. *Psychology, Public Policy, and Law*, 16(1), 39–55. doi:10.1037/a0018362.

Andrews, D.A., & Dowden, C. (2007). The risk–need–responsivity model of assessment and human service in prevention and corrections: Crime-prevention jurisprudence. *Canadian Journal of Criminology and Criminal Justice*, 49(4), 439–464. doi:10.3138/cjccj.49.4.439.

Andrews, D.A., Bonta, J., & Hoge, R.D. (1990). Classification for effective rehabilitation: Rediscovering psychology. *Criminal Justice and Behavior*, 17(1), 19–52. doi:10.1177/0093854890017001004.

Baglivio, M.T., Wolff, K.T., Howell, J.C., Jackowski, K., & Greenwald, M.A. (2018). The search for the holy grail: Criminogenic needs matching, intervention dosage, and subsequent recidivism among serious juvenile offenders in residential placement. *Journal of Criminal Justice*, 55, 46–57. doi:10.1016/j.jcrimjus.2018.02.001.

Baird, C. (2009). *A question of evidence: A critique of risk assessment models used in the justice system*. Madison, WI: National Council on Crime and Delinquency. www.researchgate.net/publication/238742845_A_Question_of_Evidence_A_Critique_of_Risk_Assessment_Models_Used_in_the_Justice_System.

Baird, C., Healy, T., Johnson, K., Bogie, A., Dankert, E.W., & Scharenbroch, C. (2013). *A comparison of risk assessment instruments in juvenile justice.* Madison, WI: National Council on Crime and Delinquency. www.ojp.gov/pdffiles1/ojjdp/grants/244477.pdf.

Basanta, J.L., Fariña, F., & Arce, R. (2018). Risk-need-responsivity model: Contrasting criminogenic and noncriminogenic needs in high and low risk juvenile offenders. *Children and Youth Services Review*, 85, 137–142. doi:10.1016/j.childyouth.2017.12.024.

Beekun, R.I., & Glick, W.H. (2001). Organization structure from a loose coupling perspective: A multidimensional approach. *Decision Sciences*, 32(2), 227–250. doi:10.1111/j.1540-5915.2001.tb00959.x.

Bernstein, A., Chorpita, B.F., Rosenblatt, A., Becker, K.D., Daleiden, E.L., & Ebesutani, C.K. (2015). Fit of evidence-based treatment components to youths served by wraparound process: A relevance mapping analysis. *Journal of Clinical Child & Adolescent Psychology*, 44(1), 44–57. doi:10.1080/15374416.2013.828296.

Bishop, D.M., & Frazier, C.E. (1992). Gender bias in juvenile justice processing: Implications of the JJDP Act. *Journal Criminal Law & Criminology*, 82, 1162–1186.

Bishop, D.M., Leiber, M., & Johnson, J. (2010). Contexts of decision making in the juvenile justice system: An organizational approach to understanding minority overrepresentation. *Youth Violence and Juvenile Justice*, 8(3), 213–233. doi:10.1177/1541204009361177.

Bollen, K.A. (2002). Latent variables in psychology and the social sciences. *Annual Review of Psychology*, 53(1), 605–634. doi:10.1146/annurev.psych.53.100901.135239.

Bonta, J. (2002). Offender risk assessment: Guidelines for selection and use. *Criminal Justice and Behavior*, 29(4), 355–379. doi:10.1177/0093854802029004002.

Bonta, J., & Andrews, D.A. (2017). *The psychology of criminal conduct.* New York: Taylor & Francis. doi:10.4324/9781315677187.

Bridges, G.S., & Steen, S. (1998). Racial disparities in official assessments of juvenile offenders: Attributional stereotypes as mediating mechanisms. *American Sociological Review*, 63(4), 554–570. doi:10.2307/2657267.

Brogan, L., Haney-Caron, E., NeMoyer, A., & DeMatteo, D. (2015). Applying the risk-needs-responsivity (RNR) model to juvenile justice. *Criminal Justice Review*, 40(3), 277–302. doi:10.1177/0734016814567312.

Brown, T.A. (2015). *Confirmatory factor analysis for applied research.* Guilford publications.

Burgess, E.W. (1928). Is prediction feasible in social work? An inquiry based upon a sociological study of parole records. *Social Forces,* 7(4), 533–545.

Case, S., & Haines, K. (2016). Taking the risk out of youth justice. In C. Trotter, G. McIver, & F. McNeill (Eds.), *Beyond the risk paradigm in criminal justice* (pp. 61–75). London: Palgrave.

Cécile, M., & Born, M. (2009). Intervention in juvenile delinquency: Danger of iatrogenic effects? *Children and Youth Services Review*, 31(12), 1217–1221. doi:10.1016/j.childyouth.2009.05.015.

Chesney-Lind, M. (1977). Judicial paternalism and the female status offender. *Crime & Delinquency*, 23, 121–130. doi:10.1177/001112877702300203.

Childs, K.K., Frick, P.J., & Gottlieb, K. (2016). Sex differences in the measurement invariance and factors that influence structured judgments of risk using the Structured Assessment of Violence Risk in Youth (SAVRY). *Youth Violence and Juvenile Justice*, 14(1), 76–92. doi:10.1177/1541204014547722.

Cooke, D.J., & Michie, C. (2010). Limitations of diagnostic precision and predictive utility in the individual case: A challenge for forensic practice. *Law and human behavior*, 34(4), 259–274. doi:10.1007/s10979-009-9176-x.

DeMichele, M., Baumgartner, P., Wenger, M., Barrick, K., & Comfort, M. (2020). Public safety assessment: Predictive utility and differential prediction by race in Kentucky. *Criminology & Public Policy*, 19(2), 409–431.

Demuth, S., & Steffensmeier, D. (2004). Ethnicity effects on sentence outcomes in large urban courts: Comparisons among White, Black, and Hispanic defendants. *Social Science Quarterly*, 85(4), 994–1011. doi:10.1111/j.0038-4941.2004.00255.x.

Dhami, M.K. (2003). Psychological models of professional decision making. *Psychological Science*, 14(2), 175–180. doi:10.1111/1467-9280.01438.

Dishion, T.J., Poulin, F., & Burraston, B. (2001). Peer group dynamics associated with iatrogenic effect in group interventions with high-risk young adolescents. *New Directions for Child and Adolescent Development*, 2001(91), 79–92. doi:10.1002/cd.6. PMID: 11280015.

Douglas, K.S., & Kropp, P.R. (2002). A prevention-based paradigm for violence risk assessment: Clinical and research applications. *Criminal Justice and Behavior*, 29(5), 617–658. doi:10.1177/009385402236735.

Douglas, K.S., & Skeem, J.L. (2005). Violence risk assessment: getting specific about being dynamic. *Psychology, Public Policy, and Law*, 11(3), 347–383. doi:10.1037/1076-8971.11.3.347.

Eckhouse, L., Lum, K., Conti-Cook, C., & Ciccolini, J. (2019). Layers of bias: A unified approach for understanding problems with risk assessment. *Criminal Justice and Behavior*, 46(2), 185–209. doi:10.1177/0093854818811379.

Ehrmann, S., Hyland, N., & Puzzanchera, C.M. (2019). *Girls in the juvenile justice system*. US Department of Justice, Office of Justice Programs, Office of Juvenile Justice and Delinquency Prevention. https://ojjdp.ojp.gov/sites/g/files/xyckuh176/files/pubs/251486.pdf.

Emerson, R.M. (1969). *Judging delinquents*. New Brunswick, NJ: Transaction Publishers.

Ericson, R.D., & Eckberg, D.A. (2015). Racial disparity in juvenile diversion: The impact of focal concerns and organizational coupling. *Race and Justice*, 6(1), 35–56. doi:10.1177/2153368715594848.

Feld, B.C. (2009). Violent girls or relabeled status offenders? An alternative interpretation of the data. *Crime & Delinquency*, 55(2), 241–265. doi:10.1177/0011128708330629.

Fiske, S.T., & Taylor, S.E. (1991). *Social cognition*. New York: McGraw-Hill Book Company.

Flay, B.R., Biglan, A., Boruch, R.F., Castro, F.G., Gottfredson, D., Kellam, S., Moscicki, E.K., Schinke, S., Valentine, J.C., & Ji, P. (2005). Standards of evidence: Criteria for efficacy, effectiveness, and dissemination. *Prevention Science*, 6(3), 151–175. doi:10.1007/s11121-11005-5553-y.

Florida Department of Juvenile Justice (2017). *Service continuum analysis, 2017*. Retrieved March 7, 2021 from www.djj.state.fl.us/research/reports/reports-and-data/static-research-reports/service-continuum-analysis/service-continuum-analysis-2017.

Floyd, F.J., & Widaman, K.F. (1995). Factor analysis in the development and refinement of clinical assessment instruments. *Psychological Assessment*, 7(3), 286–299. doi:10.1037/1040-3590.7.3.286.

Fountain, E.N., & Mahmoudi, D. (2020). Mapping juvenile justice: Identifying existing structural barriers to accessing probation services. *American Journal of Community Psychology*, 67(1–2), 116–129. doi:10.1002/ajcp.12474.

Gatti, U., Tremblay, R.E., & Vitaro, F. (2009). Iatrogenic effect of juvenile justice. *Journal of Child Psychology and Psychiatry*, 50(8), 991–998. doi:10.1111/j.1469-7610.2008.02057.x.

Glueck, S., & Glueck, E.T. (1934). *One thousand juvenile delinquents*. Cambridge, MA: Harvard University Press.

Gottfredson, D.M. (1987). Prediction and classification in criminal justice decision making. *Crime and Justice*, 9, 1–20.

Gottfredson, S.D., & Moriarty, L.J. (2006). Statistical risk assessment: Old problems and new applications. *Crime & Delinquency*, 52(1), 178–200. doi:10.1177/0011128705281748.

Graham, S., & Lowery, B.S. (2004). Priming unconscious racial stereotypes about adolescent offenders. *Law and Human Behavior*, 28(5), 483–504. doi:10.1023/B:LAHU.0000046430.65485.1f.

Green, L.W. (2008). Making research relevant: if it is an evidence-based practice, where's the practice-based evidence? *Family Practice*, 24, 20–24. doi:10.1093/fampra/cmn055.

Grove, W.M. (2005). Clinical versus statistical prediction: The contribution of Paul E. Meehl. *Journal of Clinical Psychology*, 61(10), 1233–1243.

Grove, W.M., & Meehl, P.E. (1996). Comparative efficiency of informal (subjective, impressionistic) and formal (mechanical, algorithmic) prediction procedures: The Clinical-Statistical Controversy. *Psychology, Public Policy, and Law*, 2(2), 293–323. doi:10.1037/1076-8971.2.2.293.

Guy, L.S., Nelson, R.J., Fusco-Morin, S.L., & Vincent, G.M. (2014). What do juvenile probation officers think of using the SAVRY and YLS/CMI for case management, and do they use the instruments properly? *International Journal of Forensic Mental Health*, 13(3), 227–241. doi:10.1080/14999013.2014.939789.

Hagan, J., Hewitt, J.D., & Alwin, D.F. (1979). Ceremonial justice: Crime and punishment in a loosely coupled system. *Social Forces*, 58(2), 506–527. www.ojp.gov/ncjrs/virtual-library/abstracts/ceremonial-justice-crime-and-punishment-loosely-coupled-system.

Hannah-Moffat, K. (2009). Gridlock or mutability: Reconsidering gender and risk assessment. *Criminology & Public Policy*, 8, 209–219. doi:10.1111/j.1745-9133.2009.00549.x.

Hanson, R.K., & Howard, P.D. (2010). Individual confidence intervals do not inform decision-makers about the accuracy of risk assessment evaluations. *Law and Human Behavior*, 34(4), 275–281. doi:10.1007/s10979-010-9227-3.

Harcourt, B.E. (2015). Risk as a proxy for race: The dangers of risk assessment. *Federal Sentencing Reporter*, 27(4), 237–243. https://scholarship.law.columbia.edu/faculty_scholarship/2564.

Hart, S.D., Michie, C., & Cooke, D.J. (2007). Precision of actuarial risk assessment instruments: Evaluating the 'margins of error' of group v. individual predictions of violence. *The British Journal of Psychiatry*, 190(S49), s60–s65.

Healy, W., & Bronner, A.F. (1936). *New light on delinquency and its treatment*. New Haven, CT: Yale University Press.

Heider, F. (1958). *The psychology of interpersonal relations*. New York: Wiley.

Heilbrun, K. (1997). Prediction versus management models relevant to risk assessment: The importance of legal decision-making context. *Law and Human Behavior*, 21(4), 347–359. doi:10.1023/A:1024851017947.

Hilterman, E.L., Bongers, I., Nicholls, T.L., & Van Nieuwenhuizen, C. (2016). Identifying gender specific risk/need areas for male and female juvenile offenders: Factor analyses with the Structured Assessment of Violence Risk in Youth (SAVRY). *Law and Human Behavior*, 40(1), 82–96. doi:10.1037/lhb0000158.

Holmes, B., Feldmeyer, B., & Kulig, T.C. (2020). Sentencing departures and focal concerns: The joint effect of race and gender on departures in United States district courts, 2014–2016. *Journal of Crime and Justice*, 1–25. doi:10.1080/0735648X.2020.1730933.

Howell, J.C., Lipsey, M.W., & Wilson, J.J. (2014). *A handbook for evidence-based juvenile justice systems*. London: Lexington Books.

Hu, L.T., & Bentler, P.M. (1999). Cutoff criteria for fit indexes in covariance structure analysis: Conventional criteria versus new alternatives. *Structural Equation Modeling: A Multidisciplinary Journal*, 6(1), 1–55. doi:10.1080/10705519909540118.

Hubbard, D.J., & Matthews, B. (2008). Reconciling the differences between the "gender-responsive" and the "what works" literatures to improve services for girls. *Crime & Delinquency*, 54(2), 225–258. doi:10.1177/0011128706296733.

Huizinga, D., Miller-Johnson, S., Conduct Problems Prevention Research Group, & United States Office of Juvenile Justice and Delinquency Prevention. Girls Study Group (2013). *Developmental sequences of girls' delinquent behavior*. Washington, DC: US Department of Justice, Office of Justice Programs, Office of Juvenile Justice and Delinquency Prevention. https://ojjdp.ojp.gov/sites/g/files/xyckuh176/files/pubs/238276.pdf.

Israel, B.A., Schulz, A.J., Parker, E.A., & Becker, A.B. (1998). Review of community-based research: assessing partnership approaches to improve public health. *Annual Review of Public Health*, 19(1), 173–202. doi:10.1146/annurev.publhealth.19.1.173.

Jöreskog, K.G. (1993). Testing structural equation models. *Sage Focus Editions*, 154, 294–294.

Kahneman, D. (2003). A perspective on judgment and choice: Mapping bounded rationality. *American Psychologist*, 58(9), 697–720. doi:10.1037/0003-066X.58.9.697.

Kirk, D.S. (2006). Examining the divergence across self-report and official data sources on inferences about the adolescent life-course of crime. *Journal of Quantitative Criminology*, 22(2), 107–129. doi:10.1007/s10940-006-9004-0.

Laub, J.H. (2000). A century of delinquency research and delinquency theory. In M. K. Rosenheim, F.E. Zimring, D.S. Tanenhaus, & B. Dohrn (Eds.), *A century of juvenile justice* (pp. 179–205). Chicago: University of Chicago Press.

Lee, S.Y. (2013). Testing psychometric properties and the cross-ethnic construct validity of the risk and resiliency checkup. *Youth Violence and Juvenile Justice*, 11(2), 165–177. doi:10.1177/1541204012460875.

Leiber, M.J., Brubaker, S.J., & Fox, K.C. (2009). A closer look at the individual and joint effects of gender and race on juvenile justice decision making. *Feminist Criminology*, 4(4), 333–358. doi:10.1177/1557085109338564.

Long, J.S. (1983). *Confirmatory factor analysis: A preface to LISREL* (Vol. 33). Thousand Oaks, CA: Sage Publications.

Luong, D., & Wormith, J.S. (2011). Applying risk/need assessment to probation practice and its impact on the recidivism of young offenders. *Criminal Justice and Behavior*, 38(12), 1177–1199. doi:10.1177/0093854811421596.

MacCallum, R.C., & Austin, J.T. (2000). Applications of structural equation modeling in psychological research. *Annual Review of Psychology*, 51(1), 201–226. doi:10.1146/annurev.psych.51.1.201.

Mallicoat, S.L. (2007). Gendered justice: Attributional differences between males and females in the juvenile courts. *Feminist Criminology*, 2(1), 4–30. doi:10.1177/1557085106296349.

Manktelow, K.I. (2012). *Thinking and reasoning: An introduction to the psychology of reason, judgment and decision making*. Washington, DC: Psychology Press.

Maschi, T., Hatcher, S.S., Schwalbe, C.S., & Rosato, N.S. (2008). Mapping the social service pathways of youth to and through the juvenile justice system: A comprehensive review. *Children and Youth Services Review*, 30(12), 1376–1385. doi:10.1016/j.childyouth.2008.04.006.

Meehl, P.E. (1954). *Clinical versus statistical prediction: A theoretical analysis and review of the evidence*. Minneapolis, MN: University of Minnesota.

Moore, L.D., & Padavic, I. (2011). Risk assessment tools and racial/ethnic disparities in the juvenile justice system. *Sociology Compass*, 5(10), 850–858. doi:10.1111/j.1751-9020.2011.00416.x.

Muthén, B. (2001). Latent variable mixture modeling. *New Developments and Techniques in Structural Equation Modeling*, 2, 1–33. http://statmodel.com/bmuthen/articles/Article_086.pdf

National Research Council. (2013). *Reforming juvenile justice: A developmental approach*. Washington, DC: National Academies Press.

Nelson, R.J., & Vincent, G.M. (2018). Matching services to criminogenic needs following comprehensive risk assessment implementation in juvenile probation. *Criminal Justice and Behavior*, 45(8), 1136–1153. doi:10.1177/0093854818780923.

Orton, J.D., & Weick, K.E. (1990). Loosely coupled systems: A reconceptualization. *Academy of Management Review*, 15(2), 203–223. doi:10.5465/amr.1990.4308154.

Peck, J.H., & Jennings, W.G. (2016). A critical examination of "being Black" in the juvenile justice system. *Law and Human Behavior*, 40(3), 219–232. doi:10.1037/lhb0000180.

Peterson-Badali, M., Skilling, T., & Haqanee, Z. (2015). Examining implementation of risk assessment in case management for youth in the justice system. *Criminal Justice and Behavior*, 42(3), 304–320. doi:10.1177/0093854814549595.

Piquero, A.R., Schubert, C.A., & Brame, R. (2014). Comparing official and self-report records of offending across gender and race/ethnicity in a longitudinal study of serious youthful offenders. *Journal of Research in Crime and Delinquency*, 51(4), 526–556. doi:10.1177/0022427813520445.

Price, B.R., & Sokoloff, N.J. (2004). *The criminal justice system and women: Offenders, prisoners, victims, and workers*. New York: McGraw-Hill.

Rice, M.E., & Harris, G.T. (1995). Violent recidivism: Assessing predictive validity. *Journal of Consulting and Clinical Psychology*, 63(5), 737–748. doi:10.1037/0022-006X.63.5.737.

Rodriguez, N. (2007). Juvenile court context and detention decisions: Reconsidering the role of race, ethnicity, and community characteristics in juvenile court processes. *Justice Quarterly*, 24(4), 629–656. doi:10.1080/07418820701717144.

Rotter, J.B. (1966). Generalized expectancies for internal versus external control of reinforcement. *Psychological Monographs: General and Applied*, 80(1), 1–28.

Schwalbe, C.S. (2008). Strengthening the integration of actuarial risk assessment with clinical judgment in an evidence based practice framework. *Children and Youth Services Review*, 30(12), 1458–1464. doi:10.1016/j.childyouth.2007.11.021.

Schwalbe, C.S., Fraser, M.W., Day, S.H., & Cooley, V. (2006). Classifying juvenile offenders according to risk of recidivism: Predictive validity, race/ethnicity, and gender. *Criminal Justice and Behavior*, 33(3), 305–324. doi:10.1177/0093854806286451.

Scott, E.S., & Steinberg, L.D. (2009). *Rethinking juvenile justice*. Cambridge, MA: Harvard University Press.

Serin, R.C., Lloyd, C.D., Helmus, L., Derkzen, D.M., & Luong, D. (2013). Does intra-individual change predict offender recidivism? Searching for the Holy Grail in assessing offender change. *Aggression and Violent Behavior*, 18(1), 32–53. doi:10.1016/j.avb.2012.09.002.

Shlonsky, A., & Wagner, D. (2005). The next step: Integrating actuarial risk assessment and clinical judgment into an evidence-based practice framework in CPS case management. *Children and Youth Services Review*, 27(4), 409–427. doi:10.1016/j.childyouth.2004.11.007.

Shook, J.J., & Sarri, R.C. (2007). Structured decision making in juvenile justice: Judges' and probation officers' perceptions and use. *Children and Youth Services Review*, 29(10), 1335–1351.

Sijtsema, J.J., Kretschmer, T., & van Os, T. (2015). The Structured Assessment of Violence Risk in Youth in a large community sample of young adult males and females: The TRAILS study. *Psychological Assessment*, 27(2), 669–677. doi:10.1037/a0038520.

Silver, E., & Miller, L.L. (2002). A cautionary note on the use of actuarial risk assessment tools for social control. *Crime & Delinquency*, 48(1), 138–161.

Silvestro, R. (2005). Applying gap analysis in the health service to inform the service improvement agenda. *International Journal of Quality & Reliability Management*, 22 (3), 215–233. doi:10.1108/02656710510582462.

Simon, H.A. (1972). Theories of bounded rationality. *Decision and Organization*, 1(1), 161–176. http://innovbfa.viabloga.com/files/Herbert_Simon_theories_of_bounded_rationality_1972.pdf

Singh, J.P. (2013). Predictive validity performance indicators in violence risk assessment: A methodological primer. *Behavioral Sciences & the Law*, 31(1), 8–22. doi:10.1002/bsl.2052.

Singh, J.P., Desmarais, S.L., & Van Dorn, R.A. (2013). Measurement of predictive validity in violence risk assessment studies: A second-order systematic review. *Behavioral Sciences & the Law*, 31(1), 55–73. doi:10.1002/bsl.2053.

Singer, S.I. (1997). *Recriminalizing delinquency: Violent juvenile crime and juvenile justice reform*. New York: Cambridge University Press.

Skeem, J.L., & Lowenkamp, C.T. (2016). Risk, race, and recidivism: Predictive bias and disparate impact. *Criminology*, 54(4), 680–712. doi:10.1111/1745-9125.12123.

Skeem, J.L., & Monahan, J. (2011). Current directions in violence risk assessment. *Current Directions in Psychological Science*, 20(1), 38–42. doi:10.1177/0963721410397271.

Soderstrom, M.F., Childs, K.K., & Frick, P.J. (2020). The role of protective factors in the predictive accuracy of the Structured Assessment of Violence Risk in Youth (SAVRY). *Youth Violence and Juvenile Justice*, 18(1), 78–95. doi:10.1177/1541204019837329.

Spivak, A.L., Wagner, B.M., Whitmer, J.M., & Charish, C.L. (2014). Gender and status offending: Judicial paternalism in juvenile justice processing. *Feminist Criminology*, 9(3), 224–248. doi:10.1177/1557085114531318.

Steffensmeier, D., & Demuth, S. (2006). Does gender modify the effects of race–ethnicity on criminal sanctioning? Sentences for male and female white, black, and Hispanic defendants. *Journal of Quantitative Criminology*, 22(3), 241–261.

Steffensmeier, D., Kramer, J., & Streifel, C. (1993). Gender and imprisonment decisions. *Criminology*, 31(3), 411–446.

Steffensmeier, D., Ulmer, J., & Kramer, J. (1998). The interaction of race, gender, and age in criminal sentencing: The punishment cost of being young, black, and male. *Criminology*, 36(4), 763–798.

Strand, K., Marullo, S., Cutforth, N., Stoecker, R., & Donohue, P. (2003). *Community-based research and higher education*. San Francisco: Jossey-Boss.

Sullivan, C.J. (2019). *Taking juvenile justice seriously: Developmental insights and system challenges*. Philadelphia, PA: Temple University Press.

Sullivan, C.J., Piquero, A.R., & Cullen, F.T. (2012). Like before, but better: The lessons of developmental, life-course criminology for contemporary juvenile justice. *Victims & Offenders*, 7(4), 450–471. doi:10.1080/15564886.2012.713318.

Sullivan, C.J., Strange, C., Sullivan, C., Newsome, J., Lugo, M., Mueller, D., Petkus, A., Holmes, B., Lonergan, H., & McCafferty, J. (2019). *Multi-method study on risk assessment implementation and youth outcomes in the juvenile justice system*. Submitted to Office of Justice Programs, Office of Juvenile Justice and Delinquency Prevention. www.ojp.gov/pdffiles1/ojjdp/grants/252927.pdf.

Szmukler, G., Everitt, B., & Leese, M. (2012). Risk assessment and receiver operating characteristic curves. *Psychological Medicine*, 42(5), 895–898. doi:10.1017/S003329171100208X.

Thompson, A.P., & McGrath, A. (2012). Subgroup differences and implications for contemporary risk-need assessment with juvenile offenders. *Law and Human Behavior*, 36(4), 345–355. doi:10.1037/h0093930.

Ulmer, J.T., & Johnson, B. (2004). Sentencing in context: A multilevel analysis. *Criminology*, 42(1), 137–178.

Vieira, T.A., Skilling, T.A., & Peterson-Badali, M. (2009). Matching court-ordered services with treatment needs: Predicting treatment success with young offenders. *Criminal Justice & Behavior*, 36(4), 385–401.

Viglione, J., Rudes, D.S., & Taxman, F.S. (2015). Misalignment in supervision: Implementing risk/needs assessment instruments in probation. *Criminal Justice and Behavior*, 42(3), 263–285.

Vincent, G.M., Guy, L.S., Fusco, S.L., & Gershenson, B.G. (2012). Field reliability of the SAVRY with juvenile probation officers: Implications for training. *Law and Human Behavior*, 36(3), 225–236. doi:10.1037/h0093974.

Vincent, G.M., Guy, L.S., & Grisso, T. (2012). *Risk assessment in juvenile justice: A guidebook for implementation*. Washington, DC: MacArthur Foundation. https://njjn.org/uploads/digital-library/Risk_Assessment_in_Juvenile_Justice_A_Guidebook_for_Implementation.pdf

Ward, T., & Brown, M. (2004). The good lives model and conceptual issues in offender rehabilitation. *Psychology, Crime & Law*, 10(3), 243–257. doi:10.1080/10683160410001662744.

Ward, T., & Stewart, C. (2003). Criminogenic needs and human needs: A theoretical model. *Psychology, Crime & Law*, 9(2), 125–143. doi:10.1080/1068316031000116247.

Ward, T., Melser, J., & Yates, P.M. (2007). Reconstructing the Risk–Need–Responsivity model: A theoretical elaboration and evaluation. *Aggression and Violent Behavior*, 12(2), 208–228. doi:10.1016/j.avb.2006.07.001.

Weber, J., Umpierre, M., & Bilchik, S. (2018). *Transforming juvenile justice systems to improve public safety and youth outcomes*. Washington, DC: Georgetown University Center for Juvenile Justice Reform. https://humanrights.iowa.gov/sites/default/files/media/download.pdf.

Weick, K.E. (1976). Educational organizations as loosely coupled systems. *Administrative Science Quarterly*, 21(1), 1–19.

Widaman, K.F., & Reise, S.P. (1997). Exploring the measurement invariance of psychological instruments: Applications in the substance use domain. In K.J. Bryant, M. Windle, & S.G. West (Eds.), *The science of prevention: Methodological advances from alcohol and substance abuse research* (pp. 281–324). American Psychological Association. doi:10.1037/10222-009.

Widaman, K.F., Ferrer, E., & Conger, R.D. (2010). Factorial invariance within longitudinal structural equation models: Measuring the same construct across time. *Child Development Perspectives*, 4(1), 10–18. doi:10.1111/j.1750-8606.2009.00110.x.

Zahn, M.A., Day, J.C., Mihalic, S.F., & Tichavsky, L. (2009). Determining what works for girls in the juvenile justice system: A summary of evaluation evidence. *Crime & Delinquency*, 55(2), 266–293. doi:10.1177/0011128708330649.

Chapter 7

The Next Generation of Juvenile Risk and Needs Assessment

Today, the use of systematic risk/needs assessment is a fundamental part of the juvenile justice process. Juvenile Risk and Needs Assessment (JRNA) practices echo aspects of the early juvenile court and use modern thought and technology based on more recent research to arrive at decisions about how best to intervene with individual cases and identify agency needs. With the expansion of their use and beliefs about efficacy comes the potential for profound impacts on various stakeholders—especially youths. Despite the empirical and practical evidence favoring their use, there is also significant variation in findings, even in predictive validity studies which represent the lion's share of the research. Therefore, it is necessary to take a continuous quality improvement approach in analyzing the current status of JRNA usage and identify how to move forward with policy, practice, and research.

In this chapter we summarize what we have discussed to this point in the book to reach conclusions and make recommendations for the next phase of research, practice, and policy on JRNAs. The intent in the previous chapters was to carry out a multi-faceted and comprehensive evaluation of all aspects of JRNA (e.g., validation, implementation, use, broader principles) to reach conclusions about the current state of research and practice. This work was also meant to identify potential gaps in knowledge that must be addressed to optimize the use of JRNA in the future.

Summary of Key Conclusions

We began in Chapter 1 with some general questions: First, how well does the process of reaching case-level conclusions based on JRNA work? Second, how is that information then used to reach appropriate decisions? These simple questions serve as a starting point for the objectives of JRNA and include considerations of the implementation process and potential spillover of these practices to ancillary aspects of doing juvenile justice. In that overview of JRNA, Chapter 1 offered a few key introductory take-aways that set the context for the rest of the book:

DOI: 10.4324/9780367823122-7

- JRNA is increasingly used across jurisdictions and stages of the juvenile justice process and therefore has a significant impact on youths, families, communities, and the juvenile justice system.
- JRNA intends to facilitate more systematic decision-making by using standardized assessment protocols to gather information from youths and families.
- JRNA has generated a great deal of research in recent decades that could lead to the conclusion that the use and impact of JRNA is a "settled question," but researchers and policymakers must pay attention to several additional questions about JRNA to ensure effective and equitable use, ease of implementation, and sustainability.

Chapter 2 offered an overview of key aspects of the juvenile justice system and considered where JRNA fits into that process. This chapter also covered much of the pivotal research to date on JRNA and identified key findings. The major points from Chapter 2 are as follows:

- The JRNA process is best described in three parts comprised of information gathering, scoring and classification, and decision-making. This effectively means that the JRNA logic model entails a system of interrelated parts as opposed to a single intervention or program.
- The predictive validity of JRNA instruments has been found to be moderate to strong and is mostly consistent across subgroups of youths based on race, ethnicity, and gender.
- There is, however, some variation across studies in the strength of predictive validity as well as other aspects of JRNA tool performance that have not been studied as extensively (e.g., inter-rater reliability, measurement invariance, prediction error rates and types).

Building on the general notion of a three-step process, Chapter 3 laid out the JRNA logic by considering its important inputs and outputs. We discussed the use of JRNA in juvenile justice practice. With that, Chapter 3 set the stage for further examination of key elements of JRNA to determine how it fits into the current evidence-base for quality juvenile justice practice—including how to support effective implementation. Key summary points from Chapter 3 were as follows:

- The logic model for JRNA is complex and has numerous inputs, activities, and outputs across different stages of juvenile justice.
- Effective JRNA requires solid linkages between assessments and services provided and points out that there are differential levels of support for elements of the three-step process based on factors like staffing and service availability.
- The context in which JRNA processes are embedded determines how successful a juvenile justice system is in implementation, but there has been relatively little consideration of those questions in prior research.

The research on JRNA to date is heavily skewed toward investigating aspects of the tools themselves and some basic work on how they are used in practice. Therefore, Chapter 4 sought to consider the available research and commentary on implementing JRNA and to fuse that small body of work with related insights from the growing field of implementation science. Together, those areas of research suggest a more deliberate approach to moving the evidence on JRNA to the field to support effective and sustainable use of these practices. They also identify several areas where there must be more work to support the effective use of JRNA. Key points emerging from the discussion in Chapter 4 include:

- Research on JRNA implementation is limited but suggests that it is important to have a systematic process that allows for staff input, strong change leadership, intentional rollout procedures, and continual monitoring with appropriate data systems.
- Insights from implementation science help to offer a sense of the different aspects of the three-step JRNA process that require attention, including key stakeholder groups and the inner and outer contexts for adoption and use of these practices.
- JRNA is a unique, multi-faceted process to implement, and the juvenile justice system is a unique implementation environment. This requires a sense of broader principles and findings from implementation science as well as an understanding of specific factors that can influence success in juvenile justice settings.

Like Chapter 4, Chapter 5 considered elements of JRNA policy and practice that have not received as much attention in prior research and discussion. For the most part, issues surrounding equity, fairness, and the consequences of assigning a label derived from the JRNA process (e.g., "high risk") have not been prioritized as much as the question of whether the results of the assessment tool are correlated with recidivism. This shifts the focus to the broader values of the juvenile justice system. Takeaways from that chapter include:

- JRNA is, on balance, a positive development in juvenile justice, but researchers, policymakers, and practitioners should nevertheless pay attention to questions beyond predictive validity to ensure that these practices do not bring unintended consequences.
- Among these issues is the potential for differential scoring and impact across race, gender, and age subgroups; the degree to which reassessment procedures capture change in risk and needs; and labeling and reductionism in the assessment process that may lead to distorted views of how to best respond to specific cases and juvenile delinquency more generally.

- It is important to stay mindful of the value-based elements of juvenile justice practice and identify how those are relevant to JRNA.

Chapter 6 began to turn toward ideas about the future of JRNA and focused specifically on returning to key elements that underlie actuarial practices at the heart of JRNA and associated decision-making. Key takeaway points from Chapter 6 include:

- A need to remember the underlying tenets of clinical versus statistical assessment practices and theories of decision-making from both inside and outside of justice settings in using and studying JRNA.
- The additional value of looking more deeply at JRNA in research to ask different questions about its uses and outcomes.
- The importance of the need for collaboration across juvenile justice agencies, other network stakeholders, and researchers when implementing and researching JRNA to ensure relevant objectives are fully included in the process.

Together the analysis and demonstrations from these six chapters help to establish a foundation for a series of recommendations about the policy, practice, and research around JRNA as we move to the next generation of using assessment tools in juvenile justice practice. As we have argued throughout this book, risk and needs assessment in juvenile justice can be broadly viewed as a three-step process: (1) gathering information on youths' risks and needs, (2) synthesizing that information to develop general and specific risk and need scores (e.g., risk level), and (3) using the results to reach conclusions about juvenile justice cases and facilitate effective interventions. Importantly, though, this process is embedded in a broader implementation and usage context that affects the degree to which the three-step JRNA process can be carried out according to the underlying logic. The logic model discussed in Chapter 3 describes key elements of JRNA that must be considered as a system of inputs and outputs. This also means that the implementation and usage of JRNA must be responsive to a variety of stakeholders to ensure that all aspects are addressed at some point in the process. Even in the absence of a full evidence-base on the implementation, use, and sustainability of JRNA, there certainly are some general frameworks and principles that can be utilized to ensure that those implementing and supporting JRNA processes can effectively carry out their objectives.

As described in Chapter 2, the discussion of risk and needs assessments is frequently couched in language of "generations" of tools and usage objectives (Andrews & Bonta, 2010; Andrews et al., 2006; Baird et al., 2013). Along those same lines, we identify points of consideration for the next generation of research, policy, and practice of risk and needs assessment in juvenile justice settings. These suggestions involve shoring up unresolved questions that may require backfilling in the existing evidence-base—both in terms of research and demonstrated efficacy and effectiveness in practice. This means that research should move toward a more holistic approach to JRNA, incorporating multiple aspects of the logic model that represent the inputs, activities, and outputs that are central to its effectiveness.

A Next Generation JRNA Research Agenda

Broadly, future research must be expansive in terms of covering different aspects of the logic model of JRNA but also be mindful of smaller details such as how recidivism is measured (i.e., time frame, type of reoffending), adjusted for (e.g., does it account for differential degrees of supervision?), and which variables are included in multivariate models. It is also important to assess the range of outcomes that are expected to be impacted using JRNA practices—beyond reductions in recidivism (e.g., reduced out of home placements, cost-savings). More attention should also be directed toward understanding the perspectives of youths, families, and those working in the juvenile justice system focusing on their experiences with the JRNA and juvenile justice decision-making processes as well as their usage and adherence to JRNA policies and protocols. This in turn should improve the understanding of implementation and sustainability. At the same time, researchers and practitioners must also focus on understanding the processes at work in the system and the short- and longer-term effects of JRNA on juvenile justice (and vice versa). This requires that researchers carefully consider the context of JRNA along with understanding the precise inputs and outputs relevant to individual-level decisions and how those decisions impact aggregate-level outcomes.

Logic and Theory of JRNA

To set a foundation for quality research on JRNA, it is important to embed the three-step JRNA process in the underlying theory and logic of assessment in general and how its application in the juvenile justice system fits with that logic—both in terms of the process and in using the results to make decisions about youths. As researchers have moved away from early insights on the advantages of actuarial practice in decision-making relative to purely clinical decisions, some theoretical grounding has been lost even as other empirical and technical advances have occurred. It is important to bring those insights into the understanding and practice of JRNA to move forward effectively in the future. Early work in assessment was more heavily embedded in diagnostic and clinical case explanation frameworks. As structured assessments evolved there was more attention to measurement theory and psychometrics in the assessment of instruments. Research should retain that fundamental focus on actuarial assessment and measurement even though many tools are now established and used regularly. Indeed, there is still much to be learned by considering how assessments fit with the original underlying framework for their development.

Future research and planning should also build in more realistic decision-making frameworks when considering JRNA usage and implementation. Ideas of bounded rationality, for example, should be at the center of how information is assimilated and used in juvenile justice decision-making. More can also be done to integrate focal concerns and attribution theories to integrate existing ideas and findings about decision-making into JRNA research that is often undertheorized or focuses predominantly on risk-needs-responsivity principles. It is also important to think about where effective clinical judgment fits into the JRNA process, as there is still discretion at play in JRNA systems. Structured professional judgment (SPJ) approaches have become more prominent in recent years and offer a useful framework to consider how the discretion and bounded rationality vary across JRNA instruments, practitioners, and youth outcomes.

Aggregate-level questions require greater attention. If the case-level objective of JRNA is to improve decision-making about placements and services, then improvements should be seen at the agency and system level as well. The process of juvenile justice supervision and treatment should be more effective and save costs because of the greater efficiency and appropriateness of use in justice resources. At this point, however, there is relatively little formal research that studies these questions or formally links the expansion of risk and needs assessment to juvenile justice reforms, such as reduced residential placement (Sullivan, Park, & Holmes, 2019).

Several specific ways in which research can branch out to better understand and evaluate the full logic and theory underlying application of these tools in practice have been discussed in this book. These can be divided into three types: studies of assessments, studies of assessment usage and the logic model, and implementation research. Given the degree to which they are linked, some studies may address more than one of these areas. For example, studies where researchers observe the intake interview and information gathering practices of juvenile justice officials and ask them specific questions about how they are gathering and using information to score the assessment could also observe court hearings and case meetings within juvenile courts to determine whether and how that information is used in the decision-making process.

Studies of Assessments

While evaluating the assessment tools themselves has been a primary focus of research to this point, a great deal more that can be done in that area. If the objective is to use these tools to make effective and fair decisions about cases that affect youths' lives and system practice (and resources), then it is studies aimed at validation should expand their lens to cover questions beyond just the relationship between assessment and recidivism and meet standards of psychometric evaluation. For example, what are the false-positive and false-negative rates in the use of the tools and what do the cases that are effectively classified(not) look like? Additionally, if these tools are meant to be used for case management and treatment matching then it is important to look at their various subcomponents (i.e., domains) to determine how well they can establish needs in those areas effectively. While the whole may be greater than the different components in its relationship with recidivism, the way JRNA information is used shifts when considering case management objectives. Finally, the scoring and synthesis of the items should be more realistic in terms of the potential for differential weighting and interactions among items and domains. Of course, all of this should be extended to assessment of possible gender and race/ethnicity differences in how the properties of these tools work to ensure that they are used as effectively, fairly, and equitably as possible.

The return to basic principles described in Chapter 6 requires scrutinizing the properties of assessments more closely before they are widely disseminated and used in practice. For example, the "fourth generation" of risk and needs assessment is defined by the linkage between risk and needs, case management, and treatment. This inevitably means moving beyond crude measures of predictive validity to shore up support for precise linkage between assessment and intervention. With this, more must be done to establish internal consistency and predictive validity in items that are meant to coalesce to represent risk or need—especially within domain areas that inform treatment goals. Relatedly, checks for measurement invariance across groups or over time are needed as JRNA users seek to apply assessment procedures effectively to different race, sex, and age groups (including intersectional groups) or across time (as in reassessment). In general, more attention to psychometric properties as they affect usage requires a deeper focus on analyzing all the assessment items and domains as a means of fully investigating potential effectiveness and equity in practice.

Even consideration of predictive validity studies can be expanded to include psychometric properties that might connote fairness and equity. Researchers should do more to probe error rates and discretionary overrides associated with assessment usage. Research can also focus on the way in which certain risk and need level classifications are calibrated to reach conclusions about youths as those in turn affect important case-level decisions. Given the recognition of potentially different enforcement patterns affecting youths of color and girls, it is also important to study incremental validity to disentangle static, record-based indicators within the assessment from those that connote dynamic needs to ensure that it is appropriately balanced in terms of its effects on the results for different groups of youths. Last, it is important that the items in assessments are culturally and developmentally appropriate so as not to disadvantage youths in terms of factors that are out of their control and/or which do not fit well across groups. This also pertains to the data gathering and interviewing practices used by juvenile justice personnel to conduct and score the assessment.

Studies of Assessment Usage and the Logic Model

Studies of assessment tools are informative, but also frequently decontextualized from JRNA usage. Since JRNA is already embedded in juvenile justice practice, there are inherently some long-term goals that must be considered in evaluating their effectiveness. This is meant to be an operating system for juvenile justice practice and therefore we should evaluate its effectiveness from a broader perspective and over longer time periods to determine how youths fare following their assessment (and the decisions that are made based on its results). Research should certainly expand outward from the tool into the process surrounding its use and whether that effectively meets its objectives. One clear takeaway from the few existing implementation studies available is that little attention is paid to the degree to which JRNA insight is utilized from the perspective of agencies to better serve the youths who encounter juvenile justice and make the job easier for their staff.

Staff generally seem to respond favorably to the use of these practices, but their views are contingent and complex. It is important, therefore, to generate additional research on the ways that practitioner characteristics and beliefs influence JRNA usage, and then to incorporate these findings into the planning and implementation process (Vincent, Guy, & Grisso, 2012). The working knowledge and views of line personnel should be centered during implementation and continuous quality improvement work. This also offers an opportunity to enhance buy-in by paying attention to concerns raised by practitioners. For instance, looking at the validity of a tool for a given population or revisiting items that lack face validity might be beneficial in settings where practitioners raise that issue. This should include some consideration of the ways in which JRNA leads to shifts in agency practice around placement and intervention that in turn lead to greater effectiveness and efficiency in placements and perhaps even cost savings. Given that this is meant to be a global change to practice we should presumably see effects at multiple levels of the system (as outlined in the logic model in Chapter 3) but that has yet to be assessed much.

As mentioned with respect to the underlying theory for JRNA, research should more thoroughly investigate the RNR framework as a foundation for its use. We know that there are some elements of the adult system that have uneasy transitions to the juvenile justice setting (e.g., drug courts; see

Sullivan et al., 2016). So, it is important to look more concertedly at how well the logic of JRNA fits with the reality of the juvenile justice system. This work would both assess the degree to which there may be necessary additions or gaps in that model as well as how seamlessly it reflects the goals of the juvenile justice system.

Since decisions based on JRNA are not binding, relative to the assigned risk and needs levels, examining cases where professional judgment "overrides" assessment results would be insightful in considering usage, implementation, and identifying places where research and practitioner information weighting may differ. While overrides have been studied from the standpoint of how they might undermine the utility of the assessment, they may also be revelatory about the processes that practitioners use when they look at JRNA and use its results as a decision-making tool. This type of analysis requires a multi-method study of the three-step process in the field. Researchers could observe the information gathering and scoring process to understand how information about youths is collected and weighted. Then, decision-makers' statements about the process of choosing to override the assessment results (or not) could be linked to the observations about the process—as in a cognitive interview (Boeije & Willis, 2013).

Systematically analyzing the SPJ approach, which blends clinical judgment with a structured assessment process, might also be valuable in terms of different assessment properties, buy-in and use by practitioners, and outcomes for youths and agencies. Assessment practices grew in response to the shortcomings of subjective approaches to case evaluation and related decision-making. Some, however, argue that these can be integrated effectively, and SPJ seeks to do that. The SPJ approach explicitly draws both on actuarial and clinical approaches to assessment, making it a more open system of information gathering and use than the former alone. Intensive training on youth development, empirical research, and key mitigating and aggravating circumstances are critical to ensuring appropriate structured judgments (Borum, 2003; Vincent, 2006). SPJ can account for some of the uniqueness across groups and individuals. But it also introduces more discretion into a process that is meant to reduce discretion.

More research comparing these practices in terms of fidelity to the logic model, practitioner attitudes and uptake, and youth and case outcomes is needed. With that, the field can expand upon existing research on the factors that lead to alignment with JRNA policies/RNR principles. These might include any implicit biases and variability in skills and training that may infiltrate estimates of risk and needs. This is especially important as there is an assumption of the objectivity of structured assessment that does not always account for the information gathering and synthesis that may lead subjectivity to enter the process. There have been studies of field reliability that allow for checks on consistency in application of the assessment and scoring procedures. This does not always occur in usage studies, however, so it would be valuable to look at this more deeply in both frontline personnel and those in juvenile justice administrative officials. This could also be expanded to field observation studies during administration of the assessment and integration in later decision-making. Overall, it is essential that future research fully contextualizes JRNA in the juvenile justice decision-making process to fully account for the logic model that links it to those broader objectives and tasks.

Studies of Implementation and Use

Chapters 3 and 4 identified key contextual factors in the effective implementation of JRNA. This requires attention to policy and practice from federal, state, and local agencies—both within juvenile justice and from other networked human service agencies. Baird and colleagues (2013) studied juvenile risk assessments across ten jurisdictions and recommend that clearer national standards might be useful in improving practice, particularly the fidelity of these assessments. This suggests that there are areas where federal guidelines could be beneficial. Some of the key conclusions reached in this book and outlined in this chapter could be helpful in informing such recommendations. Though juvenile justice agency practices vary appreciably both within and across states, there are very clearly points that all should consider at different stages of contemplating, adopting, implementing, and sustaining these practices.

Establishing best practices in information gathering, assessment scoring, and case management is central to ensuring fair and effective practice of JRNA in the future. This should be done in a way, however, that gives juvenile justice personnel ownership over the process and its results. Implementation must be informed by and capture the broad view of identified stakeholders. Given that JRNA is a process that affects almost every aspect of the juvenile justice system, it is essential to consider policy and practice from the standpoint of all stakeholders and multiple inputs and outputs. The dependence of the process on resources is one example of a place where more attention should be given to understand what happens to youths because of JRNA. This would include some sense of potential frustrations of juvenile justice personnel in applying the results of the assessment process to meet the needs of individual cases.

Overall, growth in this type of research requires multisite studies where organizational, staff, and youth characteristics can be considered within various implementation frameworks. Although somewhat complicated and time-consuming, such a holistic approach is necessary for understanding exactly how JRNA activities can achieve the intended outcomes in practice. To this point we have already seen how Aarons and colleagues' (2011)

Exploration, Preparation, Implementation, Sustainment (EPIS) framework can be used to organize knowledge about and evaluation of JRNA practices. Likewise, Wandersman and colleagues (2008) developed the Interactive Systems Framework (ISF) that helps to identify aspects of JRNA's logic model and usage that are helpful in analyzing how well it is implemented.

The Consolidated Framework for Implementation Research (CFIR) can be used as a foundation for further exploration of these elements of JRNA as it offers a way to describe implementation and evaluate it.[1] It is also helpful as it links to several areas that have been covered in this book. The first construct of the CFIR is *intervention characteristics*, including its complexity and evidentiary support. We have argued that this is especially important in considering the research and implementation of JRNA as it has a multi-faceted logic model that goes beyond merely collecting relevant information and then making decisions. We also critiqued the evidentiary support as being somewhat narrow and argue that this should be improved for individual assessment tools and settings—as well as the understanding of JRNA more broadly.

Like Aarons and colleagues (2011), the second element of CFIR involves the settings in which the implementation occurs. Most importantly the impact of the *outer setting* is at least partly driven by external policy and incentives. In a juvenile justice context, this could include state authorizing bills that include language about the risk and needs assessment or legislative expenditures offered to support implementation. These, in turn, are linked to the *inner setting*, which comprises several elements including the culture of the organization both generally and around implementation of new initiatives. The "tension for change" around JRNA would also be part of this component in the sense that success in implementation would likely be driven in part by whether there is a perceived need to introduce a new assessment tool or process (or one could be fostered). Relatedly, the networks of the organization would be implicated in JRNA as that may dictate the types of referrals that juvenile justice personnel could make based on usage of those processes. The compatibility between the JRNA tool and procedures also must be checked in terms of how it fits with existing juvenile justice practice.

The fourth component of CFIR is *characteristics of individuals*. Importantly, this could also comprise the degree to which personnel responsible for implementing the assessment and decision-making feel confident that they can effectively do so. An individual component of readiness for change plays a role in implementation as well. This may in part be affected by knowledge of and attitudes toward JRNA. Last, the *processes* of implementation are essential to how effectively it will be used and sustained. This includes many points discussed in Chapter 4 in terms of having systematic planning processes, engaging with key stakeholders, and cultivating appropriate leadership around the incorporation of JRNA practices into everyday routines and larger strategic initiatives. The comprehensiveness of the CFIR reinforces the importance of the spectrum of immediate (staff training and buy-in) and longer-term (sustainability) outcomes. This in turn leaves us with a reminder that there are several components that must be considered in implementing JRNA practices and—while all questions do not have to be answered at once—it is essential that these are considered in the planning process and revisited regularly.

Together, these recommendations set the groundwork for an expansive research agenda that goes far beyond aggregate rates of predictive validity. Importantly, our current analysis was limited to analyzing the various dimensions of JRNA in two important ways. First, we primarily relied on existing published studies of various aspects of the relevant practices and their implications. Second, where we were able to look at new data and conduct formal analysis, we were limited in terms of the data sources and locations to which we had access. An increased evidence-base for JRNA requires attention to the points raised next—in a variety of sites, contexts, and samples—to effectively grow the knowledge-base that researchers and practitioners have available to them. In short, while we have a great deal of confidence in the evidence-base on JRNA, there are clearly gaps that must be filled to inform research, policy, and practice in the future. For instance, there has been a great deal of published research on juvenile risk and needs assessment, however it is highly focused on establishing the validity of tools using a limited number of definitions. Researchers should expand their focus to set the stage for efficacious and fair use of JRNA in juvenile justice settings and be sure to fully embed research in the policy and practice questions that more fully evoke the logic model of JRNA.

Next Generation JRNA Policy

Fairness and equity in the juvenile justice process cannot solely be driven by risk management. These questions must be considered intentionally in determining where assessment fits into the overall process of doing justice with youths and adolescents. Relatedly, there must also be careful attention to the degree to which youths' identified needs are being met via opportunities for change without risk of unneeded further penetration into the juvenile justice system or labeling that has further deleterious consequences. It is possible, for instance, that a tool and the accompanying process assesses two groups equally well, but there are other elements in the decision-making process that affect fairness and equity, just as in the application of the assessment results (e.g., distribution of resources to support positive development across neighborhoods or higher geographic administrative units). These tools are developed, scored, and used by humans and therefore there is always a possibility that bias will enter the process. Chapter 5, for example, covered the potential that attributions about family needs might still be disproportional in relevant ways.

This means that state authorizing statutes and local policy documents should clearly spell out the purposes of JRNA in a way that covers the multi-faceted mission of the juvenile justice system and builds in provisions to ensure that these practices are used in a way that is equitable and fair. With youths, this should include consideration of the balance of static and dynamic factors in making decisions as well as the need to avoid labeling and ensure re-assessment to consider possible change over time and in response to intervention. These examples amount to a more nuanced view of the role of JRNA in the system's operations to create a greater consciousness around avoiding errors related to stereotyping and reductionism that may emerge when we lose sight of the fact that groupings do not necessarily equate to youth behavior and that youths generally have strengths and protective factors that may offset any risk profile. Developing local policy documents and clear protocols is where federal and state guidelines and best practice recommendations may be the most beneficial.

Next Generation JRNA Implementation and Usage

Suggestions for practice naturally build on insights from research and field knowledge on JRNA usage and implementation. Those in the field must focus on implementation and give careful consideration of facilitators and barriers to implementation, sustainability, and appropriate modification (especially given that JRNA is firmly entrenched in practice at this point). This review and the recent research identified several common facilitators and barriers that offer places to start for those interested in implementing, improving, or obtaining a better understanding of JRNA practices. Line personnel and end-use decision-makers must be given an authentic voice in the process to ensure buy-in, which in turn can affect the quality of implementation.

Training practices are essential in implementation. It is, therefore, important that JRNA training and professional development resources be enhanced and evaluated in the future. Certainly, it is important that users first be introduced to the basics of an assessment tool and related processes but optimizing its usefulness for case outcomes requires coverage of second level components that may move its usage past risk management and into something more consistent with a developmental approach to juvenile justice, such as holistic, strengths-based case management. Demonstrating desired use requires clarity about the case-level decisions that practitioners must make on a routine basis as that will be part of effectively engaging key stakeholders in championing the new practice (see, e.g., Howell, 2005). Such effective assessment usage might perhaps best be conveyed by example using cases identified by peers as opposed to researchers or upper-level managers. Furthermore, the effective use of these tools in practice must be developmental in nature, meaning that administrators, decision-makers, service providers, and those who monitor youths must use the information to contribute to youth development (at least as one goal). However, if there is little buy-in, aptitude, or effective services to do that, that objective will not be met. The system then is likely to default simply to a risk identification and management process or a "one size fits all" intervention approach. This must be avoided to ensure fair and effective practice of juvenile risk and needs assessment.

States and localities have started to work more on the "back end" of the JRNA process whereby the results of assessments are linked to grids of sanctions and treatments. These can be useful, but the field should work with such grids in a well thought out way to ensure that the process is fair, equitable, and evidence-based. This has the potential to improve the mapping of identified risk and needs to actual decisions about dispositions and available interventions. It also can help with monitoring use of JRNA in decision-making (process outputs) to get past an emphasis on whether the assessment is conducted as expected (bureaucratic inputs). This potential substitution and cooptation of the practice must be monitored, and individuals and the system should be pushed back to the original objectives as needed. It is, however, important that agencies are intentional about gathering insights from their personnel and other stakeholders (e.g., youths and families) to help develop the grids and associated protocols and to map out available placement and intervention options in a realistic way.

Beyond policy and technical support, the success of the three-step JRNA process is heavily dependent on appropriate placements and interventions to match the information coming from its first two steps. This is, of course, essential at the case level, but should ideally be considered at the agency, system, and jurisdiction level, too. Appropriate resources are essential in making the logic model of JRNA work fully. With this, the next phase of JRNA practice should use assessment data more effectively to argue for additional and appropriate types of resources. For example, agency administrators should highlight that a lot of the potential success of JRNA comes down to agencies being able to fully go through the logic of JRNA from start to finish on the high volume and variety of cases that it encounters. Capacity to evaluate system and program success relative to youths' initial risk and needs also allows for improved precision.

While it is easy to lament the lack of information on effective implementation of JRNA practices, there are certainly conditions in the immediate and outer implementation context that facilitate the effective introduction and integration of JRNA in juvenile justice agencies and their networked partners. Each implementation setting is apt to be somewhat different based on a variety of characteristics. Therefore, a system-wide needs assessment should be conducted, including gathering a sense of the facilitators and barriers that may affect implementation, in every agency or system that wishes to use JRNA practices. This would even be fruitful in sites that might be experiencing challenges in sustainability or which would like to improve their practices.

The Future of JRNA: Theory, Research, Policy, and Practice

As mentioned earlier in the book and in this chapter, it is important to reflect on why JRNA practices are being used in addition to how they perform on selected benchmarks. Without some principled guidance it is easy to lose sight of the multi-faceted goals of the process and the varying inputs/outputs in the JRNA logic model and the juvenile justice system. Developmental goals have been centered in the juvenile justice process in recent years (National Research Council, 2013; Scott & Steinberg, 2009) and that framework is an important piece of JRNA in practice, particularly with respect to dynamic factors that are apt to change during adolescence (Vincent, Perrault, et al., 2012).

It is important to pivot from greater understanding of JRNA properties, usage, and implementation to ensure that these practices benefit youths involved in the juvenile justice system and agencies themselves. Right now, the research and practice of JRNA is highly focused on its benefits without as much attention to limitations, costs, challenges, or unintended consequences. To some extent this is natural in adopting a practice that is believed to be—and for the most part is—an improvement on the status quo. At the same time, a focus on continual improvement requires better understanding of the ways in which assessment tools and practices can be improved for the benefit of youths and the juvenile justice system.

Sustainability is an important part of thinking about the logic and evidence for JRNA, but perhaps misses the point in some ways. Given the tendency toward inertia and path dependence it is unlikely that agencies will quickly do away with a JRNA tool and process that is not working. Instead, it is more likely that the process continues without being optimized to the benefit of youths and the juvenile justice agencies. At the extreme, this could lead to a "zombie" program or idea (Pitner, 1990) that continues with a revised objective, unrelated to quality or effectiveness. The bigger question then is the degree to which agencies that are utilizing juvenile risk and needs assessment processes are engaged in continuous evaluation and adjustment as needed to optimize the benefits to youths, their personnel, and the juvenile justice system. In a sense, this reduces to the question of whether agencies and the researchers who frequently work with them are satisfied with acceptable predictive validity statistics and—sometimes—inter-rater reliability or prefer to keep working to improve in those areas and revisit other elements of practice and policy that warrant increased attention.

Clearly, there are many steps from adoption to sustainability of JRNA in practice that must be assessed and considered within agencies that wish to optimize these processes in their systems. For practitioners and policymakers, it is essential to take a deliberate, calculated approach as several components of the JRNA logic model must be adhered to for success. Researchers must consider these elements comprehensively in studying JRNA and communicating the results of that research as well. Wandersman and colleagues (2008) identify synthesis and translation as one of the key interactional systems for implementing evidence-based practices. In turn, the way that the evidence-base is conveyed to those in the field has implications for how well it is received (Tseng, 2012). This is especially true when considering the question of external validity, or transportability, of a given tool or set of practices from one agency/setting to another (Miller & Lin, 2007). Translation affects actual performance of the tools as well as the perceptions of practitioners who are asked to implement them outside of the setting(s) in which they were originally developed and validated (Sullivan, Strange, et al., 2019).

The process of translation and, eventually, implementation is more challenging than simply having a section of the training to cover relevant research that supports the use of structured assessment. Tseng (2012, p. 3) suggests that:

> the research community needs a stronger understanding of how practitioners and policymakers engage research. This understanding should include their definitions of research, their perceptions of its relevance and quality, their preferred modes of communication, and the forces that influence their use of research.

Seminal work in evaluation and implementation science by Weiss and Bucuvalas (1980) pointed out that the uptake of evidence in policymaking was not entirely linear and tended to come as a slow seep into the policy and practice environment as opposed to a one-to-one research-to-practice pipeline. Recent reviews of justice practices have drawn on this framework in considering the movement of research to practice (e.g., Nichols et al., 2019; Zane & Welsh, 2018) and it is useful to bear in mind when considering prospects for implementing JRNA. The notion of structured assessment certainly has taken hold among managers in the juvenile justice system, but the implementation process does not end there.

The nature of what is being implemented in JRNA practices is multifaceted in its objectives and the way it is meant to serve the mission of the juvenile justice system. Depending on how the balance of decision-making based on risk and needs is framed and addressed in the implementation process, there may be more of a gravitation toward one or the other without fully balancing both. In the juvenile justice system especially, the potential downside is that risk and disposition/placement may be weighed more heavily as that is relatively easier to implement and monitor compared to identifying needs and matching them to treatment and services. This is supported by the degree to which strength-based approaches are only starting to take hold in the juvenile justice system (see, e.g., Barton & Butts, 2008; Clark, 2009; Nissen, 2006).

During implementation planning, it is essential to address how the rationale, process, and potential outcomes of JRNA are conveyed with relevant research. While some are optimistic that simply conveying the research evidence to those in the field will set the stage for effective implementation by overcoming the objections of practitioners (Bonta et al., 2001), there is inevitable variation in how that information will be received and processed (see Tseng, 2012). Panacea thinking and promotional styles can be detrimental to long-term effectiveness as they may ultimately lead to disappointment if the full promise of the new practice is not realized in a relatively short time window. Finckenauer (1982) details the potential for this to occur using the example of Scared Straight programs where justice-involved youths interact with those serving adult prison time. Sullivan and colleagues (2016) describe implementation challenges in juvenile drug courts that may preclude their effectiveness in addressing delinquency and drug use problems commensurate with the perceptions of their potential (see Berman & Fox, 2010, for more on these types of "failures" in justice policy and practice).

New approaches to risk assessment are highly compatible with the desire to reintroduce a developmental foundation for juvenile justice because risk assessment tools, although not infallible, can contribute to public safety *and* promote youth potential when used to their full potential. Modern risk assessment tools improve the ability of systems to help youths become productive members of the community because many tools evaluate not only the degree of risk, but also the factors that are likely contributing to that risk. Still, researchers, practitioners, and policymakers must address all aspects of the underlying logic of JRNA more thoroughly.

One undercurrent that has appeared throughout the book is the importance of being able to expand on what effectiveness looks like when considering JRNA. We have been clear throughout the book that effectiveness is not merely whether a given score derived from a JRNA tool predicts recidivism beyond some pre-identified threshold (i.e., p < .05 or area under the curve [AUC] > .60). We have identified some key points that must be considered to effectively implement JRNA in context. Some of them build on the work of Vincent, Guy, and Grisso (2012) and Sullivan, Strange, et al., (2019) but reflect a broader review of the theory and research that forms the foundation for these practices. We have also highlighted the range of short- and long-term goals that should be accomplished via the three-step JRNA process, all of which contribute to definitions of "effectiveness." Unfortunately, there is a tendency to implement initiatives, evaluate for a short period of time, and assume that they will continue to "work" (however that has been defined initially). The definition of effectiveness needs to be clear, multidimensional, and mindful of continuous quality improvement. This is the case for fairness and equity as well and it provides some foundation from which to consider research and evidence-based policy and practice around the use of JRNA while also highlighting some areas where we believe it would be valuable to consider effectiveness.

Thinking about the CIFR framework as it relates to JRNA, effectiveness can best be judged by considering the different aspects of the logic model relative to the implementation processes that must be carried out to move it to the field effectively. It should also be evaluated at each relevant layer such that all key stakeholders are included. This includes youth outcomes across multiple areas (beyond official recidivism) and organizational outcomes such as shifts in resource usage and cultivating new referral options that align with youth needs identified via assessment. There are also questions about adherence to information gathering and scoring protocols that can be considered in the "usage" area. Ideally, there will also be evidence of fidelity in how the tool is used to gather information and then make appropriate decisions. In situations where there are deviations, effective practice requires clear documentation to ensure that the reasoning is clear. Effective implementation and sustainability will engage stakeholders in a formal planning process, identify key needs and foster readiness to change, train personnel effectively, embrace continual quality improvement and monitoring, and adjust as needed.

The recommendations made in this chapter, which build on points encountered throughout the book, require more attention in research, policy, and practice. Ultimately, some may prove fruitless or be limited in certain ways. Nevertheless, new evidence and ways of doing things are necessary in JRNA given the somewhat stagnant state of knowledge and practice as well as the stakes for the youths who are being assessed. The general belief around JRNA practices is positive about the potential outcomes for key stakeholders—especially youth and juvenile justice agencies. Still, it is important to continue to evaluate relevant evidence-base outcomes multiple facets of the process. This necessitates an orientation toward continuous quality improvement and a willingness to be introspective about these practices. It is also essential that the foundational principles of structured assessment, juvenile justice decision-making, and the broader mission of juvenile justice are kept in mind in all discussions and research on these practices. Only with such an approach can we be sure that JRNA practices will be aligned with the goals and mission of the juvenile court which means balanced, dynamic assessment to both reduce recidivism and ensure public safety and to address youths' needs in ways that promote their development and growth.

Note

1   https://cfirguide.org/constructs/

References

Aarons, G.A., Hurlburt, M., & Horwitz, S.M. (2011). Advancing a conceptual model of evidence-based practice implementation in public service sectors. *Administration and Policy in Mental Health and Mental Health Services Research*, 38(1), 4–23. doi:10.1007/s10488-10010-0327-0327.

Andrews, D.A., & Bonta, J. (2010). Rehabilitating criminal justice policy and practice. *Psychology, Public Policy, and Law*, 16(1), 39–55. doi:10.1037/a0018362.

Andrews, D.A., Bonta, J., & Wormith, J.S. (2006). The recent past and near future of risk and/or need assessment. *Crime & Delinquency*, 52(1), 7–27. doi:10.1177/0011128705281756.

Baird, C., Healy, T., Johnson, K., Bogie, A., Dankert, E.W., & Scharenbroch, C. (2013). *A comparison of risk assessment instruments in juvenile justice*. Madison, WI: National Council on Crime and Delinquency.

Barton, W.H., & Butts, J.A. (2008). *Building on strength: Positive youth development in juvenile justice programs*. Chicago, IL: Chapin Hall Center for Children at the University of Chicago. https://jeffreybutts.files.wordpress.com/2008/08/building.pdf.

Berman, G., & Fox, A. (2010). *Trial and error in criminal justice reform: Learning from failure*. Washington, DC: Urban Institute Press.

Boeije, H.R., & Willis, G. (2013). The Cognitive Interviewing Reporting Framework (CIRF): Towards the harmonization of cognitive interviewing reports. *Methodology*, 9(3), 87–95. doi:10.1027/1614-2241/a000075.

Bonta, J., Bogue, B., Crowley, M., & Motiuk, L. (2001). Implementing offender classification systems: Lessons learned. In G.A. Bernfeld, D.P. Farrington, & A.W. Leschied (Eds.), *Offender rehabilitation in practice: Implementing and evaluating effective programs* (pp. 227–245). Chichester, UK: Wiley.

Borum, R. (2003). Managing at-risk juvenile offenders in the community: Putting evidence- based principles into practice. *Journal of Contemporary Criminal Justice*, 19(1), 114–137. doi:10.1177/1043986202239745.

Clark, M.D. (2009). Juvenile justice and a strengths perspective: Complement or clash? *Reclaiming Children and Youth*, 18(2), 21–26. https://search.proquest.com/openview/3bbf9ba814b94dd72b7ab9cb6cada61c/1?pq-origsite=gscholar&cbl=33810

Finckenauer, J.O. (1982) *Scared straight and the panacea phenomenon*. Englewood Cliffs, NJ: Prentice-Hall.

Howell, J.M. (2005). The right stuff: Identifying and developing effective champions of innovation. *Academy of Management Perspectives*, 19(2), 108–119.

Miller, J., & Lin, J. (2007). Applying a generic juvenile risk assessment instrument to a local context: Some practical and theoretical lessons. *Crime & Delinquency*, 53(4), 552–580. doi:10.1177/0011128706293689.

National Research Council (2013). *Reforming juvenile justice: A developmental approach*. Washington, DC: National Academies Press. www.njjn.org/uploads/digital-libra ry/Reforming_JuvJustice_NationalAcademySciences.pdf.

Nichols, J., Wire, S., Wu, X., Sloan, M., & Scherer, A. (2019). Translational criminology and its importance in policing: A review. *Police Practice and Research*, 20(6), 537–551. doi:10.1080/15614263.2019.1657625.

Nissen, L. (2006). Bringing strength-based philosophy to life in juvenile justice. *Reclaiming Children and Youth: The Journal of Strength-Based Interventions, 15*(1), 40–

46. https://lauraburneynissenlovessocialwork.files.wordpress.com/2012/03/bringing-strength-based-philosophy-to-life-in-juvenile-justice-settings.pdf

Pitner, N.J. (1990). *Reinventing school leadership.* Cambridge, MA: National Center for Educational Leadership.

Scott, E.S., & Steinberg, L.D. (2009). *Rethinking juvenile justice.* Cambridge, MA: Harvard University Press.

Sullivan, C.J., Blair, L., Latessa, E., & Sullivan, C.C. (2016). Juvenile drug courts and recidivism: Results from a multisite outcome study. *Justice Quarterly,* 33(2), 291–318. doi:10.1080/07418825.2014.908937.

Sullivan, C.J., Park, I., & Holmes, B., (2019). *A micro and macro-level assessment of juvenile justice placement reform in Ohio.* Submitted to Office of Justice Programs, Office of Juvenile Justice and Delinquency Prevention.

Sullivan, C.J., Strange, C.C., Sullivan, C.C., Lugo, M., Mueller, D., Petkus, A., Newsome, J., Holmes, B., Lonergan, H., & Gibbs, G. (2019). *A multi-state and multi-method study of juvenile risk assessment implementation, usage, and outcomes.* Final technical report submitted to the Office of Juvenile Justice and Delinquency Prevention.www.ojp.gov/pdffiles1/ojjdp/grants/252927.pdf.

Tseng, V. (2012). The uses of research in policy and practice. *Society for Research in Child Development, Social Policy Report,* 26, 1–16. https://knightadrc.wustl.edu/cdrtraining/traininga/.

Vincent, G.M. (2006). Psychopathy and violence risk assessment in youth. *Child and Adolescent Psychiatric Clinics,* 15(2), 407–428. doi:10.1016/j.chc.2005.12.001.

Vincent, G.M., Guy, L.S., & Grisso, T. (2012). *Risk assessment in juvenile justice: A guidebook for implementation.* Washington, DC: MacArthur Foundation. www.njjn.org/uploads/digitallibrary/Risk_Assessment_in_Juvenile_Justice_A_Guidebook_for_Implementation.pdf.

Vincent, G.M., Perrault, R.T., Guy, L.S., & Gershenson, B.G. (2012). Developmental issues in risk assessment: Implications for juvenile justice. *Victims & Offenders,* 7(4), 364–384. doi:10.1080/15564886.2012.713900.

Wandersman, A., Duffy, J., Flaspohler, P., Noonan, R., Lubell, K., Stillman, L., Blachman, M., Dunville, R., & Saul, J. (2008). Bridging the gap between prevention research and practice: The interactive systems framework for dissemination and implementation. *American Journal of Community Psychology,* 41(3–4), 171–181. doi:10.1007/s10464-008-9174-z.

Weiss, C.H., & Bucuvalas, M.J. (1980). *Social science research and decision-making.* New York: Columbia University Press.

Zane, S.N., & Welsh, B.C. (2018). Toward an "age of imposed use"? Evidence-based crime policy in a law and social science context. *Criminal Justice Policy Review,* 29(3), 280–300. doi:10.1177/0887403417694068.

Index

Note: Page numbers in *italics* represent Figures. Page numbers in **bold** represent Tables. Page numbers followed by {n} represent Notes.

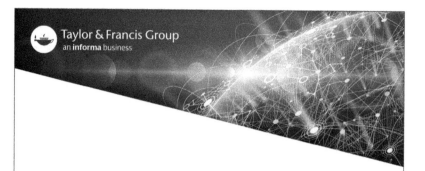

Milton Keynes UK
Ingram Content Group UK Ltd.
UKHW050146260424
441726UK00014B/88